The Meaning of Rehabilitation and its Impact on Parole

This book queries the concept of rehabilitation to determine how, on a legislative and policy level, the term is defined as a goal of correctional systems. The book explores what rehabilitation *is* by investigating *how*, at different moments in time, its conceptualization has shaped, and been shaped by, shifting norms, practices, and institutions of corrections in California. The author calls for a rethinking of theoretical understandings of the corrections system, generally, and parole system, specifically, and calls for an expansion in the questions asked in reintegration studies. The book is designed for scholars seeking to better understand the relationship between correctional systems and rehabilitation and the full scope of rehabilitation as a legislative goal, and is also suitable for use as teaching tool for historical, textual, and interviewing methods.

Dr. Rita Shah is an Assistant Professor of Criminology at Eastern Michigan University. Her research combines textual analysis with qualitative and visual methods to understand the ways in which correctional systems are socially and legally constructed. Her work has been published in the *British Journal of Criminology* and *Contemporary Justice Review* and is supported by NEH and NSF grants. Bridging the areas of criminology and law and society, her courses focus on the social construction of crime, the relationship between law and society, and issues of social justice. She received her BA in communications, legal institutions, economics, and government (CLEG) from American University and her MA in social ecology and Ph.D. in criminology, law, and society from the University of California, Irvine. In her free time, she can be found on photographic expeditions or watching football.

Routledge Innovations in Corrections

An emphasis on innovation is evident in the field of corrections. While changes in policies and public opinion regarding sentencing philosophies such as mass incarceration bump up against the reality that budgets continue to be tightened and the division of these revenues is more competitive, innovative strategies become all the more valuable. The premise behind innovation is effecting improvements without sacrificing the overall safety and security of the institution. Through research and evaluation, we seek to identify what works and what does not work.

The Angola Prison Seminary
Effects of Faith-Based Ministry on Identity Transformation, Desistance, and Rehabilitation
Michael Hallett, Joshua Hays, Byron Johnson, Sun Joon Jang, and Grant Duwe

The Meaning of Rehabilitation and its Impact on Parole
There and Back Again in California
Rita Shah

Correctional Rehabilitation and Therapeutic Communities
Reducing Recidivism Through Behavior Change
Jennifer Pealer

Rural Jail Re-entry
Offender Needs and Challenges
Kyle Ward

The Meaning of Rehabilitation and its Impact on Parole

There and Back Again in California

Rita Shah

Routledge
Taylor & Francis Group
LONDON AND NEW YORK

First published 2017
by Routledge

2 Park Square, Milton Park, Abingdon, Oxfordshire OX14 4RN
52 Vanderbilt Avenue, New York, NY 10017

Routledge is an imprint of the Taylor & Francis Group, an informa business

First issued in paperback 2018

Library of Congress Cataloging-in-Publication Data
Names: Shah, Rita, author.
Title: The meaning of rehabilitation and its impact on parole : there and back again in California / Rita Shah.
Description: New York, NY : Routledge, 2017. | Series: Routledge innovations in corrections | Includes bibliographical references.
Identifiers: LCCN 2016054972 | ISBN 9781138202191 (hardback)
Subjects: LCSH: Parole—California—History. | Criminals—Rehabilitation—California—History. | Corrections—California—History.
Classification: LCC HV9305.C2 S53 2017 | DDC 365/.66109794—dc23
LC record available at https://lccn.loc.gov/2016054972

ISBN: 978-1-138-20219-1 (hbk)
ISBN: 978-0-367-13389-4 (pbk)

Typeset in Sabon
by Apex CoVantage, LLC

To my nephew, Jaiden, for whom I strive to build a better world.

Contents

Acknowledgments

As with any project, this book would not be possible without support and mentorship from many individuals. I am especially grateful to my advisors at the University of California, Irvine, Justin Richland, Mona Lynch, and Susan Coutin, for helping me build an idea into an argument. This book benefitted immensely from their invaluable mentorship and constant reminder to search for the complexities and contradictions in everyday realities. To my mentors at Elizabethtown College, Elizabeth Newell and April Kelly-Woessner, thank you for pushing me to reach for my academic goals and strategizing with me over meals and drinks. I would also like to thank Kate Henne, Tyler Grimm, Alexandria Poole, and Emily Troshynski for their feedback on earlier drafts. Thanks to the SAGE reviewers for comments on the portions of Chapter 1 that first appeared in Shah, R. (2012). Parole. In W. R. Miller, (Ed.), *The Social History of Crime and Punishment in America: An Encyclopedia*. Thousand Oaks, CA: Sage Publications, Inc. and Shah, R. (2012). Rehabilitation. In W. R. Miller, (Ed.), *The Social History of Crime and Punishment in America: An Encyclopedia*. Thousand Oaks, CA: Sage Publications, Inc. Finally, reviewer comments from Lawrence Burke and other anonymous reviewers were invaluable in shaping the book you read today.

I am also appreciative of the many individuals who assisted me along the way. The data for this book would not exist without the wonderful archivists at the California State Archives and T. H. Pendergast Parole Museum, my undergraduate research assistant Joseph McCall, and the many parole agents who agreed to be interviewed for this study. As with most academic work, this book builds on prior projects. As such, I am grateful to Donna Selman, the Visualizing Governing Through Crime group, and various individuals commenting at conference presentations for their feedback on various versions of this project. Several organizations also helped bring this book to fruition. The National Science Foundation (SES-0921943), the American Society of Criminology Fellowship for Ethnic Minorities, the UCI Center for Organizational Research

Graduate Student Fellowship, and the UCI Dean's Dissertation Data Gathering Fellowship all supported data collection. Additional funding through the UCI Dean's Dissertation Writing Fellowship, Elizabethtown College Faculty Research Grant, and Elizabethtown College Junior Leave were instrumental in writing and completing the book. Special thanks goes to the team at Routledge, particularly Ellen Boyne and Eve Strillacci, for navigating the book through the publication process.

Finally, I would like to thank my friends and family for their constant love and support. Most importantly, I thank my mom, Nalini Shah, for always standing by me and helping me find my way in the world. To my sister and brother-in-law, Deepa and Sanjay Khetan, your never-ending reminder to shoot for my dreams helped get this book over the finish line. I cannot thank you three enough.

Introduction

> *Whoever wishes to foresee the future must consult the past; for human events ever resemble those of preceding times. This arises from the fact that they are produced by men who ever have been, and ever shall be, animated by the same passions, and thus they necessarily have the same results.*
>
> ~*Machiavelli*

Bullshit. That's what Red called it. A bullshit word. "A made up word. A politician's word" (Marvin & Darabont, 1994). But a bullshit word with a purpose: "so young fellas like yourself can wear a suit and a tie and have a job" (Marvin & Darabont, 1994). As described by Morgan Freeman's character in the movie rendition of *Shawshank Redemption*, the term "rehabilitation" is just that: a term. What is most interesting about this description is the time in which it is expressed. The movie is set in a time when rehabilitation was the overarching goal of correctional systems nationally and, presumably, when it had a very pointed meaning and purpose. Red's definition, however, is more in line with when the movie was released (Marvin & Darabont, 1994), when rehabilitation was indeed a bullshit word, as it was deemed unattainable.

This was not the first time Red is asked this question, but this response was the first to earn him release on to parole. One could argue the parole hearing members agreed with his definition. One could also argue he was released because of the remorse he showed about the crime he committed. The combination of Red expressing frustration at the term "rehabilitation" and sorrow over his past and the perspective of a changed man highlight the ways in which rehabilitation—as a concept—can have different meanings that resonate at different times.

In many ways, the temporal contradictions highlighted by *Shawshank Redemption* tell the story of rehabilitation in US corrections. Even in the moment when rehabilitation was the very purpose of correctional systems, questions arose regarding the efficacy of the goal. These questions eventually led to a rejection of rehabilitation, but, as several scholars argue (Lynch, 1998; Hutchinson, 2006; Robinson, 2008; Phelps, 2011), it never truly went away. Even within Shawshank Prison, glimmers of rehabilitation are clearly seen (e.g., expansion of the library, opportunities to obtain a GED). Decades after the movie was released, these glimmers seem to be expanding as state and federal governments are re-emphasizing a shift back towards rehabilitation (e.g., Second Chance Act of 2007[1]; Lawrence, 2013).

Yet, Red's view of rehabilitation as a bullshit term still resonates. Perhaps it is because the meaning of the term is rarely questioned (Raynor & Robinson, 2005) or provided (Maruna, 2011; McNeill, 2012), even during a time of renewed calls for rehabilitating offenders. When rehabilitation is discussed, the meaning often echoes that offered in the movie: "it means you're ready to rejoin society" (Marvin & Darabont, 1994). As Phelps (2011) notes, rehabilitation programs today tend to focus on reentry and recidivism reduction. As Phelps also finds, however, these programs used to focus on much wider goals. The contradictions highlighted in *Shawshank Redemption* echo questions raised by this seeming return to rehabilitation about the true meaning of rehabilitation, how that meaning changes over time, and how these changes may impact the current focus on rehabilitation.

This book queries the concept of rehabilitation to determine how, on a legislative and policy level, the term is defined, or if is indeed a bullshit word. This book argues that while current understandings of rehabilitation are not incorrect, they are incomplete and do not line up with the implicit definition found in the legislation. The way in which we conceive of rehabilitation in everyday discourse is missing key components of how it is conceived in legislation and policy directives across time. Specifically, rehabilitation is defined as a process that requires assistance of some form to achieve two distinct goals: 1) a change for the better (an end to criminal activity), which is necessary to achieve 2) a return to a former state (return of all legal rights). Second, the meaning of rehabilitation is not as static as current discourses assume. Rather, the process is unsettled and ever changing; as a result, the goal and meaning of rehabilitation is always in flux. Rehabilitation is reframed to fit within the existing correctional philosophy and while it at times fell from the forefront, it never truly disappeared. These shifts do not occur in a vacuum, however. Today's version of the legislative understanding of rehabilitation is different from, but connected to and based on, prior versions of the construct.

In making these arguments, the book calls for a rethinking of theoretical understandings of the corrections system, generally, and parole system, specifically. The very way in which scholars and criminal justice practitioners understand the concept of rehabilitation is misaligned with how the legislative discourse defines it. Rehabilitation is not simply about ending criminal activity. The legislative histories suggest a call to restore rights lost upon conviction before one can be fully rehabilitated/reintegrated—a process that can take decades. Legal barriers do not just make reintegration difficult; they make it impossible. By focusing on ending criminal activity, current correctional practices maintain and justify a system that creates second-class citizenry.

Thus, this book calls for an expansion in the questions asked in reintegration studies. We cannot fully understand challenges to reintegration without understanding how rehabilitation is *actually* defined within legislative discourse and the role of parole as described in the legislative history, nor can we understand the effectiveness of parole in achieving rehabilitation without a fuller understanding of its meaning. Studies of parole's effectiveness tend to focus on its ability to impact recidivism rates, which assumes a correctional rehabilitation definition (e.g., Gottfredson, Mitchel-Herzfeld, & Flanagan, 1982; Jackson, 1983; Solomon, Kachnowski, & Bhati, 2005; Schlager & Robbins, 2008; Ostermann, 2013; Vito, Higgins, & Tewksbury, 2015). If rehabilitation as a legislative end means something other than—or in addition to—correctional rehabilitation, the majority of studies on the effectiveness of parole are providing an incomplete and perhaps inaccurate picture. If criminal justice scholars and practitioners want to truly reduce recidivism (and thus reduce crime), we have to rethink our study of and implementation of rehabilitation practices and call for broader policy changes to ensure returning individuals are able to regain their full citizenship status (e.g., restore voting rights; elimination of criminal record).

To better understand the meaning of rehabilitation in the United States, California served as the case study for three reasons. First, the moments in which the shifts towards, away from, and back to rehabilitation occur were explicitly specified in state legislation. The shifts did not occur as suddenly or as concretely as the laws indicate, but two statutes (SB 42 The Uniform Determinate Sentencing Act and SB 737 The Governor's Reorganization Plan, discussed in Chapters 3 and 4, respectively) provide natural cut-points in a timeline of an ever-evolving correctional system.

Second, in 2005, California became the first state to re-emphasize rehabilitation with legislative changes that restructured the correctional system (California Department of Corrections and Rehabilitation Expert Panel on Adult Offender Reentry and Recidivism Reduction Programs [CDCR Expert Panel], 2007). This move "back" to a statewide policy of rehabilitation provides an avenue by which to question the nature and scope of rehabilitation. Additionally, changes made in California's correctional system are often copied by other states. Hence, understanding the meaning of rehabilitation in California can potentially provide insights into the meaning of rehabilitation in other states.

Third, the shifts in rehabilitation in the correctional system as a whole had an interesting impact on the state's parole system. At its inception, the system was a bureaucratic tool enabling the release of inmates. As the parole system grew, it adapted to meet the needs of the larger correctional system. Parole became a key tool for achieving rehabilitation (Simon, 1993; Petersilia, 2003) and eventually shifted to focus on case management and surveillance (Simon, 1993). The renewed call for rehabilitation appears to be a (re-)emergence of rehabilitative policies that remained on the books but were largely unpracticed between 1977 and 2000 (Lynch, 2000). Efforts to implement a rehabilitation-oriented parole system face particular challenges in light of the current state of California's corrections policies and practices. Emerging within a broader structural context in which punishment has been fundamentally, perhaps irrevocably, transformed (Garland, 2001; Simon, 2007), the reassertion of rehabilitation as a goal today may mean that this contemporary incarnation is quite different from any prior one. These shifts provide an avenue by which to understand whether and how rehabilitation changed over time.

Ultimately, this book aims to develop an understanding of the sociocultural forces and meanings surrounding the rehabilitative ideal at various moments in the history of California's correctional system, and specifically California's parole system, with an eye towards understanding the forces and meanings surrounding the most recent rise of the rehabilitative ideal after 2005. Using documents relating to various statutes, documents surrounding the practices of California's parole system, and interviews with parole agents, the goal of this book is to understand what rehabilitation *is* by investigating *how*, at different moments in time, its conceptualization has shaped, and been shaped by, shifting norms, practices, and institutions of corrections in California.

Scholarly Understandings of Rehabilitation

Conversations on rehabilitation often focus on two factors: 1) the role of rehabilitation in correctional systems; and 2) how rehabilitation might be defined. Rehabilitation, as a response to criminal behavior, is a relatively new concept. The notion that offenders could change was not a part of punishment regimes until the 1800s, when punishment moved from being directed at the body to directed at the soul (Rothman, 1971; Foucault, 1975/1977). In the early 1800s, many reformers believed the only cure for criminality was to place offenders in isolation. Although jails and prisons existed at this time, there was little support these institutions could result in the type of repentance necessary for a criminal to be welcomed back to the greater society. New institutions were built with the view that "remov[ing] the offender from all temptations and substitute[ing] a steady and regular regimen would reform him"

(Rothman, 1971, p. 82; see also, Garland, 1985). These new facilities, called penitentiaries, required individuals to seek penitence and salvation and remain locked away until redemption occurred (McNeill, 2012). The length of time one was incarcerated varied. As Lombroso argued, punishment should be based on the dangerousness and type of the criminal and that "[c]rime is like an illness that requires a specific remedy for each patient" (quoted in Rafter, 2009, p. 219).

This was the first sign of rehabilitation as an aspect of the correctional system and this new form of punishment was predicated on the idea that people could change. Yet, correctional systems had not embraced the language of rehabilitation. Scholars note this did not occur until the mid-1900s when criminological theories began arguing criminal offenders were a product of their environment. This shift allowed rehabilitation within corrections to grow in favor. The rehabilitative ideal, often referred to as the clinical or medical model of corrections, gained strength during the 1940s through the 1960s. Allen (1959, p. 227) notes this version of the rehabilitative ideal is "sharply distinguished from earlier expressions" for two reasons: 1) the emergence of "scientific disciplines concerned with human behavior" and 2) the dominance of the rehabilitative ideal in

> theoretical and scholarly inquiry, to such an extent that in some quarters it is almost assumed that matters of treatment and reform of the offender are the only questions worthy of serious attention in the whole field of criminal justice and corrections.

As argued in Chapter 2, this view of rehabilitation framed the correctional system such that time spent in prisons and on parole was, in and of itself, seen as causing rehabilitation.

This fierce attachment to the rehabilitative ideal would not last long. Even in moments when rehabilitation was the main goal of corrections, the very structure that allowed rehabilitation to flourish was questioned by the public, academics, and legislators. These critiques centered on three things: 1) the notion of rehabilitation itself; 2) the indeterminate sentencing structure; and 3) the punishments carried out in the name of rehabilitation.

First, as Allen (1981) notes, a cultural shift occurred in which society lost faith in social institutions (e.g., schools and families) once thought to shape one's moral character. This shift led to a general lack of faith in the malleability of individuals, which raised questions of the very premise of the rehabilitative ideal. The public also began viewing those in rehabilitative programs as incapable of change (Allen, 1981). Critiques of rehabilitation came from individuals across the political spectrum. Liberals argued the rehabilitative ideal helped justify longer sentences;

conservatives argued it "weakened the punitive mechanisms of the state" (Rotman, 1990, p. 109). Radical criminologists claimed that rehabilitation, if it was possible, was an excuse to avoid making the structural changes necessary for rehabilitation to be effective long term (Rotman, 1990). Without changes within society, returning citizens would return to the same conditions that initially propelled them into crime. Radical criminologists also critiqued the discretionary power associated with indeterminate sentencing and the ineffectiveness of correctional institutions. They stated rehabilitation was "a means to cloak the mechanisms of social control through which prisons were perpetuating unjust structures of power" (Rotman, 1990, p. 116).

The second major critique centered on the indeterminate sentencing structure, which was justified as necessary to ensure individuals obtained the proper amount of rehabilitation while in prison. Liberals argued indeterminate sentencing led to abuses of power by sentencing and correctional officials; conservatives argued indeterminate sentencing led to increased leniency (Rotman, 1990). While the liberal and conservative critiques were polar opposites, both favored moving away from indeterminate sentences.

The final critique centered on the types of punishments and treatments used. Some treatments, such as shock therapy (Rotman, 1990), were criticized for being inhuman, abusive, and intrusive. As these treatments grew out of favor, the rehabilitative ideal was held responsible for such harsh approaches. Questions also arose as to whether one could "volunteer" for such programs if release was determined in part by successful completion of these treatments. Morris (1974) argued the coerced nature of treatment within prisons failed to achieve the goal of change because, unlike antibiotics, treatment programs do not work without the cooperation of the prisoner, undermining the very assumptions of the medical model.

Many treatments were also found to be ineffective. Much to Richard McGee's chagrin, the multiple studies he conducted in California showed the organization of the parole system had little-to-no impact on parolee outcomes (Glaser, 1995), which raised questions as to parole's ability to effect change. Possibly the most damaging study was Martinson's (1974) meta-analysis on the effectiveness of correctional programs nationwide. Although the study found some programs were promising, the general conclusion was that no program worked consistently to reduce recidivism (Farabee, 2005). These findings led to the public losing faith in the correctional system, in those authorizing rehabilitation, and in deciding what constituted rehabilitation and who decided what constituted a cure (Allen, 1981).

While rehabilitation was growing out of favor, there was an increasing emphasis on the impact of crime on the victim. There was also a developing view that crime resulted from a lack of social controls (rather than social depravation). Because of these factors, governing officials began shifting the use of prisons and parole in the 1970s towards controlling and managing convicted individuals rather than attempting to rehabilitate them. This culture of control (Garland, 2001) permeated everyday life such that the "technologies, discourses, and metaphors of crime and criminal justice" are now embedded in the language of governance (Simon, 2007, p. 4). As this form of governance became embedded within society, it emphasized the need to control those viewed as the dangerous class, creating a vicious cycle.

The shift towards control also led to a risk management model, referred to as the new penology (Feeley & Simon, 1992), to the exclusion of any form of rehabilitation. In order to control the criminal population, correctional systems began utilizing actuarial tools to determine who should be released, who should be in programs, and who to be most concerned about. Unlike rehabilitation, which focused on changing or reforming *individuals*, contemporary penality focused on minimizing the risk posed by *groups* of people (Feeley & Simon, 1992). As discussed in Chapters 3 and 4, such attempts led to an increase in the surveillance of parolees and greater reliance on drug testing and statistical risk analyses.

O'Malley (1996) argues the shift towards control and risk management and away from rehabilitation within corrections is also related to rise of neo-liberalism. In particular, it seems to match a movement towards responsibilization, that is the reliance on individuals to address issues of crime control and prevention and a detachment of government's involvement (Garland, 1996; Rose, 2000; Hannah-Moffat, 2001). This reliance on individuals furthers the notion they needed to ensure themselves against adverse situations in order to protect themselves from crime (O'Malley, 1996). Hannah-Moffat (2001, p. 166) argues that similar shifts in Canada's treatment of federal female offenders meant "[o]ffenders are now seen as being responsible for their own reform," or, as Nikolas Rose (2000, p. 324) argues, "responsible for their own destinies." Furthermore, neo-liberalism's focus on rational actors who weigh costs and benefits allows for a view of those who commit crimes as making the choice to do so, reducing the need for treatment programs. As criminals are no longer influenced by outside factors, they are now responsible for choosing to no longer commit crimes. As will be discussed in Chapters 3 and 4, this move towards responsibilization impacted the ways in which the state intervenes with parolees and the meaning of rehabilitation.

Others argue, however, that even at times when punishment and risk management are the main focus, the shift did not occur immediately and that the notion of rehabilitation is present in some way. For example, Lynch (1998) found that, in practice, parole agents functioned as more than "risk managers" and the practice of punishment does not fall in line with all of the theoretical tenets of the new penology. Cullen and

Gendreau (2000) argued that correctional systems nationwide continued to use and expand programs, particularly those that addressed drug and alcohol addiction. Phelps (2011) also challenged the prevailing belief that support and funding for programs in prison disappeared over night. Rather, she found that it was not until the 1990s that support for inmate programs changed and that funding shifted away from academic programs and towards reentry preparedness programs. Rehabilitation programs were reframed as necessary to eliminate one's risk when released to the community.

Similarly, Kelly Hannah-Moffat (1999) argues the use of risk assessment has reframed rehabilitation such that criminological risk is now framed as criminological needs. She and her colleague note that reframing risk in this way enables correctional systems to focus on the treatment of criminological needs, which "lower[s] recidivism and, consequently, risk" (Maurutto & Hannah-Moffat, 2006, p. 442). This is particularly true of risk assessment tools, such as the Level of Service Inventory (originally called the Level of Supervision Inventory), the use of which shifted from determining the required level of supervision to the required level of treatment and programming even when the different versions of the assessment itself were fairly similar (Maurutto & Hannah-Moffat, 2006).

These studies provide support for Hutchinson's (2006) argument that punishment and rehabilitation are "braided" together. Punishment and rehabilitation cannot be separated, though one may be more prominent than the other. Indeed, Allen (1981) speculates that while the use of rehabilitation declined during the late 1900s, its use may not have disappeared entirely, and likely shifted from a central role to a peripheral role. As argued in Chapter 3, rehabilitation remained a part of the parole system as a tool of supervision, even at times when it seemingly disappeared from the correctional system as a whole.

Furthering this idea, Robinson (2008) argues the concept of rehabilitation in the United Kingdom and Wales did not disappear and then reappear; rather, it evolved over time. In the 1950s and 1960s, rehabilitation was viewed as a form of welfarism and was understood as designed to benefit the returning citizens' lives. During the "Nothing Works" period of US corrections in the 1970s to 1990s, Robinson notes that rehabilitation evolved into a risk management tool. Treatment programs were viewed as a way of reducing an individual's criminogenic risks and assist in preventing future crimes. Today, rehabilitation is reframed as a tool for the improvement of society, risk management, and as a form of punishment. Thus, rehabilitation is used as a means of providing the greatest good to the greatest number of people by managing and maintaining risk, reducing recidivism, and providing alternatives to incarceration (e.g., community sanctions) (Robinson, 2008). As argued throughout the book, California does reframe rehabilitation in ways similar to

Robinson's findings; unlike Robinson's findings, however, rehabilitation has always been used a form of punishment.

Regardless of the role of rehabilitation within correctional systems, it is unclear what rehabilitation means as a goal of the criminal justice system (Maruna, 2011; McNeill, 2012) and the term is rarely critically examined (Raynor & Robinson, 2005). Theories abound as to its definition. Among them are claims that rehabilitation is best understood as 1) an elimination of criminal behavior or the causes of criminal behavior; 2) an undoing of criminal convictions; or 3) an ongoing event. For some, rehabilitation is "simply the absence of new criminal behavior" (Joan Petersilia, as quote in Shaughnessy, 2007) or the causes of criminal behavior (Raynor & Robinson, 2005). Also called correctional rehabilitation, this theory views rehabilitation as an end goal. The specific means of achieving this goal are not discussed, but some scholars argue factors important to achieving recidivism reduction include repairing relationships, restoring one's status in the community (Raynor, 1997; Raynor & Robinson, 2005), and establishing stable employment (Simon, 1993). The role the state plays in achieving correctional rehabilitation is unclear. Goodman, in his study of California Fire Camps, argued, "Rehabilitation as such is nothing more, and nothing less, than a bridge to society: the state provides the basic (and sometimes modest) infrastructure, and the individual decides whether or not to cross it" (2010, p. 342). Precisely what this infrastructure looks like is unclear, though Goodman does note that many in the fire camps found access to drug rehabilitation, work skills, and educational programs to be especially useful.

Forsyth (1987, cited in Maruna, 2011) argued there is a difference between reform and rehabilitation. Reform requires a change in character; rehabilitation requires a restoration of one's reputation and citizenship status (see also Raynor & Robinson, 2005). This type of rehabilitation, known as legal or judicial rehabilitation, calls for an undoing of the collateral consequences of a conviction, such as eliminating the stigma, returning legal rights (e.g., right to vote), and restricting computer records (Maruna, 2011). Echoing Cesare Becarria's notion of the "requalification of citizens" (McNeill, 2012), some scholars argue legal rehabilitation is an important step in reintegrating returning individuals and could potentially reduce recidivism (Uggen & Manza, 2006; Maruna, 2011). Maruna (2011) also argues that rehabilitation without a restoration of rights is not rehabilitation at all and that such restoration should be swift and public. As he states (2011, p. 99), "If reintegration is to be meaningful (and effective in removing stigma) it presumably requires comparable levels of symbolism and ritual as punishment itself."

For others, rehabilitation is an ongoing effort that may be achieved in numerous ways. This view of rehabilitation, called generic rehabilitation in this piece, comes from non-criminological fields such as psychological and physical therapies and usually encompasses four principles: 1) it is a process; 2) it is viewed as a change for the better; 3) it implies a return to a former state (e.g., a mobile state after an accident; in this case, a return to the community); and 4) it implies the intervention of some other party (Raynor & Robinson, 2005). For criminological purposes, the process of rehabilitation may result in "the restoration of a former state . . . [or] the acquisition of skills, and the establishment of rank, rights and responsibilities previously denied" (Lewis, 2005, p. 123). Even for those who may not seek "official" forms of intervention (e.g., therapists, support groups, drug rehabilitation programs, education or job skills classes, or parole agents), some assistance exists through the support of friends, family, and community members (Maruna, Immarigeon, & LeBel, 2004).

While most theories of rehabilitation focus on the individual, social rehabilitation takes into account the social context in which offenders are returning. Social rehabilitation is "a process by which the offender takes his or her place in society" (Robinson & Crow, 2009, p. 124). Echoing the radical critique of the rehabilitative ideal, social rehabilitation calls for addressing needs such as housing and employment so returning citizens are able to reenter society and addressing the needs of the community to which offenders are returning so they may remain in the community. It also requires (re-)establishing social relationships (McNeill, 2012). Achieving social rehabilitation requires changes to the social structure and implementation of new social policies.

These theories of rehabilitation are not necessarily mutually exclusive. Rehabilitation could be both a process and an end goal, and the goals may include an elimination of criminal behavior and a restoration of legal rights (i.e., reform and rehabilitation; Maruna, 2011). What is unknown is whether the offender is a passive recipient of rehabilitation (Rotman, 1986) or an active participant (Maruna, Immarigeon, & LeBel, 2004). As argued throughout the book, rehabilitation as a legislative goal seems to be a process that requires correctional (change for the better) and legal (return to former state) rehabilitation to be successful. What this process looks like, and the role the state plays in the process, varies over time.

Parole as a Case Study for Rehabilitation

In many ways, this book is a history of parole in California and studies its creation and evolution through the centuries. The pieces of legislation that focus on California's correctional system broadly were analyzed with an eye towards understanding how the larger changes impact the parole process. As Jonathan Simon's (1993) *Poor Discipline* shows, studying parole is a useful means of studying larger changes within corrections. Simon focuses on the ways in which changing political and economic structures impacted the practices of parole. In turn, these changes give insight to the ways punishment and correctional systems change over time. In this book, the question becomes, how can tracing the history of parole help us understand the meaning of rehabilitation?

Parole—particularly in California—can provide unique insight into the meaning of rehabilitation specifically because of its role within corrections. As an arm of the correctional system, parole is intended to provide assistance to returning individuals as they transition to the community and provide a means of early detection and sanction of potentially deviant behavior (Piehl & LoBuglio, 2005). Thus, parole functions as a state-mandated reentry program that combines the goals of rehabilitation, social reintegration, and recidivism reduction through surveillance. At times, these goals are at odds with each other and the on-the-ground practice of parole often depended on which goal took priority (Berecochea, 1982; Messinger, Berecochea, Raums, & Berk 1985; Simon, 1993; Petersilia, 2003).

The parole system exists within, and its goals are dependent upon, the larger context of the correctional system. While the correctional system includes both the prison and parole systems, these two systems are loosely coupled in that they are responsive to each other but maintain separate identities and some relative autonomy (Hagan, Hewitt, & Alwin, 1979). This coupling plays a key role in the day-to-day activities of parole. While the history of parole is about maintaining public safety through ensuring rehabilitation, how parole accomplishes this goal is linked to the correctional system as a whole but not necessarily the prison system. The failures and successes of parole say very little about the failures and successes of prisons and vice versa. The role of parole administrators and parole agents are largely independent of prison administrators. Thus, while changes in the correctional system—and correctional philosophy specifically—impact both prisons and parole, it does so in different ways.

As the correctional philosophy shifts, so does the role of rehabilitation. For parole, the shift may not have led to the elimination of rehabilitation, as it seems to have within prisons. As Lynch (1998; 2000) found, parole agents want to focus on rehabilitation even at times when the official rhetoric does not support it. Studies on the effectiveness of parole during the new penology also focus on parole's rationale as a rehabilitative program (e.g., Jackson, 1983). The rise of risk assessment tools also has a distinctly rehabilitative tone as they are used to determine the programs and services deemed necessary to ensure parolees stay out of prison.

Thus, a study of the history of parole in California is, in many ways, a study of rehabilitation in California corrections. Parole's consistent focus on service and programming offers a unique lens by which to understand what rehabilitation means within correctional structures. In order to understand why parole focuses on services and programming, it is necessary to understand how it maintains its role within the larger correctional structure. As argued throughout the book, the parole system frames itself as a rehabilitative tool within an ever-changing correctional landscape. How it maintains that frame requires understanding rehabilitation within correctional structures as a whole. In turn, studying the relationship between parole and rehabilitation also highlights how and to what extent the shifts in rehabilitation within the correctional system impacts the practices of parole.

A Note on Methods

As the parole system is embedded within the larger correctional system and governed by legislative directives, data were selected from both legislative files that govern the larger correctional system and parole-related files that provide the policies and procedures of the parole system specifically. Archival files offer a uniquely advantageous method of analyzing law and legal institutions, as "files capture . . . all the life, the struggle, and speeches that surround decisions" (Vismann, 2008/2000, p. 10). Files illuminate the story behind the laws passed and the impact of the law. A study of the files also provides insight into what was changed over multiple iterations and contested points within the arguments also become part of the story (Riles, 2006). These files were collected from the T. H. Pendergast Parole Museum in Diamond Bar and the California State Archives in Sacramento.

To understand larger organizational changes and the role of rehabilitation within those changes, analysis focused on six laws that highlight key moments in the story of rehabilitation in California corrections: 1) 1943 Certificate of Rehabilitation (SB 904); 2) 1976 Uniform Sentencing Law (SB 42); 3) 1978 Parole expansion bill (SB 1057); 4) 2005 Legislative Amendment's to the Governor's Reorganization Plan for the Department of Corrections (SB 737); 5) 2009 Non-Revocable Parole (SB X3 18); and 6) 2011 Public Safety Realignment (AB 109 and AB 117). The 1943 law was passed not only at a point when rehabilitation was the driving force of corrections, but also at a point when the country was embroiled in an economic depression and war. The 1976 bill stated that the "purpose of prisons is to punish" and effectively eliminated rehabilitation as a purpose of the correctional system as a whole. The 1978 bill sought to address perceived flaws established in the Uniform Sentencing Law and was introduced by the parole agent's professional organization to bolster and, arguably, preserve the parole system. The 2005 bill was designed to be the first step in reforming the correctional system so as to reinstate rehabilitation as a major focus of the system. Finally, the 2009 and 2011 bills brought dramatic changes to California's parole and correctional systems. The 2009 bill changed how and to whom the parole system applied. The 2011 bill changed how individuals were sentenced and released. Both of these bills changed who partook in various aspects of the rehabilitation process, potentially changing or limiting the process for thousands of California's offenders. Files relating to these six statutes were analyzed to understand how these laws came about and the potential impact of the legislative changes created by these statutes.

To understand the impact of correctional changes on the parole system, analysis focused on five main parole-related document types: 1) parole models; 2) parole agent manuals; 3) parolee handbooks; 4) internal memos; and 5) reports from various paroling authorities (see Table 1.1 for a timeline of paroling authorities). These documents represent all three levels and subjects of the parole process: administrators, parole agents, and parolees. Each of these documents, in some way, constitutes and is constituted by the work of parole and encompasses the purpose of parole. The parole models are developed on the administrative level as a way to lay out what they would like parole to be and how to accomplish that goal. It is supposed to act as a frame for the work of parole that can be adjusted as necessary. The parole agent manuals inform the agents of the policies and procedures that are to inform their daily work lives and inform how they do their job. They are the documents that tell parole agents what to do, or not do, in various situations. The parolee handbooks are created for the parolees and include information on what they should do to be "successful." Internal memos provided agents and administrators with new policies or clarification on existing policies. Finally, reports from the various paroling authorities provide a rather

Table 1.1 California Paroling Authorities

Years	*Board*	*Notes*
1893–1930	State Board of Prison Directors	Parole responsibilities were added to the board's existing role
1930–1944	Board of Prison Terms and Parole	Took over paroling responsibilities from the State Board of Prison Directors
1944–1977	Adult Authority	Created under the 1944 Prison Reorganization Act
	Women's Board of Prison Terms and Parole	Responsible specifically for female prisoners and parolees
1977–2005	Parole and Community Services Division	Created under SB 42; merged responsibility for male and female parolees
2005–present	Division of Adult Parole Operations	Created under SB 737

unique view of the parole system. They are often used to report on the progress made with regards to changes within the parole system, as well as provide the frame by which the legislature should view the (necessity of) the parole system.

Unfortunately, not all of the desired files were located. As Vismann (p. xiv) reminds us, "files themselves become an object of legal regulation." In this case, part of the regulation includes at what point certain files are added to the state archives. Specifically, California State Archives have a limited number of files for legislation passed before 1945. As a result, files on two key pieces of legislation (1917 Indeterminate Sentencing Bill; 1944 Prison Reorganization Act) were unable to be located. In these cases, archival documents that mentioned these two laws and secondary sources provided information on these bills. Additionally, files following the 2005 reorganization are limited. Many aspects of legislative files do not become archived until after the authors of the bill and governor under which the bill passed have left office. While many files are now available following the departure of Governor Schwarzenegger, some files are incomplete and many of the files of laws passed under Governor Brown are not available. The depth by which I am able to analyze the correctional system before the mid-1940s and after 2005 is limited. Documents located at the T.H. Pendergast Museum were donated by former parole agents or acquired from the California State Archives. As the museum was not established until 2003, most of the donated files are from the mid-1900s forward and the acquired files suffer the same limitations as files from the state archive.

The limited files from both archives made it difficult to find files relating to female parolees. As noted in Table 1.1, two separate boards once supervised female and male parolees. Files from the Women's Board of Prison Terms and Parole are extremely limited; it is unclear if the documents describing the parole practices and procedures of men also describe those of women. Even after the two boards were combined back into one, the documents are usually gender neutral, making it difficult to know whether men and women were treated equally in practice. Sadly, this means the story of parole in California is mostly the story of male parolees.

Furthermore, parole-related documents published and distributed after the reorganization have not been placed in the archives and only a few documents were available from other sources, limiting the ability to discern how the reorganization impacted the way policies and procedures were officially expressed to parole agents after 2005. To fill in this gap, semi-structured interviews were conducted with parole agents throughout Southern California from December 2009 to June 2010 to gain a better understanding of the impact of legislative changes on current parole practices. Interviewees were identified through snowball sampling, which began with two agents known to the author who then recommended other agents to be interviewed, and so on. Approximately 30 interviewees were identified in this way, but many potential interviewees (including two individuals in an administrative position) did not respond to requests or declined to participate.

Three women and eight men were interviewed for a total of 11 interviewees. The interviewees' time working in parole ranged from 2–30 years, with the majority working 20 years or fewer. The parole agents worked either in Region III, which covers most of Los Angeles County, and Region IV, which covers parts of Los Angeles, Orange, Riverside, and San Diego Counties. The agents from Region IV were concentrated in Orange County and a small part of Los Angeles County. Unfortunately, no interviews were conducted with agents from Riverside or San Diego Counties. At the time of the interviews, seven interviewees were parole agents, one was a unit supervisor, and three were retired. The eight agents employed were based in three offices and the three retired agents worked in multiple offices across both regions.[2] The parole agents were able to discuss how the reorganization impacted their day-to-day activities and impacted the overall culture of parole in a way that cannot be conveyed through the official rhetoric of the parole-related documents. They also provided valuable insight into the current meaning of rehabilitation and how agents interpret and implement the goal of rehabilitation.

The snowball sampling method and small sample size, however, are the biggest weakness of the interviews, as it is difficult to discern how representative the interviewees are to the greater agent population. The snowball method also did not lead to potential interviewees in northern California, so it is not known if there are differences across geographic regions. Furthermore, it is unknown whether the views represented by those interviewed were the same as or substantially different from those who did not respond to requests.

Outline of this Book

This book offers an historical story of parole and rehabilitation within California corrections. The story begins in Chapter 1 with the origins of parole. This chapter discusses the creation of parole in California and the growth of its bureaucracy up to the end of the 1930s. The remaining chapters are organized chronologically and thematically. The first half of each chapter analyzes key legislative statutes that signal a break from the past and how those laws changed California's correctional system. The second half of each chapter analyzes the meaning of rehabilitation as expressed in those legislative changes and parole-related policy documents that followed these changes. Within this section, each chapter traces various aspects of the rehabilitative process and how they changed over time.

Chapter 2 begins with the 1940s for several reasons. First, it was not until the 1940s that the parole bureaucracy as we know it today was fully in place and was capable of surveilling and assisting returning individuals on a regular basis. Second, the 1940s saw a major shift in the role of rehabilitation within the correctional system. While the Indeterminate Sentencing Law implemented release based on rehabilitative progress, the 1943 Certificate of Rehabilitation provided a means of declaring one was rehabilitated and the 1944 Prison Reorganization Act placed an explicit emphasis on developing a treatment program from the moment one walked into a prison. Combined, these legislations brought rehabilitation to the forefront of the correctional system. Third, the 1940s ushered in a broader view of criminals as sick and in need of treatment that was shared by many working within California corrections. The medical model provided the framework by which the discourse of rehabilitation was able to gain support. It also allowed for the rehabilitative process to be framed as a cure that is prescribed and administered by both in-prison employees and parole agents. Although individuals were supervised while on parole, supervision itself was viewed as a tool for ensuring the appropriate services were offered to the parolee and ensuring the parolee was progressing in the rehabilitative process. The rehabilitation of convicted individuals does not appear to be an end in itself. Rather, it was the means by which to achieve public protection. The use of rehabilitation in this way allows it to be vulnerable to changing legislative goals and allows rehabilitation to be reframed as the goals change. Faith in the medical model did not last long and the criticisms and concerns raised regarding the effectiveness of the rehabilitative process are discussed.

Chapter 3 continues the historical timeline and covers the mid-1970s through the 1990s. This time period was particularly key for California corrections, as the mid-1970s legislatively established a turning away from rehabilitation and altered the rehabilitative process. This legislative declaration was followed shortly thereafter by an expansion of parole supervision and a new parole model that placed a greater emphasis on surveillance and supervision over assistance and social work. This change was supported by a rejection of the view that individuals were sick and needed treatment and that prison and parole was that treatment. The decline in the rehabilitative ideal also paved the way for the increased dependence on determining an individual's risk level and the amount of surveillance necessary to protect the public. Yet, rehabilitation did not disappear. It was reframed as a means of addressing individuals' needs, especially while on parole, thereby reducing their risk to society. Rehabilitation was also reframed so it became a tool for supervision and as a form of surveillance. Some agents continued to argue for support for the social work aspects of their job and academics continued to carry out research to determine which rehabilitation programs worked best for which individuals. The changes in correctional philosophy led to massive overcrowding and rising budgetary costs, both of which set the stage for a reorganization of the correctional system and a (re-)emphasis on rehabilitation.

This reorganization and (re-)emphasis is discussed in Chapter 4, which focuses on 2000 to 2005. Although the reorganization of the Department of Corrections did not occur until 2005, efforts to revamp the parole system were in place as early as 2001. It was not until Governor Schwarzenegger was elected, however, that there was a push to reorganize and reform the corrections system as a whole. While this reorganization passed in 2005, multiple concerns were raised as to the ability of the reorganization to effect actual reform. Although the rehabilitative process still exists, it occurs in an altered manner. Many of the parole agents interviewed raised questions regarding the ability of the parole system to rehabilitate anyone and at least one agent questioned whether everyone was in need of being rehabilitated or if they needed something else. The relationship between rehabilitation and supervision was also altered. Now, supervision was a tool of rehabilitation and rehabilitation was a tool of supervision, forming a feedback loop. In this way, supervision and rehabilitation are not just "braided," but also mutually constituted.

Chapter 5 focuses on polices passed to support the legislative goal of rehabilitation. While the reorganization was to lay the groundwork for change, prison overcrowding hampered rehabilitative efforts. Years of lawsuits also brought the prison system under federal oversight. Both the 2009 corrections bill and the 2011 Public Safety Realignment were attempts at addressing California's massive prison overcrowding and bring the state in line with court-ordered mandates. Both laws altered who was under state jurisdiction—though in different ways—and thus eligible for the state's version of the rehabilitative process. Who had access to the parole component of the process changed in 2009 with the implementation of Non-Revocable Parole while the 2011 Realignment changed who had access to both prisons and parole. These changes suggest the correctional system may not be the only avenue for achieving rehabilitation and that some individuals may not need to participate in the process at all.

The final chapter is a conclusion, of sorts. The beginning serves as a way to tie the history of rehabilitation together; discuss the differences, similarities, and connections across the four time periods; and explore the impact these changes have on parole. The chapter ends with a discussion of what rehabilitation means within California corrections and implications of this meaning for offender rehabilitation broadly. In discussing the story of rehabilitation in California, the conclusion highlights the need to reevaluate the correctional structures as they exist and the lack of social structures in place if the goal of rehabilitation is truly desired.

Notes

1 For the full text, visit www.govtrack.us/congress/bills/110/hr1593/text.
2 While quotes throughout the book are taken word-for-word from the transcripts, ellipses are used to indicate when portions of a quote were deleted for brevity. Names of interviewees were changed to ensure confidentiality.

Chapter 1

Building a Parole Bureaucracy

Inception to 1930s

[P]ractical, everyday experience teaches policemen that when these honor men are released and are not properly supervised, many relapse and are soon picked up for other serious crimes.

—August Vollmer, first police chief for Berkeley, CA, 1923

The term "parole" often elicits images of a prisoner making his case for early release before a panel of individuals. This view of parole is a relatively new concept. Although inmates were chosen for early release from the inception of the parole system, it was not until the 1930s that a board was established specifically to review and determine an inmate's eligibility for early release. Rather, parole in California began as a way of addressing prison overcrowding and inconsistent sentences.

Parole in California was first implemented in 1893 (Berecochea, 1982). Prior to this, prisoners left confinement by escaping, upon completion of their sentence, or by executive clemency and pardons. Sentence lengths for similar crimes varied widely and executive clemency was the only way to address "the excessive sentences of most state prisoners" (Messinger, et al., 1985, p. 73; Berecochea, 1982). The time spent determining who should be released combined with public backlash over the number released prevented the governor and the directors of the California State Prison from releasing many people (Berecochea, 1982). Parole was introduced as the solution with the added benefit of addressing prison overcrowding (Berecochea, 1982; Messinger, et al., 1985; Glaser, 1995).

Eligibility requirements focused on granting parole to those who would not be a danger to the community (Berecochea, 1982). The newly established law prohibited those convicted of first- or second-degree murder and those with a prior prison commitment from being paroled. It required all others to serve at least one year in prison. The pre-release requirements included: 1) good behavior in prison for at least six months; 2) age younger than 40; 3) a legitimate job waiting upon release; and 4) a security deposit to cover the costs of returning to prison should the parolee violate his or her conditions (Berecochea, 1982). After release, the conditions of parole were based on the idea "that a person who would lead a life consistent with these rules would not engage in criminal behavior" (Berecochea, 1982, p. 116).

At this time, the parole system was not equipped to handle the roles of surveillance or rehabilitation. These roles were left to the community, especially local law enforcement (Simon, 1993). In order to maintain tabs on released prisoners, parolees were required to submit monthly reports to state officials signed by his or her employer and local law enforcement (Berecochea, 1982). Because the community at large, along with the parolees, was responsible for ensuring they did not commit additional crimes, the conditions of parole were limited, as "a truly noncriminal parolee would abide by these rules as a matter of course. Failure to abide by them would mark the parolee as being a criminal at heart, as might other signs of criminality" (Berecochea, 1982, p. 118). These requirements were likely in place to reassure the public that the board was not releasing dangerous individuals; they also hint at the possibility of parole as a tool for assisting individuals in maintaining legal compliance and moving towards a life where compliance is not simply a means of avoiding prison.

Over a decade after the inception of parole, California saw a shift in the purpose of parole (Berecochea, 1982; Messinger, et al., 1985; Simon, 1993). The first sign of a shift was the establishment of a parole bureaucracy designed to control parolees and provide services (Messinger, et al., 1985). The bureaucracy was established in 1908 with the introduction of the first parole officer, who was located in San Francisco (Berecochea, 1982; Messinger, et al., 1985). In 1909, the State Board of Prison Directors developed the first *Rules and Regulations for the Paroling of Prisoners* (State Board of Prison Directors, 1909). This document described the process by which wardens were to determine who should and should not be paroled. The board chose individuals based on who they "saw as being good citizens who had done wrong but who were to be trusted" (Berecochea, 1982, p. 116) and distinguished "between those convicts who were criminals at heart and those who were not" (Berecochea, 1982, p. 69). Wardens also looked at prison behavior, educational and vocational programs, and patterns prior to conviction (State Board of Prison Directors, 1909). These considerations highlight the first paradigm of parole as described by Edward Whyte, the first parole officer (Dill, 1967). He argued release on to parole was a humanitarian effort that allowed men who committed crimes a chance at regaining self-respect and becoming useful members of society. It would also save the state money through reduced prison costs and raise money through taxes paid by parolees (Dill, 1967).

Once released, parolees were required to submit monthly reports to the parole agent in San Francisco and to a local law enforcement officer as often as the release board required (State Board of Prison Directors, 1909). In 1912, the parole bureaucracy expanded with a second parole officer based in Los Angeles. As there were only two officers for the entire state, it was not possible for them to provide direct monitoring and supervision of parolees. Early parole in California was a system of suretyship, where behavior was maintained through community controls and a desire to meet the expectations of one's community (Simon, 1993). The agents were mostly "paper pushers" (Berecochea, 1982; Messinger, et al., 1985). It was up to the individual to lead a law-abiding life and the community monitored conditions of release.

In 1917, California implemented the Indeterminate Sentencing Law. Under this law, the purpose of correctional custody was rehabilitation and the power to determine sentences was moved to the parole board. The law was designed to determine who should be paroled based upon expert determination that one was rehabilitated. The law followed three basic ideas: 1) individualized responses to the criminal; 2) length of custody responsive to the success of custodial treatment; and 3) supervised release as essential for both public protection and rehabilitation (Simon, 1993). This was the first time rehabilitation officially became a part of the correctional philosophy.

In 1922, Whyte (cited in Dill, 1967) described a new rationale for the parole system. Release onto parole, with its requirement of employment and supervision, was viewed as improving the chances an individual would do well once released from prison. As Dill (1967, p. 13) noted, in his *History of the Parole System in California*, "For the first time, parole begins to be justified as a method of protecting community interests, not merely as a method of reducing public expenditures on prison maintenance." There were concerns, however, that the existing structures were insufficient to meet this new goal. August Vollmer, the first police chief of Berkeley, argued, "practical, everyday experience teaches policemen that when these honor men [paroled and probationed individuals] are released and are not properly supervised, many relapse and are soon picked up for other serious crimes" (Vollmer, 1923, p. 11). Vollmer argued supervision should be a key component of parole (and probation). He also suggested the police were not equipped to properly supervise these individuals and that more help was needed.

The parole department, however, had not expanded much beyond two parole agents and continued to rely on community members to supervise and monitor the behavior of released individuals. The only mandate was employment. The regimented and disciplined nature of industrial employment was believed to be the best way to reintegrate and normalize released individuals, not only because those who worked were considered "normal," but also because work was punitive and provided a strong means of social control (Simon, 1993). A reformed parolee would be able to get and maintain a job; a non-reformed parolee would not. Thus, there still was not a need for direct supervision.

While the Indeterminate Sentencing Law placed rehabilitation as the purpose of correctional custody, there was some concern over the correctional system's ability to achieve this rehabilitation. In *Prison and the Social Sciences*, a seven-page document that discussed the role the social sciences played in addressing crime and criminal behavior, one unknown author (1924, p. 6) wrote, "Rehabilitation of a family or individual is attended to with much danger, and care must be exercised lest through unscientific methods we reap a harvest of degenerates of the Jukes and Kellikak [sic] type."[1] While those on parole were not deemed criminal at heart (unlike the Jukes and Kallikaks), there was a fear that improper "treatment" would push those in prison towards further criminal behavior. The same author (1924, p. 7), however, also indicated, "[s]cientists are better informed regarding this difficult question, and are rapidly improving their technique to segregate the reclaimable and worth-while from the socially unfit." This suggested faith in the ability to scientifically understand and implement the path to rehabilitation was growing.

In 1931, the parole bureaucracy expanded to include the newly created Board of Prison Terms and Parole, which took over the fixing of prison terms and the granting/suspending of parole—powers previously held by the State Board of Prison Directors. By this time, the parole staff had expanded to 14 agents, but there was simply no way for them to directly supervise all of the paroled men. As such, the Board of Prison Terms and Parole (1933, p. 9) recommended an increase in the number of supervising agents "to permit a closer check of conditions . . . and to gain a more intimate knowledge of his daily life after his release." This recommendation signaled the expansion of supervision over parolees.

The Board of Prison Terms and Parole (1933, p. 10) further solidified supervision as part of the second rationale of parole, stating:

> Whatever the motives may have been for the original establishment of the parole system, this Board considers the primary purpose of parole to be an attempt to give an added degree of protection to society. Parole extends the supervision and control exercised over a person to that most trying period immediately following release from a penal institution.

The purpose of parole was no longer to alleviate criticisms of the clemency process or save the state money (at least not officially). It was now a means to supervise released individuals as they transitioned into life outside of the prison walls and protect the public. It was unclear precisely how parole agents supervised or controlled parolees, as the monthly reports submitted by parolees were the only consistent form of contact with a parole agent.

As the correctional system developed and expanded, faith in using the system as a rehabilitative tool also developed. During the 1930s, the belief was growing that a prisoner was "one whom society has been unable to control" and, while prisons were not the most appropriate location for rehabilitation, "the prison and its officials must undertake the job of rehabilitation and reformation" (Board of Prison Terms and Parole, 1933, p. 11). The State Board of Prison Directors (1936, p. 13) reported:

> As we consider the proper function of a prison, we are increasingly of the opinion that, where possible, rehabilitation of prisoners as a basis for restoration to useful citizenship is more effective for the inmate and more important to society than the concept of punishment.

The board argued the use of employment within prisons was the most important factor in rehabilitating inmates and that little has been done to provide such employment opportunities. The board also noted the majority of inmates would eventually be released and it was necessary to ensure they would not commit new crimes. Although the board does not use the term risk, the adoption of rehabilitation also took a distinctly risk management tone as the purpose of rehabilitation was to protect the public by "minimizing the likelihood of some new crime being committed" (State Board of Prison Directors, 1936, p. 13). To help reduce this risk, California prisons developed treatment programs that segregated and classified individuals based on individual situations; a plan was then developed based on this classification. For the most part, in-prison employment was viewed as the key to rehabilitation and this belief carried into the parole system (State Board of Prison Directors, 1936).

The parole system was also showing more signs of embracing rehabilitation and providing assistance to those leaving prisons. There was a growing recognition that release from prison into the community "is always a hard one" as it "is almost impossible to take up life where [the ex-prisoner] had left off and the job of gathering up loose ends and starting anew is a difficult and hazardous one" (Board of Prison Terms and Parole, 1933, p. 10) and that the "road to rehabilitation is fraught with many handicaps" (State Board of Prison Directors, 1936, p. 109). In response, more parole offices were created and the number of parole agents increased. In 1936, California developed local field staff, centered in San Francisco and Los Angeles, who had the capacity to meet with and directly supervise parolees (Simon, 1993). Although some counties still relied on local sheriffs to monitor the employment of parolees (State Board of Prison Directors, 1936), it was at this point the role of supervision and service began to shift from the communities to the paroling authority (Simon, 1993). A program that started as an alternative to executive clemency and means of maintaining the size of prisons "gradually developed a distinctively rehabilitative rationale" (Bottomley, 1990, p. 325) with the ability to provide surveillance and assistance (Messinger, et al., 1985; Bottomley, 1990). The parole agents were not directly responsible for the rehabilitation of a parolee, but they were to provide all opportunities for rehabilitation to the parolee and be available to him and his family should they desire advice or assistance (Board of Prison Terms and Paroles, 1933).

For all of the changes made to the parole system, the main focus remained public safety and it was viewed as a system separate from prisons. It was not until the 1940s and the development of the medical model, however, that the prisons and parole system combined to develop a continuum specifically designed to carry out the rehabilitative process. The next chapter discusses this move towards a more rehabilitative system, the growth of the relationship between the prisons and parole systems, and how rehabilitation was defined under this system.

Note

1 The Jukes and Kallikaks (misspelled in the quote) were pseudonyms for two families that became poster families for the eugenics movement of the late nineteenth and early twentieth centuries. The Jukes were painted as a family in which criminality was inherited and the Kallikaks were painted as a family in which mental retardation was inherited. For more information on the Jukes, see Dugdale, 1877. For more information on the Kallikaks, see Goddard, 1912.

Chapter 2

The Rise of the Rehabilitative Ideal

1940s to Mid-1970s

It would be heartening and perhaps effective, if the parolee could view his experience and relationships as if the paroling agency were a group of medical specialists who . . . had determined that the acute stage of infection was past, that institutional care was no longer needed and the services of the community doctor would now suffice.

~Ervis Lester, member of the Adult Authority, 1952

The early 1900s were an interesting time for the parole system, as the economic downfall of the 1930s created a logistical nightmare for the releasing authority. From its inception, California's parole system relied on employment as key to social normalization (Simon, 1993). As such, parolees were required to obtain employment prior to release, report to the place of employment immediately upon release, and obtain verification from the employer once a month (Berecochea, 1982). The Great Depression, however, prohibited many parolees from obtaining jobs. Parolees approved for release were often held in prison for failing to meet all of the conditions necessary for release. The parole system was no longer an efficient means of reducing overcrowded prisons, addressing inconsistent prison sentences, or providing an alternative to the pardon process. This, in turn, meant the parole system lacked a purpose.

Changes in the post-WWII era also changed correctional systems (Garland, 1985). The development of the field of criminology came with new theories of criminal behavior that centered on the idea of criminals as socially maladapted and therefore capable of being cured. The rise of social work and social security implemented systems in which assistance was provided by the state. These larger changes created an atmosphere in which government agencies were deemed responsible for criminal offenders, thus creating a new correctional philosophy—known as penal welfarism (Garland, 1985). Penal welfarism argued for a system of penality based on the ideas that "social reform together with affluence would eventually reduce the frequency of crime" and that the "state is responsible for the care of offenders as well as their punishment and control" (Garland, 2001, p. 38–39).

The rise of penal welfarism created an opening for California's parole system. Those leading the parole bureaucracy began arguing that, given the government's role in assisting offenders, parole was an integral aspect of the criminal justice system. In its annual report to the governor, the Board of Prison Terms and Paroles (citing President Roosevelt, 1941, p. 4) argued that because of the difficulties individuals faced upon release—such as finding housing, reconnecting with family and friends—parole was "the most promising method of terminating a prison sentence." The Board of Prison Terms and Paroles (1941, p. 11) also argued releasing individuals onto parole, where they must be employed and supervised and may be "returned to prison for unsatisfactory conduct without the necessity of a new conviction," was far better for public protection than release without parole supervision. As such, the Board of Prison Terms and Paroles (1941) decided that no one should be released from prison *except* on parole. While release in the early decades of the parole system was reserved for those already deemed to be rehabilitated, "[t]his Board is therefore of the opinion that while prison life constitutes a period of reclamation, parole itself completes the actual rehabilitation of an institutional case" (Board of Prison Terms and Parole, 1943, p. 12). This reversal allowed administrators to frame parole as a separate and necessary component of rehabilitation and corrections.

Supervision was viewed as the essence of parole (Parole Officer's Report, included in Board of Prison Terms and Paroles, 1941) and necessary to rehabilitate offenders. Local law enforcement and community members were not enough. Six additional local parole offices were established in January 1941, bringing the total of local offices to 10.[1] The Parole Officer's Report stated the decentralization of supervision enabled supervising officers to become better acquainted with community resources and services, thus expanding services provided to parolees. Supervision was not necessarily viewed as a means of watching a parolee's movements, but as a way of guiding parolees towards various services and ensuring they took advantage of the services. In this way, supervision became the means by which parole ensured rehabilitation.

WWII and Parole

For prisoners waiting to be released on to parole who could not obtain a job, the beginning of the 1940s brought an unexpected change. Because of the United States' role in developing and supplying defense equipment to the Allied Forces at the beginning of World War II, war-related industries were booming and required a steady increase in employment. Many firms were requesting "the parole of skilled mechanics and craftsmen among the prisoners" (Board of Prison Terms and Paroles, 1941, p. 11). In response, the board adjusted sentences and parole release dates of some inmates—based on their record, prison conduct, and opportunity for rehabilitation—so they could work in the national defense industries.

After the United States entered World War II, the Board of Prison Terms and Parole (1943) argued the paroling of inmates to the Armed Forces and war-related industries would be profitable to both the released individual and the government. The number of individuals held back from release because of a lack of employment virtually disappeared. Placement in defense jobs and on farms was to be the first type of employment considered for parolees. For many parolees the type of crime for which they were convicted barred them from enlisting in the armed forces or getting employment in war-related industries. The only option for these individuals was a full pardon. There was some concern, however, that the process took too long. There was also criticism the process was being mired by political considerations (Unknown, 1943, February 16; Warren, 1943, March 12; Wood, 1943, January 6). Woodward (1943, January 4, p. 1), then Judge for the San Joaquin County Superior Court, argued:

> Pardon me if I show a lack of judicial restraint in expressing a gratuitous opinion. One cannot help but suspect that this board is tinged with some sort of class prejudice or leftist ideology. It seems that if an applicant for a pardon can get the backing of certain labor leaders; or, if he is so fortunate as to belong to the Communist party, or if he is an exponent of what is sometimes called the new liberalism—if he falls into any of these categories it is not difficult to anticipate what the advisory Pardon Board will do.

Wood (1943, January 6) also noted that whether one chooses to apply for a pardon was often determined by access to funds and the right people.

In response to these concerns, legislators created a means by which returning citizens could be declared "rehabilitated" without needing a formal pardon. In 1943, the California State Legislature passed SB 904, which created the Certificate of Rehabilitation.[2] This certificate was to serve as "a procedure for the restoration of rights and the application for a pardon" (Reed, n.d., p. 1). In order to apply for a Certificate of Rehabilitation, a convicted individual must "live an honest and upright life, conduct himself with sobriety and industry, exhibit good moral character, and conform to obey the law during the period of rehabilitation" (State of California Office of Legislative Counsel, 1943, May 4). A judicial council then reviewed the application. If the application was denied, often for "violation of law," the judicial council may set a new period of rehabilitation and the case would be reviewed again at that time. If the application was approved, the certificate provided a formal means of proving that one had completed the rehabilitative process and restored most legal rights to the offender.[3]

The application process was also designed to eliminate disparities of the pardon process. First, it prohibited "the soliciting, collection and payment of any fees whatever in connection with the procedure" (Unknown, 1942, p. 1) and made such solicitation a misdemeanor (State of California Office of Legislative Counsel, 1943).[4] Second, approval of a certificate resulted in an automatic recommendation for a full pardon and the governor was able to approve the pardon solely on the approval of the certificate. In this way, convicted individuals without the means of hiring assistance were arguably able to apply for a full pardon. Thus, the majority of prisoners approved for parole were able to obtain employment and be released from prison. Perhaps more importantly, all parolees now had the opportunity to prove their rehabilitation.

The creation of the Certificate of Rehabilitation seems to be the first step in a larger emphasis on rehabilitation. In 1944, the state legislature reorganized the correctional system in California. This reorganization "recognized the need for rehabilitative treatment of offenders committed to the prisons of California" (Adult Authority, 1972, p. 4) and developed the Department of Corrections, Board of Corrections, Adult Authority, and Women's Board of Prison Terms and Paroles. The Adult Authority, which replaced the Board of Prison Terms and Paroles, was now responsible for the setting of terms and release of male inmates on to parole.[5] The reorganization legislation developed four main purposes of the correctional system (Adult Authority, 1972, p. 4):

1. A comprehensive study of [sentenced men's] problems.
2. A broad program of treatment.
3. Release to parole if and when they [sentenced men] were deemed ready.
4. Parole supervision aimed at completing their rehabilitation and protecting society.

Combined, these goals were designed to create a continuum of treatment and services for convicted felons from the time they entered prisons until they were discharged from parole (Adult Authority, 1972). At least in writing, the 1944 reorganization affirmatively linked release onto parole as a time where individuals could complete the rehabilitation they began in prison.

Following the reorganization, the Adult Authority (1945) developed a new guiding document entitled, *Philosophy, Principles, and Programs of the California Adult Authority*. Within the document, the Adult Authority

(1945, p. 2) stated, "protection of society is the aim and purpose of the penal system. It does not believe that punishment alone is truly protective. Only when prisoners are rehabilitated as well as punished, does the penal system solve its problem." While rehabilitation was the rationale behind the prison and parole systems, it was not viewed as an end for its own sake. Rather, rehabilitation was the best mechanism by which to achieve the goal of public protection.

In order to maintain public protection, parole was seen as the only safe way to release prisoners. Just as the Board of Prison Terms and Paroles found supervision to be the essence of parole, so too did the newly established Adult Authority. Then Attorney General Earl Warren (quoted in Drucker, Gordon, & Bixby, 1944, p. 8, underline in original) argued, "Supervision *is* parole." Yet, the Adult Authority also acknowledged that parole agents were primarily social workers, not peace officers (Gordon, 1946) and that, while legislation authorized parole officers to act as peace officers, they should not "broaden their range of activities to include routine police work" done by other state apparati (Adult Authority, 1947, p. 33). It is not clear the precise limits such a view placed on agents, but it seems to imply that agents were not to engage in arrests of parolees or investigations of potential criminal acts as parole agents do today. Furthermore, supervision was an aspect of parole service (Drucker, Gordon, & Bixby, 1944), not a function separate from the provision of services. Supervision was used not only to ensure parolees followed their conditions of parole and did not commit new crimes, but was also the means by which the need for certain services was determined. The new paroling authority reiterated and re-emphasized the role of supervision within parole that was originally stated by the 1941 Parole Officer's Report.

The tools of supervision and surveillance were framed as a mechanism to achieve rehabilitation. Rehabilitation itself was framed in such a way as to disguise the punishment inflicted upon parolees. Treatment, supervision, and conditions of parole were all framed as a means of addressing the needs of the parolee, and yet, they were also things that parolees were forced to participate in. Failure to participate in programs or comply with the conditions and surveillance of parole resulted in a return to prison and this threat of return was used to gain compliance. While the various aspects of parole were framed as a way of assisting the parolee, they were also extensions of penal control over the parolees and continued punishment for the criminal conviction.

Parole After WWII

Although the 1940s saw the establishment of a correctional system centered on rehabilitation, it was not until the 1950s and 1960s that the ideal of parole as a tool for rehabilitation took center stage (Simon, 1993).

After World War II, the number of jobs available declined again and employment was no longer a requirement of parole. It was at this point that the "discourses of rehabilitation finally [moved] to the center of parole" and the system began emphasizing treatment, classification, and training (Simon, 1993, p. 66). In order for the discourse of rehabilitation to take hold and be a politically viable argument, the parole system stigmatized the parolee as being different "from the rest of us which provides the possibility for return and normalization" (Simon, 1993, p. 70). Key administrative leaders, including Director of Corrections Richard McGee (1958), began describing parolees as maladjusted and needing readjustment through supervision and guidance of parole agents. These discourses also included describing the parolee as a psychological or emotionally sick person (Lester, 1952) or troubled (Parole and Community Services Division, 1969). This framing of parolees allowed the parole system to embrace a medical discourse emerging nationally. As Simon (1993, p. 65) argues, the emergence of the clinical model seems to fit a natural progression, as the parole system "had been surrounded by a clinical discourse of diagnosis, treatment, and rehabilitation" and embraced the ideas of treatment and rehabilitation from its inception, even when the original practices did not address these ideas.

The clinical discourse framed every aspect of parole. Parole agents were described as local therapists (Lester, 1952) who made diagnoses and reported on the case's prognosis (California State Personnel Board, 1958). The parolee was equated to a patient and the parole agent to the physician, as noted by Ervis Lester (1952, p. 12–13), a member of the Adult Authority:

> It would be heartening and perhaps effective, if the parolee could view his experience and relationships as if the paroling agency were a group of medical specialists who, upon staffing his case, had determined that the acute stage of infection was past, that institutional care was no longer needed and the services of the community doctor would now suffice. The parole agent would become the therapist to prescribe treatment for the period of convalescence. In such a situation appropriate rapport could be established easily. Parole rules, sweetened psychologically by the supervisor, would be resisted as "bad medicine" no more than bitter herbs, sugar-coated by the corner druggist, are resisted by the physically ill.

The imagery of prisons as hospitals and parole as medicine eloquently captures the medical/rehabilitative discourse. The cure for criminal behavior was time in prison followed by the methods of the parole system as applied by the skilled parole agent. A medical framing invokes images of an individual who must take his medicine (conditions of parole) if he wishes to leave the care of the state or risk becoming sick and needing further institutional care (i.e., a return to prison). The hope of achieving this type of buy-in from parolees also indicated a desire for parolees to become willing subjects of the carceral regime and avoid resisting the assistance forced upon them by parole agent.

This reframing of parole and the rehabilitative discourse propelled treatment as the most important function of the parole system, superseding surveillance. Lester (1952) argued the threat of revocation does little to deter parolees from committing violations, but the guidance and support of a parole agent provided parolees with hope that they may live a socially acceptable life. The parole agent's job was described as someone who "[c]ounsels parolees, helps them to understand their problems, and adapt the treatment program to the individual" (California State Personnel Board, 1958, p. 1) and whose resources included a positive client relationship, individual counseling, and a flexible treatment plan (Unknown, 1967).[6]

Parole supervision was akin to the watchful eye of a doctor (Lester, 1952, p. 17–18):

> The surveillance work of a parole agent will be carried out in the same spirit that a physician watches a polio patient make his first attempt to walk alone. The spirit of this watchfulness is marked by a sincere interest in assisting the patient to continue on the road to recovery and certainly not in the finding an excuse to send the victim of this dread disease back to the hospital.

Supervision was the best tool to determine a course of treatment. A return to prison was used only when necessary (presumably only if the parolee was determined to be still too "sick" to be in the community or when the "disease" of criminal behavior returned). Every effort was made to keep a parolee in the community and continuing on the path of treatment and rehabilitation (Unknown, 1976, September).[7] The Adult Authority conducted several studies to determine the best way for the parole system to achieve this rehabilitation. The studies hoped to determine maximum caseloads, parolee-parole agent pairings, and other structural adjustments that would result in the lowest recidivism rates (Glaser, 1995). Research, it was believed, was the key to determining the best structure necessary for achieving the goals of rehabilitation and treatment (McGee, 1958) and determining how to best classify and treat parolees (Unknown, 1967).[8] The Adult Authority also developed the first Parolee Outpatient Clinics (POC), free psychological clinics for parolees run in conjunction with the parole agents, to help address a parolee's mental and emotional needs (Dunbar, 1965). Although the language of risk management had not yet been embraced by California's correctional system, the development of POC seems to be the first sign of managing risks by managing needs (e.g., Hannah-Moffat, 1999).

In the 1960s, the Adult Authority also implemented programs such as halfway homes, work furlough programs, and early discharge for redeemed parolees (Glaser, 1995). Each of these changes was meant to introduce standardization, scientifically sound practices, and drug rehabilitation as critical parts of the parole process (Simon, 1993). The work furlough programs were run by community correctional centers established by the Department of Corrections. These programs provided transitional housing and employment opportunities for inmates who did not have adequate community resources upon release (Unknown, 1963)[9]. The programs were also used "as an alternative to return to the institution" for those having serious problems adjusting in the community rather than being sent back to prison (Unknown, 1970, July 22; Unknown, 1976, September),[10] instilling the notion that rehabilitative programs could be used as a form of punishment (a la Robinson, 2008) even though it was not described as such. The work furlough program's main objective was to improve the chances that one would be successful on parole (Unknown, 1975, January 10).[11] While at least one study showed that the work furlough program increased parole failure, the parole administrators reasoned it was due to some other circumstance and not the fault of the work furlough program (Parole and Community Services Division, 1976, May 11). While the Adult Authority used research to justify its actions, it also remained committed to its own programs as a key component in achieving rehabilitation regardless of what the research showed.

While parole supervision continued to increase its role in the rehabilitation process, belief in the view of prisons as an optimal location to begin rehabilitation began to fade. Procunier (1971) argued the artificiality of prisons made rehabilitation within the walls difficult. This questioning of prisons as a rehabilitative mechanism bolstered the view that parole was necessary to achieve rehabilitation. As the Task Force on Probation and Parole (1972, p. 16) noted, "Most penologists believe that the principal way in which a man learns to live in the community in conformance with society's demands is to be in the community." The Department of Corrections still believed both incarceration and parole must be used to achieve rehabilitation, but parole was becoming equal to, if not more important than, prisons as a rehabilitative tool.

What is Rehabilitation?

California's view of rehabilitation was twofold. First, it viewed rehabilitation as a way of maintaining punishment and control in the community. As Robinson (2008) argues, rehabilitation in the 1950s and 1960s in the United Kingdom and Wales was designed to benefit the lives of returning citizens. California's prison and paroling authorities also framed rehabilitation in this way, but did so to disguise the punishing aspects of the parole system. This was accomplished by framing supervision as a tool of assistance and rehabilitation. In doing so, supervision provided a means by which to detect compliance with the conditions of parole. Failure to follow the conditions of parole or to complete treatment programs, detected through supervision, was grounds for revocation and a return to prison, which enacted greater punishment. When parolees were sent to programs as an alternative to a return to prison, the programs themselves became a tool of punishment for non-compliance. Thus, the two prongs of rehabilitation—supervision and service—both served to extend punishment into the community.

Second, California's reorganization of its correctional system implied rehabilitation was an ongoing effort that could be achieved through in-prison treatment and parole supervision. At this time, California corrections encompassed all four principles of this theory: 1) it was a process; 2) it was viewed as a change for the better; 3) it implied a return to a former state; and 4) it implied the intervention of some other party (Raynor & Robinson, 2005). The notion of reforming the offender and turning him into a socially adjusted person (change for the better) mimicked the goals of a correctional rehabilitation. The idea of completing the process by restoring all of the civil rights lost upon imprisonment and reintegrating back into society (return to former self) mimicked the goals of a legal rehabilitation. California's correctional administrators believed neither of these goals could be achieved without some form of state intervention. Interestingly, the official rhetoric of the rehabilitative process remained the same, even as the practices of parole changed across this period (see Simon, 1993).

The Process

The medical model implied an individual's deficiencies could be improved or even "cured." Individuals under control of the corrections system were viewed as "inadequate human beings, emotionally unstable, morally irresponsible, and socially maladjusted" (McGee, 1958, p. 11; see also Lester, 1952; Unknown, 1957, March 8) and in need of reformation (Drucker, Gordon, & Bixby, 1944). The way to ensure this reformation was to implement a treatment plan specifically designed for the individual that began in prisons and continued through parole.

The total time spent in an institution and on parole was referred to as the "correctional process" or "rehabilitation process." Lester (1952), then member of the Adult Authority, described parole as "the continuation of the training and treatment process started in the institution" and later referred to the "rehabilitation process" in a paper presented at the Annual

Congress of Corrections National Probation and Parole Association. In a letter to the parole board, then-Director of Corrections McGee (1958) also referred to the "correctional process" to describe the control and adjustment of offenders following conviction, a term that was repeated by the Department of Corrections (1964a) in a report on proposed changes to the parole system. This sentiment was further expressed in 1974, when the Inmate Committee for Higher Education (p. 11) argued:

> Implied here is the concept of rehabilitation as a process which is begun in the penal institution and continues upon release. The institutional phase constitutes educating the individual to the personal and social forces which brought him to prison, so that he might better manage these factors upon release. The re-entry phase continues the educational phase adding dimensions of a reality situation in which the individual can begin actual implementation of his newly acquired insights, while involved in a supportive program to which he can turn for support against the pressures of "cultural shock unique to men being released from long periods of cultural isolation."

Lester (1952, p. 2) argued that once an inmate entered prison, the process was "fairly simple. The inmate is a psychological sick person. He is taken to an institution for treatment." This treatment might include prison employment, education, recreation, and other programs (Board of Prison Terms and Parole, 1943) designed to address an individual's perceived deficiencies. As individuals spent time in prison and progressed, they were constantly evaluated and re-evaluated to properly develop a program that addressed their needs (Drucker, Gordon, & Bixby, 1944; Parole Task Force, 1967).

The process was not without challenges. While prison staff were to guide prisoners on their "road to rehabilitation," it was possible inmates did not follow the larger social belief that they were sick and might resist the guidance (Lester, 1952, p. 2):

> Among the obstacles lying in the path of reformation is the attitude of the inmate. He doesn't feel like a patient being treated for emotional illness. He feels like a prisoner being punished because he got caught while others more fortunate are getting by with similar conduct every day. It is only natural that his first reaction would be largely colored by suspicion and distrust. Much resistance must be overcome before he can be oriented to accept incarceration as treatment.

As such, prisoners needed to buy in to the idea of the prison, and the punishment placed upon them, serving as a treatment center. Buying in also meant ignoring the inconsistency with which those who commit crimes are sentenced to treatment in the first place.

There was also acknowledgement that treatment in prison had its limits. As Walker (1962) notes, even if inmates were able to get past their concerns and bought in to the treatment, prison sub-cultures sought to pull individuals away from rehabilitation. Additional concerns included the artificial nature of the prison environment (Procunier, 1971) and the "culture shock" that may occur upon release from a lengthy stay (Inmate Committee for Higher Education, 1974). Thus, the individual should be released at the opportune moment: "When the maximum benefits from institutional therapy have been received [the inmate] is released on parole to convalesce in the community under the care of a local therapist, the parole agent" (Lester, 1952, p. 2). Parole was viewed as the optimal location to complete rehabilitation (Board of Prison Terms and Parole, 1943) and the final step in the correctional process (Lester, 1952). Release on to parole was only granted when inmates showed they were "on the road to recovery" and making progress (Lester, quoted in the *Soledad Star News*, Unknown, 1957, March 8). In order to be released on to parole, inmates must show a response to and significant progress on the institutional treatment program, a change in personal attitude, and a general preparedness to live in the community (Department of Corrections, 1964b), which included having a job and residence lined up (Drucker, Gordon, & Brixby, 1944; Department of Corrections, 1975). A parole board then reviewed each case and decided whether an inmate met these goals.

Once on parole, supervision was aimed at helping parolees complete their rehabilitation and adjust to living in the community (Adult Authority, 1945, February 9; Adult Authority, 1947). Just as in prison, the parole agent must determine a treatment program for the parolee. This treatment plan was supposed to include an analysis of progress made to date, suggestions of activities that would assist with rehabilitation, and possible solutions to domestic problems (Adult Authority, 1947). Also just as in prison, parolees were to be constantly re-evaluated and adjustments were to be made to the treatment plan and conditions of parole as necessary (Adult Authority, 1947).

Parolees were placed on one of three levels of supervision—maximum, normal, and minimum. All parolees began at maximum supervision (Board of Prison Terms and Parole, 1941) and were moved to normal supervision only after they "become sufficiently adjusted and ha[ve] made sufficient progress to justify such a reduction" (Adult Authority, 1947, p. 47). Similar guidelines were used when moving a parolee to minimum supervision. Movement between levels occurred at the discretion of the parole agent. The goal was for supervision to be gradually lessened until the parolee achieved full freedom and discharge (Board of Prison Terms and Parole, 1941).

Transition through the levels of supervision and discharge from parole was not necessarily smooth. Failures occurred and they, especially returns for technical violations, were often viewed as a "successful phase of parole work," as it was an indication the parole system was working and accomplishing its goals of public protection (Department of Corrections, 1964a, p. 89). For some, failures and partial failures—especially as they relate to unsatisfactory conduct with regards to conditions of parole (Board of Prison Terms and Parole, 1943)—were inevitable "due to the personality and character defects of inmates" (Lester, 1952, p. 16). Some of these failures were caused by alcoholism or "a complete lack of understanding of the moral and social concepts of life in a civilized community" (Board of Prison Terms and Parole, 1943, p. 24). When failures occurred, parolees were returned to prison for further treatment (Department of Corrections, 1964a). It was also believed that some parolees may need to be maintained on parole longer than the determined discharge date if the parolee had not made the expected progress (Adult Authority, 1947) and that others should never be released from parole supervision (Board of Prison Terms and Parole, 1943). This raised questions as to how or when an individual was actually released or moved to a lower level of supervision. The requirements for movement and discharge were rather vague and interpretation of the requirements varied from agent to agent. Furthermore, the re-evaluation of the treatment plan could potentially create a situation where the needs or goals of treatment were never fully met, as completed goals could simply lead to new goals. In this way, the rehabilitative process remained never-ending, particularly while on parole and, to some extent, in prison. It also created a situation where progress could potentially lead to more punishment as the re-evaluation could determine that more progress or a return to prison was necessary, providing justification for keeping the parolee under state control.

Discharge also did not guarantee an end to the rehabilitation process. Parolees were discharged only when they "made a satisfactory response to a definite program, and that further supervision is not necessary for continued progress and complete rehabilitation" (Adult Authority, 1947, p. 65; Department of Corrections, 1964a). Even upon discharge, parolees were not viewed as fully rehabilitated, only that they had progressed enough to now be responsible for their own completion of the process. Ostensibly, the process ended only upon the granting of a Certificate of Rehabilitation, as it "permits the ex-convict who has made good to have an official court finding that he has rehabilitated himself in the satisfaction of society" (Adult Authority, 1947, p. 84).

Change for the Better

One way the process was deemed successful was to determine whether the individual had changed for the better. As one was not expected to leave prison fully rehabilitated, one was not expected to leave prison fully changed. Rather, the inmate needed to show improvement in certain areas while the Adult Authority determined whether someone was suitable for release. Two episodes of a television program that aired parole board hearings (covering a total of four hearings) provide some insight into the process of how suitability is determined (Television Memories, 1957).[12] In each episode, the show takes the viewer inside a prison to watch actual parole hearings. Two hearings were shown in each episode, with each episode focusing on either San Quentin or Folsom prison. During the episode, the viewer watches a conversation between the parole board (composed of three men) and the inmate being considered for parole, as well as the conversation that occurs between parole board members when determining to release or hold the inmate. Though it is difficult to know how representative these four hearings were of all parole hearings, they indicate the hearings covered a variety of topics when interviewing inmates up for parole. Topics included the conviction offense, the inmate's family life, and programs in which he participated while in prison. All four decisions were based on the perceived amount of "progress made." In the two cases that parole was denied, the decision was based solely on the view that not enough progress was made. In the two cases that parole was granted, the decisions were based on specific factors that indicated that progress was made. One gentleman earned parole because "he's beginning to get some insight into his behavior," while the other gentleman earned parole because "[h]e's accepted the program. He's come a long way from the chap he was when he came in" (Television Memories, 1957). The hearings seemed to last for roughly thirty minutes and decisions seemed to be made within a minute or two after the inmate left the room. It is unclear how such short interactions can provide the board members with adequate information to make a decision.

Parole manuals from the 1970s also provide insight into how board members were to determine suitability for release. The suitability criteria included reviewing psychological reports to determine an inmate's past and present mental status (State of California, 1976). Additional evaluation reports required the board members to determine an inmate's "sincerity and motivation for improvement; his understanding of his emotions, drives and feelings; and evidence of his willingness and ability to exercise self control" (Adult Authority, 1972, p. 7). In short, inmates must show evidence that they have changed for the better (State of California, 1976), have a changed attitude, and have new plans for the future (Task Force on Probation and Parole, 1972).

Once on parole, individuals were expected to continue their improvement. If it was true that "the home, school, church, or society in general, have failed to teach these individuals the basic principles of living" and that "the average parole failure is distinguished by a complete lack of understanding of the moral and social concepts of life in a civilized community" (Board of Prison Terms and Parole, 1943, p. 24), then the conditions of parole and assistance by parole agents were supposed to address these issues. Prisons focused on improving the mental abilities and technical skills of individuals; parole supervision ensured the change for the better included the ability to live socially acceptable lives within the community (McGee, 1958).

As the purpose of parole was to ensure public protection through rehabilitation, arguably the most important goal of living a socially acceptable life included the ability to maintain self-control and lead a law-abiding life (Lester, 1952), echoing the theories of correctional rehabilitation (Raynor & Robinson, 2005). While release from prison was also predicated on the reasonable belief that the inmate could lead a crime-free life, parole supervision was in a position to ensure public safety by "preventing, or reducing the likelihood of, further illegal behavior" (Parole Task Force, 1967, p. 7). A successful parolee was defined as one who stayed in the community and was not sent back for a new crime or technical violation (Department of Corrections, 1964a; Task Force on Probation and Parole, 1972). Thus, discharge from parole was permitted only after the parolee was viewed as no longer being a danger to the public and would no longer commit crimes (Adult Authority, 1972; Task Force on Probation and Parole, 1972). This echoes the definition of correctional rehabilitation, which calls for an elimination of criminal behavior and the causes of criminal behavior.

Change for the better also implied having acceptable social habits and living according to social rules (Adult Authority, 1945, February 9; Adult Authority, 1947; Lester, 1952; Adult Authority, 1966, October 31), making good, being thrifty (Board of Prison Terms and Parole, 1943), thinking objectively (Unknown, 1957, March 8), behaving as a good citizen (Adult Authority, 1947), becoming a constructive person (Department of Corrections, 1964a), and adjusting "to the complexities and competition of everyday living" (McGee, 1959, p. 2). Simon (1993) argued that the disciplinary power of industrial labor was essential to normalization in the time period when the parole bureaucracy was still forming and expanding. Official documents from the 1940 to 1960s suggest this faith in employment continued well into the middle of the century. Maintaining employment was considered a main aspect of a socially acceptable life (Board of Prison Terms and Parole, 1941; Board of Prison Terms and Parole, 1943), as it allowed the individual to become self-reliant (Board of Prison Terms and Parole, 1941) and care for one's family (Board of Prison Terms and Parole, 1943; Department of Corrections, 1964b), ultimately becoming "a taxpayer instead of a tax drain" (Department of Corrections, 1964b, p. 9). And yet, the only objective measure of indicating a parolee had achieved a socially acceptable life was whether or not the parolee was re-arrested or re-convicted and there is little to indicate that achieving the other measures of success precluded a continuance of criminal behavior.

Return to Former Self

Another way the process was deemed successful was to determine how well an individual reintegrated back into society as a community member with full civil rights. Although these individuals were once a part of the community, they were supposedly returning as better individuals who were now capable of being good citizens and following social norms. The return as changed individuals would enable parolees to reintegrate into the community without further criminal behavior and with socially accepted behaviors. Successful parolees were ones whose success could not be publicized, "because their success depends upon their status being generally unknown" (Board of Prison Terms and Paroles, 1941, p. 32; see also, Board of Prison Terms, 1943; Procunier, 1971). The return to a former state not only implied returning to the community, but also maintaining that reintegration in such a way that an individual's prior supposed deficiencies were unknown, as they may have been before conviction.

Perhaps the biggest indication of returning to a former self was the restoration of civil rights lost while incarcerated. Unlike the theory of legal rehabilitation (Raynor & Robinson, 2005; Maruna, 2011), for California, a restoration of civil rights did not in itself constitute rehabilitation. Instead, civil rights were gradually restored as one showed signs of rehabilitating and full correctional rehabilitation (i.e., a sufficient amount of time away from offending) was necessary to earn back all of one's civil rights. Some rights, such as the right to marry or divorce, would only be restored to the parolee upon approval of the Adult Authority (Adult Authority, 1947; Adult Authority, 1972). In 1973, the Adult Authority issued Resolution 199, which expanded the automatic restoration of civil rights to include those rights needed to perform certain acts, such as opening bank accounts or obtaining a driver's license (Adult Authority, 1973, February 27), arguably to make the rehabilitative process easier and smoother once on parole. In 1975, the conditions of parole (Adult Authority, 1975, February 19) reminded parolees that their civil rights have been suspended in prison, but that some rights (e.g., employee rights such as worker's compensation and unemployment insurance) were automatically restored upon release.

Upon final discharge, almost all remaining civil rights were restored and the parolee could apply for a Certificate of Rehabilitation. It did not, however, restore the rights to vote, to hold office, or to act as a trustee, as this was not possible without a full pardon (Adult Authority, 1947). The pardon finalized the return to a former state as all rights of citizenship were finally restored to the released offender. The pardon, however, was dependent on no longer committing crimes, suggesting a change for the better was necessary to return to a former self.

Intervention of Other Party

In order for the rehabilitative process to be effective, the correctional and paroling authorities believed it was necessary for other parties to intervene and assist with the process and that such assistance came in the form of parole agents. Walter Gordon (1946, p. 10), then chairman of the Adult Authority, argued assistance was needed because the transition from prisons to parole was too difficult to handle alone:

> If you had someone tell you every day for ten years or more, or even one year or more, what you were to do in the morning, what time to get up, what time you would have breakfast, when you would eat lunch, what time you would go to work, what time you would go to bed, etc., you could easily understand how difficult it would be for those individuals who are already regimented to make an adjustment on the outside without help from the parole officers.

The Inmate Committee for Higher Education (1974, p. 6) repeated this sentiment several decades later in a presentation at a training meeting for California corrections officers:

> Then suddenly, as if emerging from some quiet dark primitive backward culture where he has been isolated in a casket-like prison cell for a seemingly lifetime, the inmate is surrounded by an avalanche of motion. Thus, the former inmate begins an ever increasing crescendo of culture shock that can bring the most intrepid ex-felon to his knees, and cripple the strongest of wills.

Prisoners not only lived in an artificial environment (Procunier, 1971), but they also became used to living in this environment, making it difficult to successfully transition to a new environment. The Board of Prison Terms and Parole (1941) also argued that because the stigma of a prison record cut off returning citizens from law-abiding friends, they were more likely to return to a criminal life. Thus, the philosophy of California's correctional system was that parolees needed assistance if they hoped to reintegrate into society and complete their rehabilitation (Department of Corrections, 1964a), regardless of whether or not they wanted the assistance.

This belief may also explain why all parolees were automatically placed on the maximum supervision level (Adult Authority, 1947). Doing so allowed agents to closely monitor potential criminal behaviors and needs. As the risk to public safety decreased and the parolee showed signs of adjustments, the role of the parole agent was gradually removed (Adult Authority, 1947). Once again, supervision was framed as a tool for achieving rehabilitation rather than an end itself and more strict supervision was reserved for those needing the most assistance.

As Gordon (1946) argued, parole officers were the best people to assist with the transition, but they were not the only one. The parole agent was expected to be familiar with all of the helpers in a parolee's life (e.g., family, friends, community leaders, etc.) in order to better understand the parolee and thus better understand how to help (Parole Task Force, 1967). In the early 1970s, the parole agent manuals also indicated agents were expected to work with other agencies, such as welfare agencies (Department of Corrections, 1975) and community centers, designed to "initiate and facilitate a community reintegration process" (Unknown, 1970, July 22, p. 3). Thus, there was an acknowledgement that state intervention was a necessary (see also Garland, 1985, on penal welfarism), but not sufficient, condition for "curing" convicted individuals of their deficiencies.

Criticisms of Rehabilitation and Parole

The focus on rehabilitation as the main purpose of California's prison and parole system lasted from the early 1940s until the mid-1970s. The Adult Authority worked to ensure the community had faith in the both the system and the parolee. It argued (Adult Authority, 1947), "Without this confidence the parolee would not be given the economic and social opportunities that are requisite for his rehabilitation." Yet, questions surrounding the true effectiveness of this model were creeping in to policy and program discussions even as the Adult Authority continued to affirm that the essence of parole was supervision and rehabilitation was the key to protecting society (McGregor, 1945, February 9; Adult Authority, 1947). Among those criticisms was the ability of parolees to "partake in intoxicating liquors . . . and especially that the Parole Officers are no longer allowed to take men into custody for excessive drinking" (Holoubek, 1949, May 16, p. 2) and the parole board members' ability to discern dangerous parolees. In a letter to Governor Warren, Reid (1949, July 27, p. 1)[13] asked:

> Do not the members of your board have enough intelligence to realize that a smart criminal will always behave well in prison so long as escape from punishment is the reward for such behavior? The record

> of our parolees and repeated crime by the parolee is a disgrace to the state and a menace to the welfare of the public.

The concern over parolees posing a threat to the public was echoed by Price (1949, March 26, p. 1),[14] who stated, "Too high a percentage of early releases have proved that habitual criminals are thrown out on the public as a menace." The Adult Authority responded to such criticisms by noting that parole was not leniency, but a continuation of the indeterminate sentence and extended the supervision provided behind prison walls into the community (McGregor, 1945; Gordon, 1946).

While rehabilitation, particularly within the parole system, was supported officially, there were reasons to believe it was not being achieved in practice. A 1951 letter from a warden at Folsom prison to McGee, then director of the Department of Corrections, presented one view of the success of the rehabilitative process (Figures 2.1a and 2.1b). As the letter and photo indicate, this one particular inmate had been sent to Folsom on

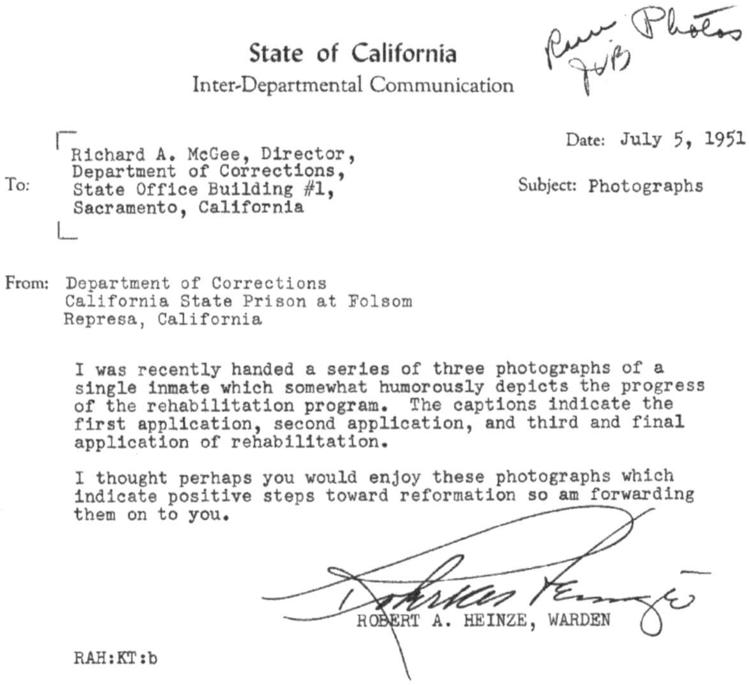

State of California

Inter-Departmental Communication

To: Richard A. McGee, Director,
Department of Corrections,
State Office Building #1,
Sacramento, California

Date: July 5, 1951

Subject: Photographs

From: Department of Corrections
California State Prison at Folsom
Represa, California

I was recently handed a series of three photographs of a single inmate which somewhat humorously depicts the progress of the rehabilitation program. The captions indicate the first application, second application, and third and final application of rehabilitation.

I thought perhaps you would enjoy these photographs which indicate positive steps toward reformation so am forwarding them on to you.

ROBERT A. HEINZE, WARDEN

RAH:KT:b

Figure 2.1a A Letter to Richard McGee, Director of the Department of Corrections, Regarding the Rehabilitation of an Inmate

Reprinted with permission from the T.H. Pendergast Parole Museum

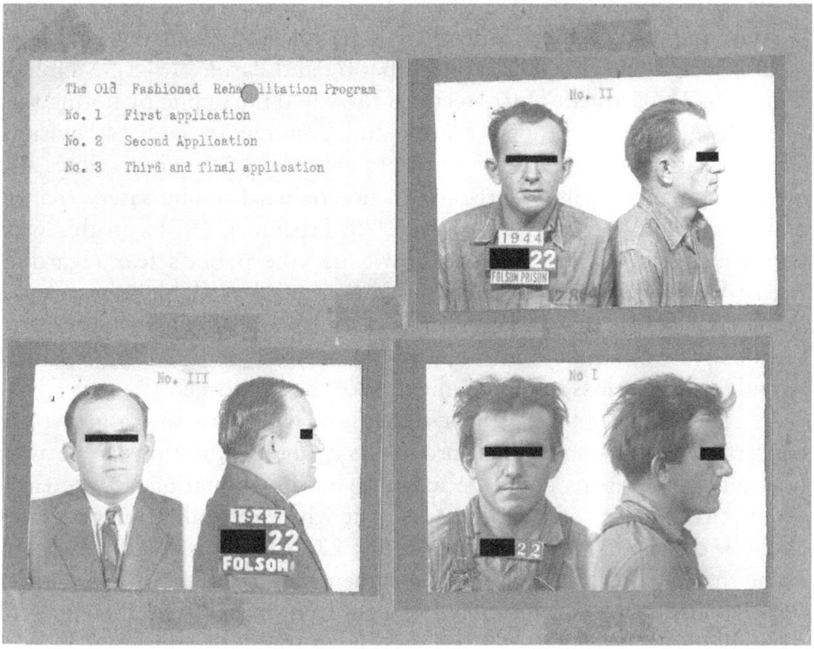

Figure 2.1b The Photographs Accompanying the Letter to Richard McGee

Reprinted with permission from the T.H. Pendergast Parole Museum

three different occasions for three "applications" of rehabilitation. While it is unknown whether the inmate returned on a new crime or a violation of his conditions of parole, the presentation of the rehabilitative process seems to indicate that it had not worked. As the letter noted, it "humorously depicts" rehabilitation and indicates "positive steps" towards reformation; yet, embedded in this humor was a critique of rehabilitation and its perceived ineffectiveness, at least with this particular case.

A revision of the penal code in 1970 addressed this criticism head on. As the penal code revision staff stated (Nelson, 1970, March 10, p. 2):

> We conceive a major goal in this area of code revision to be the affirmation that community treatment through parole is a generally indispensable part of the correctional management of felony offenders, contributing to public protection rather than being a form of leniency as is so often charged, and having innumerable advantages over incarceration so far as the achievement of rehabilitation is concerned.

On the other hand, there was also an acknowledgement that some released individuals would commit further crimes, that the public would be the victims, and that, as more individuals were released, this risk to the public also increased (Task Force on Probation and Parole, 1972). Members within the Department of Corrections reassured the public by noting that "objective statistical results" (Parole and Community Services Division, 1970, p. 1) showed the effectiveness of parole in assisting individuals and a reduction in returns to prison had not reduced public safety (Parole and Community Services Division, 1970; Procunier, 1971). In this way, corrections officials not only acknowledged the public's fear regarding released individuals, but they also used every tool available to assure the public that parole was a successful and necessary component of the corrections system, ideally ensuring public outcry did not raise to levels that would result in a loss of employment or of the department.

As concerns over the parole system grew, the 1970s saw a growth in concerns over the correctional process as a whole. Questions arose as to how effective prisons could be at achieving rehabilitation. In the early 1970s, prisons were still viewed as a place where rehabilitation programs could be delivered (Unknown, 1970, July 22), but a consensus was developing that prisons as a place of punishment can do little more than offer *opportunities* for rehabilitation and could not actually be the *cause* of rehabilitation (Procunier, 1971; Task Force on Probation and Parole, 1972). This distinction is an interesting one and suggests that, during the heyday of the clinical model, prisons themselves were viewed as a rehabilitating mechanism and that the very nature of being removed from society would rehabilitate someone. Beginning in the 1970s, this was no longer the case. Critics of prisons as a rehabilitative tool argued the artificial environment prevented them from being an ideal location of rehabilitation, particularly if the prison was very large and individualized programs were difficult to achieve, and that those who were rehabilitated did so by their own motivations (Procunier, 1971). Then-Governor Brown was cited in a *Newsweek* article (Howard, Lubenow, & Lesher, 1975, February 10, p. 36) as saying, "We face a real problem with prisons. They don't rehabilitate, they don't deter, they don't punish, and they don't protect." This growing concern led to a greater emphasis on the role of parole within the larger correctional system.

Although parole was seen as a key factor in achieving rehabilitation, rehabilitation seems to be slightly lower on the list of priorities for the organization granting parole than one would expect. In a 1973 policy statement, the Adult Authority (1973, March 27, p. 1) listed the following priorities of parole in order of importance:

1. The protection of society;
2. The punishment of the offenders: to make the punishment fit the criminal rather than the crime;

3. The deterrence of offenders (by the punishment imposed) and of others (by example of the punishment imposed on the offender);
4. To rehabilitate those who are amenable to and capable of it.

This list of priorities presents an interesting example of the conflicting role of the Adult Authority. Its priorities reflect both its role in punishing convicted individuals and in determining who got paroled. Yet, the rehabilitation of offenders, whether in prison or on parole, was its last priority and suggested not all offenders could be rehabilitated. While the difference in importance between the priorities may not be that large, correctional rehabilitation (i.e., change for the better) was the first priority with legal rehabilitation (i.e., return to former self) placed on the backburner. Policy required this: "Felons committed to prison should be kept until there is a reasonable cause to believe they can lead crime free lives in society. Doubts should be resolved in favor of public protection" (Adult Authority, 1973, March 27, p. 1). This is especially interesting as rehabilitation was framed as a means of achieving public protection and this framing justified rehabilitation as the dominant theory of California's correctional system. Yet, it seems the board needed some assurance the offender would not be a threat to the public before continuing rehabilitation in the community. This expectation seems contradictory given the increasing belief that prisons cannot rehabilitate someone.[15]

Multiple surveys of parole agents also raised questions as to the ability of parole to achieve rehabilitation. For example, a 1970 survey (cited in Newland, 1976, p. 13–14) found the following:

> In this survey, the majority of parole agents felt that the effectiveness of the parole Division was moderate to very low in the rehabilitation of parolees or in protecting the public from parolees. Also, regarding the most effective methods to achieve the goals of the Parole Division, California parole agents said that there was a conflict between the parole agents and the Division policy. A majority felt that Division case supervision requirements prevented contacts with parolees according to the agents' evaluation of case needs; and the result was insufficient contact with some cases, and unnecessary contacts with others.

Two later surveys reflect the same findings. Both a 1972 and 1976 study of parole agents found the conflict between the casework role of providing services and surveillance role of providing public protection impacted their daily activities. Studt (1972, cited in Newland, 1976, p. 18) found the conflicting roles created additional work-related stress and that agents were "required to have a 'superhuman' range of competence, dealing with all possible parolee problems" while rarely having access to the necessary resources.

Newland (1976) found agents spent only about 7 percent of their time providing rehabilitative casework and a majority of their time (56.6 percent) on routine activities (e.g., preparing reports, required contacts, etc.). Newland also found that while 80 percent of agents believed the purpose of parole was to protect the public, they were divided as to whether this was accomplished through surveillance, casework, or a combination. Over half of the agents also desired more security measures, such as firearms, security cars, and police training, which seems contradictory to their suggestion that requirements such as college degrees and casework/service-oriented training should be mandatory when hiring agents. While it is possible these responses break down between those who support surveillance and those who support casework as the most effective way of controlling parolees, the study does not provide this data.

Finally, criticisms of rehabilitation were also developing amongst legislators and academics. Questions arose as to the legitimacy of methods used in the name of rehabilitation. Morris (1974) questioned whether one could "volunteer" for such programs if release is predicated on successful completion of these treatments and that forced participation fails to actually achieve the goals of change. As Rotman (1990) notes, treatments such as shock therapy were carried out in the name of rehabilitation. Particularly in respect to California, Milford (1973, p. 86) criticized the correctional system as the "total, arbitrary, and despotic power" of prison and paroling authorities that allowed for the continuation of such practices as floggings, solitary confinement, and indefinite sentences in prisons and on parole, practices that she argued were morally unacceptable. As these treatments grew out of favor, rehabilitation was held responsible for such harsh treatments, leading many to critique the rehabilitative approach. Furthermore, legislators on both sides of the political spectrum were calling for more definitive sentences. Liberals argued that indeterminate sentencing led to abuses of power by sentencing and correctional officials and that the rehabilitative ideal helped justify longer sentences; conservatives argued that indeterminate sentencing led to increased leniency and that rehabilitation "weakened the punitive mechanisms of the state" (Rotman, 1990, p. 109). While liberals and conservatives had differing views on the goals of definitive punishments, the result was a decline in the support of rehabilitative policies.

Although studies on the effectiveness of rehabilitation were conducted throughout this time period, the findings were mixed. Richard McGee's multiple studies showed the organization of the parole system had little to no impact on parolee outcomes, suggesting the parole system had little to do with an individual's rehabilitation (Glaser, 1995). Finally, in 1974, Robert Martinson published a report on the effectiveness of correctional programs nationwide. In his report, Martinson conducted a meta-analysis of 231 studies and covered a range of both in-prison and in-community treatment programs, including vocational, educational, psychological, and medical programs. The study also looked at the effects of sentencing and being placed on parole regardless of other treatment. Although the study found that some programs were promising, the general conclusion was that no program worked consistently to reduce recidivism (Farabee, 2005). This report raised serious concerns about rehabilitative programs and resulted in a lack of faith in the correctional system and loss of legitimacy among those authorizing rehabilitation (Allen, 1981). Further, the lack of faith in the system led to questions of the effectiveness of penal-based therapy. Questions arose as to who decided what constituted rehabilitation and who decided what constituted a cure (Allen, 1981). Combined with the already-growing critiques of rehabilitation from correctional and legislative leaders, the study seemed to be the final straw.

The growing skepticism towards rehabilitation and increase in surveillance within the parole system led to dramatic changes in the late 1970s. These changes were implemented in 1976 through legislation that revamped California's correctional system and reversed the state's correctional philosophy. The next chapter discusses how this law came about, its impact on the parole system, and its impact on rehabilitation within California corrections.

Notes

1 Unfortunately, none of the documents from this or later periods indicated when additional parole agents and parole offices were established, meaning there is no way of knowing at which point the bureaucracy expanded to the point of handling the parole capacity as it does today.

2 The bill also included an emergency clause that allowed the law to go into effect immediately, which allowed for the immediate processing of applications (Unknown, 1942) and the immediate enlistment of those approved. The rationale behind this portion of the bill is unclear. As Simon (1993) notes, the US Congress removed the bans on felons serving in the Armed Services in July 1941. Thus, paroled and discharged felons could have enlisted in the Armed Services regardless of the Certificate of Rehabilitation. It is possible, however, that this restoration of rights made it easier for convicted felons to obtain employment in war-related industries that were related to, but not directly under control of, the US military. Unfortunately, none of the documents in the legislative files for SB 904 fully explains this clause.

3 A parolee needed permission from their parole agent before most rights (e.g., marry, divorce, obtain a driver's license) could be restored. The Certificate of Rehabilitation was meant to restore the remaining rights not approved (or requested) by the parole agent. The rights to vote, hold office, or act as a trustee could only be restored with a full pardon.

4 In support of this aspect of the bill, the State Bar of California noted it was ready and willing to provide legal services to those preparing their application for free (Weil, 1943, March 20).

5 Unfortunately, documents for the Women's Board of Prison Terms and Paroles are unavailable and it is unclear the extent to which policies and procedures for the men's and women's paroling authorities overlapped.
6 These resources were described in a report by the Parole Task Force, which reviewed the parole system and made recommendations for improvement. The unknown author seems to be a member of the task force.
7 The desire to maintain parolees in the community was discussed in a statement regarding the purpose of the Central City Community Center, a community-based program designed for those having a hard time adjusting in the community upon release or as an alternative to a return to prison.
8 These resources were described in a report by the Parole Task Force, which reviewed the parole system and made recommendations for improvement. The unknown author seems to be a member of the task force.
9 The development and purpose of community correctional centers was discussed in a statement to Walter Dunbar (then director of the Department of Corrections), Richard McGee (then administrator of Youth and Adult Corrections), and Edmund "Jerry" Brown (then governor of California).
10 The use of work furlough programs as an alternative to a return to prison was discussed in a statement regarding the purpose of the Central City Community Center, a community-based program designed for those having a hard time adjusting in the community upon release or as an alternative to a return to prison.
11 The purpose of work furlough programs was discussed in a memo to E. Reimer, then a California police chief.
12 Unfortunately, no information is available about the production company, when and on what channel the show aired, or why the show was created.
13 Reid appears to be a private citizen.
14 Price appears to be a private citizen.
15 Interestingly, while the section of this parole agent manual (adopted in 1975) does not provide specific criteria by which to determine suitability for release (beyond "an unreasonable risk of danger to society would not be posed by releasing him"), it does note several specific factors that may be considered when determining one's unsuitability, none of which include in-prison behavior. The 1976 Administrative Code does include reports regarding an inmate's "adjustment, accomplishments, readiness for release and plans for release" (State of California, 1976, Article 3, Sec. 2286) as information considered for release; the list of example factors indicating unsuitability still focus on the conviction offense and risk of criminality and not on in-prison behavior.

Chapter 3

The Fall of Rehabilitation

1970s to 1990s

> *The Legislature finds and declares that the purpose of imprisonment for crime is punishment.*
>
> *~SB 42, Uniform Sentencing Act, 1976*

In 1976, California was the first state to reject rehabilitation as a correctional philosophy. The implementation of determinate sentencing ended a 32-year experiment with the medical model. The shift away from rehabilitation did not occur overnight and likely began in the late 1960s when changes were made to the focus of sentencing laws. As Barker (2009) notes, then-Governor Reagan signed into law an increase in penalties for crimes that caused great bodily harm. In doing so, he introduced the idea of determining sentences based on the impact to the victim rather than the therapeutic need of the offender. This bill was the first focused on the crime, rather than the criminal.

Public support for offender rehabilitation was also waning. Barker argues California's political culture of populism and direct democracy created a culture where "crime is perceived as a moral failing of individual responsibility rather than a result of poor schooling, bad parenting, unfair labor markets, or other forms of social inequality" (Barker, 2009, p. 50; see also Allen, 1981). If social inequalities that resulted in personal deficiencies were no longer viewed as the cause of crime, than the rehabilitative rationale no longer made sense. Rather, "the prison as retribution makes moral sense" (Barker, 2009, p. 51).

In the late 1970s, California legislators formally called for a shift to determinate sentencing; those supporting the shift echoed the belief that crime was not caused by personal deficiencies and questioned the rehabilitative ideal. Several state senators and representatives of state departments criticized the idea of offenders being "sick" and raised concerns about the ability of correctional officials to determine when one was ready for release. Prisoners also criticized the ability of paroling authorities to fairly administer the indeterminate sentencing system. Families, employment, and schooling were still considered when determining parole releases, but there was uncertainty as to the predictability of who would be positively impacted by those factors and who would not (Assembly Committee on Criminal Justice, 1975, October 11). These arguments, along with others reminiscent of critiques of the rehabilitative ideal on the national level, brought about the end of indeterminate sentencing structures.

Two legal challenges that altered the way the parole system operated in the early 1970s also led to the rejection of indeterminate sentencing. In 1972, the Supreme Court of the United States determined in *Morrissey v. Brewer* (408 U.S. 471 [1972]) that parolees have some due process rights when faced with a parole revocation. In 1975, the Supreme Court of California determined in *In re Rodriguez* (14 Cal. 3d. 639) that the Adult Authority must set an initial term the prisoner will serve soon after the prisoner is incarcerated. This term could be decreased, but it could not be increased. While the workings of the Adult Authority were altered by both decisions, *In re Rodriguez* had the effect of forcing the Adult Authority to move towards a more determinate structure in practice, even though the laws had not yet codified this change. When determinate sentencing was codified, the bill's author argued, the "legislation simply adopts the Supreme Court's line of reasoning and sets a release date on the basis of the crime the individual has committed" (Nejedly, 1976, August 24, p. 1).

Reframing Corrections

The official rejection of both the indeterminate sentencing structure and the rehabilitative ideal occurred with the passage of SB 42 in 1976. This was quickly followed by SB 1057 in 1978, which addressed perceived weaknesses in the way SB 42 dealt with parole. Combined, these two bills led to dramatic shifts in the way the prison and parole systems operated in California. They did not completely eliminate the rehabilitative ideal from the correctional system (Barker, 2009; Phelps, 2011), but they did put in place an official discourse that no longer supported the ideal and the structures that led to a significant shift away from rehabilitation.

1976: Passage of SB 42

The Uniform Sentencing Law (aka Determinate Sentencing Law) was introduced in 1974 by Senator Nejedly (R-Contra Costa County), a former district attorney for Contra Costa County, as a way of addressing the perceived link between indeterminate sentences and increased prison violence. The bill initially retained the indeterminate sentencing structure, but reduced the amount of potential discretion available to the parole board (Health and Welfare Agency, Department of Corrections, 1976).

After multiple revisions and wholesale changes, the law abandoned the rehabilitative ideal as the purpose of imprisonment, discarded the Indeterminate Sentencing Law, and minimized the role of the parole system within corrections.

The main purpose of the law was clear: it "finds and declares that the purpose of imprisonment for crime is punishment. This purpose is best served by terms proportionate to the seriousness of the offense and with provision for uniformity in the sentences" (Unknown, 1976, August 17, p. 2). This marked a stark split from the previous time period and unquestionably abandoned the notion that prisons were for rehabilitation. It also marked a clear shift to determining punishment by focusing on the crime rather than the criminal. This shift occurred for a number of reasons.

The heart of the indeterminate sentencing structure was the belief that scientific knowledge could be used to predict when someone was rehabilitated and ready to be a part of the community again. Those supporting the shift to the determinate sentencing structure, including Professor Monahan (1975, April 15) from the University of California, Irvine and Senator Nejedly (n.d.), argued the notion that correctional officials can predict who would and would not be violent if released was a fallacy. Senator Nejedly (1975, June 12) argued there was simply no way to predict human behavior or know when someone was rehabilitated. Los Angeles City Attorney Pines (1976, August 25) and Senator Nejedly (n.d.) also criticized the indeterminate sentencing structure because it had done little to ensure public safety while others argued it "has achieved no rehabilitation" (Unknown, n.d. a, p. 4). The medical model was also criticized as officials argued "that the inmates aren't really sick. There really is no treatment in the medical sense for what they've got and it is difficult or impossible to tell if they have 'recovered'" (Health and Welfare Agency, Department of Corrections, 1976, p. 3). The growing lack of faith in rehabilitation and the major doctrine of the medical model resulted in a call to "end the 'indeterminate sentence fantasy'" (Welsh, 1975, p. 1).

A second major critique of the indeterminate sentencing structure was the impact of the discretion and arbitrariness involved in setting sentences. As several prisoners related in letters to Senator Nejedly, indeterminate sentencing was marred by an inability of men to administer justice "with an even hand," the potential for abuse of power by Adult Authority members, and average prison sentences longer than the national average (Unknown, 1975, February 25; Unknown, 1975, April 1).[1] The Coordinating Council of Prisoner Organizations (1975) also criticized the medical model for resulting in inconsistent and lengthy sentences that had a destructive influence on the prisoners' lives. The Health and Welfare Agency of the Department of Corrections (1976) summarized others who critiqued the inability for inmates or their families to plan for release because it was impossible to know when one would be released.

The inability of inmates to know what must be done to earn release also resulted in frustration and anxiety (Health and Welfare Agency, Department of Corrections, 1976), which led to increased levels of prison violence[2] (Citizens Advocating Legislative Leadership, 1975, April 11; Portman, 1976).

The determinate sentencing structure also eliminated the parole board's power to determine sentences, eliminating the constitutional questions raised in *In re Rodriguez*. Rather, the law established a means by which judges would choose a sentence from a limited and pre-determined set of guidelines. Upon conviction, the judge had three choices of sentence lengths, which varied depending on the conviction charge.[3] The judge must choose the middle term unless mitigating or aggravating circumstances warranted choosing one of the other terms (Unknown, 1976, August 17). The term options were legislatively determined (Unknown, 1975, August 14). The judge may also impose sentence enhancements, also determined by the legislature. These included an enhancement for each prior felony or use of a deadly weapon while committing the crime (Unknown, 1975).[4] The legislature also implemented a "good time" system, whereby inmates may reduce part of their sentence by remaining free of disciplinary charges and/or participating in programs (Unknown, 1975, February 25). While good time credit could be lost, it was "limited to a maximum of three months for lack of good time and up to one month for lack of participation" (Legislative Analyst's Office, 1976, p. 2). Good time credit banked every eight months resulting in a possible 50 percent reduction in time served.[5] The establishment of good time credit harkened back to the use of program participation prior to implementation of the Indeterminate Sentencing Law. Both time periods used program participation as a means of determining whom to release early (see State Board of Prison Directors, 1909), but who determined release differed, with prison wardens making the decision before the 1940s and legislators making the decision after 1976.

The parole system also faced numerous changes as SB 42 greatly diminished the role it played within the correctional system. First, the legislature eliminated both the Adult Authority and the Women's Board of Terms and Parole and created the Parole and Community Services Division (P&CSD) and the Community Release Board (CRB). P&CSD oversaw the parole of both men and women, determined who should be waived from parole supervision, and addressed parole revocations. The CRB, placed under P&CSD, determined release of those sentenced to life with the possibility of parole (Unknown, 1975, May 14; Unknown, n.d. a). Combining the Adult Authority and Women's Board of Terms and Parole was a move to decrease costs and the Department of Finance (1976) estimated doing so would save $2.5 million. Initially, SB 42 limited parole supervision to two years for non-lifers and five years for lifers

(Unknown, 1975, August 14), but this was reduced to one and three years respectively (Unknown, 1976, April 22). At the one- and three-year marks, each case was reviewed and, unless continuance was adequately justified, the parolee would be discharged. Parole revocation was limited to six months and did not count against time on parole. For example, a parolee who served six months on parole and was revoked for six months would be discharged upon completion of the revocation sentence (Unknown, 1976, April 22). As discussed in a document provided to the governor entitled *Benefits of SB 42, as amended April 22, 1976*, the short parole and revocation periods eliminated the "life on the installment plan" occurring under the indeterminate sentencing structure (Unknown, 1976, April 22). James Smith (1978, March 13, p. 3), a lecturer at the University of California, Davis, School of Law, argued the parole system failed at both its law enforcement aspects and social service aspects, a fact not lost on those who created SB 42, as it "limited the irrelevant and redundant surveillance or control aspect of parole by reducing the impact of parole revocation." This new sentencing structure carried large support, including from the California Department of Justice, Correctional Counselors Association, and California Employees' Association, particularly for its abilities to ensure and plan release (Unknown, 1975) and to reduce uncertainty and anxiety.

The new scheme was not without its critics, however. Los Angeles Representative Norman Boyer (1976, September 13) argued the legislature was not the appropriate body for determining the sentences and that qualified individuals working in the corrections system were better able to determine when one should be released. In a document entitled *Staff Concerns over SB 42* found in the Assembly Committee on Criminal Justice file, one individual argued the Legislature "has neither the temperament, the continuing interest, nor the insulation from political pressures that are necessary to establish—and to maintain over the years—a rational sentencing structure" (Unknown, n.d., b, p. 1). A joint letter from the Prisoners Union and ACLU to then-Governor Jerry Brown argued the shift to determinate sentencing and "tough on crime" stance was little more than an opportunity for both the legislature and governor to earn political capital (Bycel, 1976, May 17). Many—including the California Probation, Parole, and Correctional Association and the California Attorneys for Criminal Justice—expressed concerns over the likelihood that sentence lengths would increase over the years because of political pressure and highly publicized criminal events (Fitzharris, 1975; Green, 1976, August 2).[6]

Concerns were also raised that some would be released regardless of whether or not they should be. Attorney General Michael Franchetti (1974, December 18) provided an example of a convicted robber who threatened to kill a key witness upon release and that such individuals need to be kept in prison until such desire for revenge had dissipated. Others feared those who were less culpable would be punished more harshly than needed (Woodmanswer, 1974, December 5), especially women. As one bill analysis argued (Unknown, 1976, April 22), women served less time on average than men, and the switch to determinate sentencing would unnecessarily increase sentences for women, a rather prescient concern given the dramatic rise of female inmates after the passage of determinate sentencing schemes nationwide (e.g., Mauer, Potler, & Wolf, 1999; Kruttschnitt, 2010). This bill analysis (Unknown, 1976, April 22) also suggested the Uniform Sentencing Law did not even analyze women's terms and based its sentencing structure solely on statistics derived from men's terms, thus perpetuating the male-dominated orientation of the Department of Corrections. A senior consultant for the Assembly Committee on Criminal Justice (Ullman, 1976, June 14) called the bill a "male chauvinistic document" for eliminating all members of the Women's Board of Terms and Parole but retaining all members of the Adult Authority, which focused on and was comprised of men.

The majority of those opposing SB 42 focused on the overall sentencing structure. While some judges felt the sentences were too short and too lenient (Allen, 1976; Stahl, 1976; Woodworth, 1976), most felt the sentence lengths were already far too long (Magnani, 1976 September 15; Fries & Schooler, 1976, July 1; Citizens Advocating Legislative Leadership, 1975, April 11). The ACLU (Bycel, 1976) argued the prison terms would be longer than the average sentences under the indeterminate sentencing structure and many argued the presumptive sentence should be the lowest term possible, not the middle term (Bycel, 1976; Unknown, n.d. a). The sentencing structure was also criticized for not having a clear philosophy and "no consistent relationship between the harm done to society and the penalties proposed" (Citizens Advocating Legislative Leadership, 1975, April 11, p. 2).

Critics also argued the enhancements would make the sentences even longer. Concerns centered around enhancements for prior convictions in that they drastically increased the sentence length and presented the possibility that such enhancements constitute double jeopardy (Shonholtz, 1975; Citizens Advocating Legislative Leadership, 1975, April 11; Silliman, 1976). A spokesperson for the Committee for Prisoner Humanity and Justice (Silliman, 1976) argued this enhancement was contradictory to the theory of determinate sentencing, as time in prison was still partially based on prior behavior, linking back to indeterminate sentencing. A similar critique was raised by the Citizens Advocating Legislative Leadership (1975, April 11) regarding the programming requirement to earn a month of good time credit, as such a requirement was deeply rooted in the now discredited medical model. Critics raised fears that this requirement would force inmates to participate in programs and deteriorate the quality of the programs for those who chose to enroll as part of their rehabilitation (Citizens Advocating Legislative Leadership, 1975, April 11; Shonholtz, 1975; Bycel, 1976; Unknown, n.d. a).

Critiques of the parole system centered on two arguments: 1) the role of parole had been far too limited and 2) parole was inconsistent with the determinate sentencing philosophy. First, many critics, including the executive director of California Probation, Parole, and Correctional Association and the director of the Department of Corrections, felt that public protection was diminished by limiting parole to one year for most individuals (Fitzharris, 1976; Enomoto, 1976, March 30). Arguably, this critique was a means of saving departmental funds. J. J. Enomoto (1976, March 30), then director of Corrections, also felt the reduced time on parole would lead to a reduction in control over those who were not adjusting well and to a greater emphasis on providing services and a reduction in supervision. It was not clear why this would occur or why an emphasis on services was problematic. Senator Nejedly (n.d.), however, argued the bill included a provision to protect the resources allocated to parole functions and that such changes would increase supervision and surveillance of parolees. This was to be accomplished by a decrease in parolee-to-agent ratios, though how this decrease was achieved was not discussed.

Second, several individuals questioned whether parole even had a role in a determinate sentencing structure. One analyst argued that whether parole fits depended on the use of good time. As Shonholtz (1975) explained, if good time was used to reduce time spent in prison, then parole can be used to monitor the individual for the remainder of the sentence, maintaining its role of "custody without walls." If, on the other hand, it was used to reduce the actual sentence length, than parole did not have a place in the system and those who completed their sentence should be discharged (Shonholtz, 1975). The Citizens Advocating Legislative Leadership (1975) and the ACLU of Southern California (Bycel, 1976) argued that as SB 42 rejected the medical model, there was no longer a philosophical justification for parole. Regardless of the multiple arguments and critiques against SB 42, it was signed into law in 1976 and went into effect on July 1, 1977. As predicted by many of the critics, changes to the legislative terms came quickly (Griset, 1991). One of the first major changes was to the parole provision, which was amended in 1978 through SB 1057.

1978: Passage of SB 1057

Although SB 42 presented a major shift to the sentencing structure and correctional philosophy in California, the parole system was barely discussed. Charles Swim, then president of the California Probation, Parole, and Correctional Association, felt the parole provisions included were "*almost* an afterthought" (Swim, 1978, p. 1, emphasis in original) and the language of SB 42 implied that parole was a second sentence, thus prompting challenges of double jeopardy (Swim, 1977, May 10; see also, Unknown, 1977, June 16). Some feared the lack of discussion about parole, limited time individuals were to serve on parole or in prison for revocations, and the very nature of SB 42 left parole vulnerable to being abolished. Edward Davis (1977, May 11, p. 1), then Los Angeles chief of police, argued that while parole was not technically abolished, it was eliminated "for all practical purposes."

In 1978, the California Probation, Parole, and Correctional Association, a professional organization that represented prison guards and probation and parole agents, sponsored SB 1057, the purpose of which was to "maintain the institution of parole as part of the California correction system" (Unknown, 1978, October 10, p. 1) and bolster the system from legal challenges. The bill fulfilled five major objectives: 1) clarified the purpose of parole; 2) abolished parole waiver; 3) lengthened time served on parole; 4) lengthened time served for parole revocations; and 5) implemented re-parole.

First, the bill stated the purpose of parole was public protection, the parole period was added to the incarceration, and it was part of the determinate sentence, thus avoiding issues of double jeopardy. The bill also established both services and supervision as an effective means of achieving public protection. This continued the role of services and supervision under the medical model, as both served to achieve rehabilitation, which in turn achieved public protection. This suggested rehabilitation was still an important component of the parole system, even if it was not emphasized in name or in practice. It was believed the bill "provides, for the first time, a well defined reason and purpose for the parole function" (York, 1977) and that without it "we will be at the mercy of a sentencing and rehabilitation system that has been totally removed of its working parts" (Davis, 1977, May 11, p. 1).

On the other hand, the author of a document entitled *Parole* in the Senate Finance Committee file questioned whether the main purpose of the bill was to maintain employment of those working in the parole system, rather than protect the system itself (Unknown, n.d. d). Given that the country was coming out of a deep recession, it was very possible the California Probation, Parole, and Correctional Association introduced the bill for the purpose of maintaining jobs for its members, thereby enabling the organization to maintain its existing numbers and membership dues. As Gilmore (1999) argued, this rationalization also seems to be a precursor to the expansion of California's prisons system in response to surpluses of labor, land, state capacity, and capital that occurred in the 1980s.

Second, SB 1057 addressed parole waivers. Under the Uniform Sentencing Law, the Community Release Board reviewed cases and waived parole for some individuals. This echoed the indeterminate sentencing structure, as two individuals with identical situations may end up with different outcomes. Concerns were raised that such a system might violate equal protection "because one is subject to re-incarceration for parole violation while the other fears no such sanction" (Unknown, n.d. c, p. 3). The ability to waive parole also contradicted SB 42's emphasis on uniformity. As such, SB 1057 abolished the practice of parole waiver and California created a system where everyone released from prison was required to spend time on parole, even if only for one day.

Two main aspects of SB 1057 were the lengthening of time spent on parole and time spent in jail or prison for a parole revocation. SB 1057 increased parole terms to the lengths originally proposed under SB 42: three years for those serving non-life sentences and five years for those serving life sentences. The Community Release Board maintained its ability to provide an early discharge to a parolee for good cause. Supporters of the bill argued lengthening the time spent on parole would enable parole agents to more effectively assist individuals in reintegrating into society and better protect the public. Questions remained, however, as to whether the increased time period was necessary if, as the author of SB 42 argued, the period immediately following incarceration was key (Nejedly, n.d.)—a charge repeated by more recent reentry scholars (Nelson, Deess, & Allen, 1999; Visher, Kachnowski, La Vigne, & Travis, 2004; Visher & Courtney, 2007). Additionally, there were no known studies on the effectiveness of increasing time on parole and some offenders (particularly sex offenders) did not recidivate until after they were effectively reintegrated into society and presumably off parole (Clanon, 1976, September 14). Supporters of the bill responded by citing Martinson's and Wilks's (1977) paper that argued parole supervision reduced recidivism rates compared to release without any supervision. The use of Martinson is particularly ironic as his prior article, which was misinterpreted as claiming "nothing works" to rehabilitate offenders, was a key factor in the rejection of rehabilitation. Supporters of SB 1057 also argued that as most parole violations occurred within 24 months, limiting time on parole to one year did not protect the public in most cases (Unknown, n.d. c). It was not clear, however, whether these violations were technical violations or the commission of a new crime, raising questions as to the extent that public protection was harmed with a lower parole period.

The Parole Agents Association of California (n.d.) argued lengthening revocation periods would ensure individuals who violated parole would receive more than a slap on the wrist, thus protecting the public. The association also argued increasing time limits would enable revoked parolees to serve time in prison, rather than jail, where individuals had access to in-prison treatment programs. The author of a document summarizing the bill for the Senate Justice Committee (Unknown, n.d. c) argued the six-month revocation term was not enough of a "stick" to be used against parolees as a means of keeping them in line. The same author argued a longer revocation time ensured parolees accused of committing a new crime would still spend time in prison, especially when the DA was unable to proceed in a case for various reasons,[7] and that parole agents were able to prevent crimes by removing those who were committing technical violations (Unknown, n.d. c).[8] Thus, the bill changed the revocation limits from a maximum of six months to a choice of three terms: six, twelve, or eighteen months (Unknown, n.d. e).

Finally, SB 1057 altered the way a parole revocation impacted someone who is re-paroled. Under the Uniform Sentencing Law, time served for a parole revocation did not impact the parole clock. Following the implementation of SB 1057, time spent in prison for a parole revocation started the parole clock over again. The objective was to ensure that all parolees served at least one year under supervision and "would give added weight to the sanction against parole violation thereby better assuring control" (Unknown, n.d. c, p. 3). This created a system by which getting discharged from parole became incredibly difficult, depended on the discretion of the parole agent and his response to violations, and reinstated a system of "life on the installment plan." It was also probable the change in time served on parole and the change in re-parole led to higher caseloads as more parolees were added each year and negated Nejedly's intent of reducing caseloads under SB 42.

Although many supported these changes to the parole system (members of Parole Agents Association of California, multiple law enforcement personnel, and California Probation, among others), many opposed it. Much of the opposition came from groups such as the State Bar organization and Attorneys for Criminal Justice, who argued SB 1057 has not shown that longer time on parole decreased recidivism, that it would undermine the Determinate Sentencing Act, and that it would reallocate funds needed for other aspects of the criminal justice system. With respect to cost, similar concerns were raised by the Department of Finance, which also opposed the bill. An analysis conducted by the Department of Finance for then-Governor Jerry Brown noted that, given the multiple changes presented under SB 1057, the number of people on parole would greatly increase, thereby increasing costs substantially (Legislative Analyst's Office, 1978, April 17). Regardless of these concerns, SB 1057 was signed into law and went into effect January 1, 1979.

Reframing Parole

SB 1057 set the stage for drastic changes within the parole department for decades to come. Charles Swim, president-elect of the Parole Agents

Association of California, argued, "the Department of Corrections has for a number of years overemphasized the service role of the Parole Agent. We happen to believe that the supervisory role of the agent is more important for public protection" (1977, May 10, p. 1). SB 1057 created the path by which to push away from services and towards a strictly supervision-based system. Multiple letters from agents to senators encouraged support for law enforcement and the supervision and surveillance functions of parole with little or no mention of the service aspect, indicating that parole should be focused solely on the supervisory role (York, 1977; Addiego, 1978; Fitzharris, 1978; Swim, 1978).

Yet, Swim also stated SB 1057 emphasized public protection without "neglecting the service aspects of an agent's duty," suggesting that while supervision was top priority, the service aspect would not be neglected. Some supporters of the bill argued the emphasis on supervision created the means by which to ensure parolees received adequate services and rehabilitative programs. In a letter to Assemblyman Maddy (who served on the Assembly Committee on Criminal Justice), then-Chairman of the San Mateo County Juvenile Justice Committee William Addiego (1978, p. 1) argued, "This legislation will provide extended parole supervision for serious offenders and parole violators, which will certainly allow for greater community protection and increased rehabilitation services for those individuals." The Parole Agents Association of California (1978, February 27) argued the extended length of supervision would ensure changes in behavioral patterns. While rehabilitation and the provision of services were diminished as a priority, they were reframed to support the need for greater supervision. As predicted, the costs of parole increased substantially (Department of Corrections, n.d.)

Impact on Parole Manuals

A review of parole manuals immediately before and after 1976 revealed the most immediate impact of SB 42[9] was consolidation and reorganization of the various manuals. These manuals provided the guidelines by which those working in the parole system were to do their jobs and included specific guidelines on how to develop agent-parolee relationships, determine who was to be released and why, and determine who to send back to prison. The changes made to these manuals were in response to changes at both the legislative and administrative levels. The reversal in correctional philosophy following the passage of SB 42 should have provided insights to the agents as to how the rejection of rehabilitation was to be addressed at the parole level. Yet, the biggest changes to the manuals was in who was told what.

Prior to 1976, two known manuals existed: 1) parole agent manual and 2) parole revocation procedures manual. Because the parole agents were heavily involved in the release of inmates, including verifying and approving release plans, the parole agents were provided with manuals for navigating both the release process and the supervision process. The 1975 parole agent manual (Department of Corrections, 1975) included information on the suitability and unsuitability criteria used to determine release, procedures for release upon approved parole plan (RUAPP), and information regarding services available, such as cash assistance and the Parolee Outpatient Clinic. On the other hand, the 1977 parole procedures manual (Parole Policy and Procedures Committee, 1977), which was revised per SB 42, did not include much of this information. Although agents were still involved in verifying information on a parole release plan and suggesting alternatives, neither the agent nor the Community Release Board had a say in whether an inmate was released. Thus, there was no reason for the agent to be familiar with issues of suitability/unsuitability or RUAPPs. Rather, this information was now found in a new manual, the Parole Board Rules (Department of Corrections, 1977), aimed specifically at members of the Community Release Board, as it was this board's responsibility to determine release for those serving an indeterminate sentence, whether under the old scheme or under the new scheme for those serving a life sentence with the possibility of parole.

Additionally, prior to 1976, parole revocation procedures were discussed in a manual separate from the parole agent manual. It was not clear why this was the case, but given that a violation meant continuing the sentence in prison as opposed to a return as a sanction, the parole agents may not have been very involved in the revocation procedures at that time. The revocation procedures manual was likely reserved for the board members who were in charge of revocation hearings. This separation was not seen after 1976. Rather, both the 1977 parole procedures manual and parole board rules address violations. The agent's manual focused on reporting violations and the board's manual focused on determining revocation. This shift signaled that parole agents were now looking for specific, revocable behaviors, foreshadowing a larger emphasis on surveillance over services.

Although the audience for the manuals changed, the language used before and after 1976 did not change much. In some cases, the language was identical. The lack of changes to the manuals suggests the policies and procedures for the parole agents did not actually change with the passage of SB 42 and that some level of services was still provided to parolees. The largest change was an increase in the discussion on revocations and revocation procedures, once again implying a shift towards a greater reliance on supervision. The change in correctional philosophy had some, but not a large, initial impact on the practices of parole, further emphasizing the relative independence of parole and loosely coupled (Hagan, Hewitt, & Alwin, 1979) nature of the parole and prison systems.

Introduction of a New Parole Model

During the development of SB 42 and SB 1057, the paroling authority was in the midst of a three-year evaluation that began in 1975. The results of this evaluation indicated criticism of parole centered on "unclear purposes, excessive discretionary decision-making at the Board and field levels, arbitrary and inequitable treatment of adult offenders, and lack of observable results" (Parole and Community Services Division, 1978b, p. 2). The findings led to a new parole model implemented in January 1980 that was meant to address these concerns and build on the changes already created through SB 42 and SB 1057. The new model utilized comprehensive assessments and release plans, adjusted controls and services based on the parolees' needs; focused on "what works, for whom, and when"; and emphasized (undefined) results (Parole and Community Services Division, 1978b). These recommendations echoed many of the tools utilized under the medical model, which were arguably eliminated with the passage of SB 42.

The biggest change was a shift towards specialization and away from generalization. Prior to implementation of the new parole model, parole agents worked as generalists: "Caseloads were assigned on the basis of geography and each agent was expected to perform all of the case-related functions necessary to accomplish the organization's objective" (Veit, 1986, p. 3). The new plan introduced functional specialization by field staff, which broke down the varying aspects of parole (e.g., case management, case assessment, providing services) across multiple agents (Simon, 1993) and created a team approach to each case. This resulted in two types of cases: 1) supervision emphasizing controls where the primary concern was public safety and 2) supervision emphasizing services where the primary concern was readjustment to community life (Parole and Community Services Division, 1978b). The rationale was that not all individuals were good at all things, so functional specialization enabled an agent to achieve the greatest outcomes in his or her area of specialization, which increased effectiveness and efficiency (Parole and Community Services Division, 1978b). It was not clear why public safety and readjustment were viewed as mutually exclusive.

There were some concerns this shift to functional specialization would result in internal backlash from staff who were resistant to change (Parole and Community Services Division, 1978b). This fear seemed well founded, as an article in the newsletter for the Parole Agents Association of California claimed many agents who were hired as generalists enjoyed the social service aspect of parole and found satisfaction in the public protection aspect as well and argued, "[a]s time progressed, the agent became quite adept in handling both roles. In fact, one role was usually dependent upon the other" (Unknown, 1979, June, p. 5). This agent's statement echoed the ways in which supervision was used as a tool of rehabilitation prior to the switch to determinate sentencing and suggested the coupling of supervision and rehabilitation would continue, though perhaps in an altered form, if the agents were allowed to continue work as generalists. Given that rehabilitation (and by extension supervision) was used as a means of achieving public protection, the agent's statement furthered the argument that parole agents need to perform both roles in order to assure public safety, as one cannot achieve public protection or supervision without also performing some sort of social service to the parolee.[10]

What is Rehabilitation?

Rehabilitation as an ongoing event still existed, but SB 42 and SB 1057 altered the process in significant ways. The purpose of prisons was now punishment, at least rhetorically;[11] prisons were no longer part of the rehabilitative process. Parole became the main system by which rehabilitation was achieved. The changes brought on by SB 1057 led parole to focus more heavily on surveillance, relations with law enforcement, and drug testing (Veit, 1986). Parole agents were no longer supervising parolees to ensure they were making strides in the rehabilitative process; they were now surveilling to ensure compliance with conditions of parole. By claiming a focus on supervision, surveillance, and control, parole agents claimed they were focusing more directly on public protection, rather than just being service providers.

Maintaining the service-provider aspect of parole, however, enabled rehabilitation to be reframed as a tool of supervision, particularly as treatment providers were to report to parole agents when parolees were viewed as a risk to society. Then-Assistant Deputy Director Edward Veit (1983) even claimed the parolee's therapist was a crucial team member in monitoring the parolee's behavior and determining whether his behavior warranted a return to custody. Some conditions of parole also required program participation, especially the Parolee Outpatient Clinic and drug treatment programs, supposedly to ensure factors that led to the parolee's criminal behavior were eliminated. Non-compliance with conditions of parole was grounds for revocation, which provided an incentive for offenders to seek out their own rehabilitation to meet their conditions and avoid punishment. Rehabilitation was also reframed as a tool for managing risks, much as it was in the United Kingdom and Wales during this time period (Robinson, 2008). The treatments parolees were required to attend were based on factors that put them at risk for committing new crimes. If the programs were successful, they would reduce the parolees' risk, thereby reducing harm to society. If they failed, parolees were returned to custody, which also reduced harm to society.

Treatment programs were also used as intermediate sanctions for parole violations (Unknown, 1990; Legislative Analyst's Office, 1991), continuing the use of rehabilitation as a form of punishment.

The retention and reframing of rehabilitation provided credence to maintaining parole under the determinate sentencing regime. Initial concerns of parole violating double jeopardy highlighted the way parole, and by extension rehabilitation, was a second punishment carried out in the community. SB 1057 solidified this punishment by making parole an automatic part of the determinate sentence. The use of treatment programs, mental health therapists, community services, and special conditions extended carceral control into the community under the guise of rehabilitation. The reframing also changed the extent to which the state was responsible for rehabilitation. Agents were to provide opportunities for rehabilitation, but no longer forced change. Agents were now monitoring for failure rather than providing greater assistance. As one agent argued, a successful parole agent was one who returned a majority of parolees to prison rather than releasing a majority off parole (Scherb, 1993).

Changes to the Process

One major change to the rehabilitative process involved a shift away from prisons participating in the process. For those inmates who were sentenced under the old indeterminate sentencing system or were sentenced to a life term with the possibility of parole, there were some signs that prisons still played a role in the rehabilitative process. News coverage about parole board decisions suggested the board still based release on rehabilitative efforts made within prisons and on parole (Associated Press, 1979, October 12). Manuals and administrative codes developed after 1976 (Department of Corrections, 1977; Parole Policy and Procedures Committee, 1977; Board of Prison Terms, 1988) still included signs of remorse, plans for the future, and institutional behavior as indicators when determining if an individual was suitable for release.

After 1976, however, the purpose of these indicators changed. For example, prior to SB 42, institutional behavior indicated "sincerity and motivation for improvement" (Adult Authority, 1972); after SB 42, institutional behavior indicated an "enhanced ability to function within the law upon release" [Board of Prison Terms, 1988, Ch.3 Art. 5 §2281(d)(8)]. While the Community Release Board still reviewed an individual's past and present mental state along with many other factors (State of California, 1976), the purpose was to determine the risk an individual would pose upon release. The same factors used by the releasing authority to determine whether the individual changed for the better were now being used to determine one's risk (i.e., whether the individual was a threat to the public and able to lead a law-abiding life), rather than to determine improvement in the welfare or character of the individual. Rehabilitative progress was now reframed as a way of determining one's risk to society, rather than one's propensity to continue self-improvement in the community.[12]

On the other hand, those sentenced under the determinate sentencing system who did not receive life sentences were released at the end of their term regardless of the progress made within prison. Prisons still provided rehabilitation programs, but participation only accounted for one-fourth of good time credit and was not required to earn release. Parole became the part of the system mostly responsible for reintegrating and rehabilitating individuals convicted of a crime (Unknown, 1976, April 22; Otten & Lee, 1978, March 5).

Following the passage of the Uniform Sentencing Law, the parole system in California began to slowly move towards a law enforcement mentality with an emphasis on supervision over services. Officially parole administrators maintained that while the purpose of parole was public protection, the practice of parole was a mixture of both supervision and services. This official stance was expressed both externally and internally. In a directory developed for law enforcement and service agencies (Department of Corrections, 1981) and in an announcement for employment (L'Ecluse, 1993), the Department of Corrections described the parole agent's job as protecting the public and helping the parolee reintegrate into the community through a myriad of tools such as counseling parolees and their families, assisting parolees with such things as employment, and arresting parolees if necessary.

In practice, however, there was greater emphasis on supervision and a move to describing parole agents as law enforcement, implying a synonymous relationship with police officers. Beginning in the mid-1970s, the Parole Agents Association, the labor union representing parole agents at the time, filed suit against the state to allow agents to carry firearms. In 1978, the Shasta County Superior Court sided with the agents and required the state to allow parole agents to voluntarily carry guns (Keve, 1979; Veit, 1979). This decision eventually led to guns becoming a standard and required part of a parole agent's uniform. The push towards the ability to carry guns by the Parole Agents Association is particularly telling in terms of how the parole agents view their role. As Keve (1979, p. 433) found in a nationwide study on gun use perspectives by probation and parole officers, the perceived need of firearms depended on "the overall philosophy of the role and function of the probation or parole officer which has developed in the particular agency." He found that agencies that place a "heavier emphasis on community protection in terms of surveillance, control, and police-type actions when violations are detected" felt weapons were a requirement to do their job (Keve, 1979, p. 433). At least two other studies supported this claim and found that as weapon use increased, role conflict decreased, with the agents viewing themselves as law enforcement agents (Sigler & McGraw, 1984; Sigler, 1988). These studies suggested that, at the very least, the Parole Agents Association's leadership viewed the role of parole agents as law enforcement officials with little focus on the social work aspects of their job.

Articles and memos geared towards parole agents seemed to confirm this shift towards supervision. Shortly after the passage of the Uniform Sentencing Act, an article published in the *Correctional Peace Officer* (the newsletter for the California Peace Officers' Association) discussed a project implemented to "test control methods of parole supervision" (Marks & Lander, 1983, p. 17). The High Control Project placed parolees on a caseload focused on strict surveillance and supervision and did not appear to include any services. The high control caseload "represented a law enforcement approach to supervision . . . [and] emphasized pre-arrest rather than post-arrest investigation" (Marks & Lander, 1983, p. 19). The pre-arrest investigations included undercover surveillance of parolees and the use of vehicles with car-to-car radios that enabled the agent to call other law enforcement groups for back up. The project found that such practices significantly increased the likelihood of determining criminal activity or violations of the conditions of parole. Although the project ended in March 1980, "[l]essons learned from the project have been incorporated to an extent in parole supervision as it currently exists" (Marks & Lander, 1983, p. 35, 37). This again suggested an increased emphasis on surveillance over services.

Additionally, Veit proposed in a memo to the Deputy Director that the Division consider increasing the working hours of parole agents to include weekends and holidays (Veit, 1981). The recommendation was made to respond to potential criticism regarding "the importance of a parole program that chooses to ignore allocation of critical staff resources to the time periods which most parolee crime is occurring" (Veit, 1981, p. 2). By increasing field supervision hours, parole agents would presumably be able to increase supervision on parolee activity and either prevent crimes from occurring or catch them in the act.

This increased reliance on arrests and supervision was also reflected in the training and equipment required by the parole system. When discussing the impact of the large increase in the parole population, Veit (1986) noted the division was lacking the necessary resources, including parole offices, staff, safety equipment, and vehicles. He did not, however, mention the need for greater access to services and programs, whether offered through the parole office or through the community. The reliance on supervision was also reflected in policy. For example, the 1988 Parole Revocation Guidelines manual (Board of Prison Terms, 1988) listed several factors that provided good cause for maintaining someone on parole at the time of one's discharge review. Three of the five factors focused on criminal activity and revocations while on parole and one explicitly listed "special need of continued supervision for the safety of the parolee or the public" [Board of Prison Terms, 1988, Ch. 5, Art. 3., Sec. 2535(d)(5)], but there was no discussion of the need for continued services and assistance.

The disconnect between an official commitment to service and on-the-ground realities of a lack of resources and training on providing service was rarely discussed in official documents. One of the few documents that discussed these differences was a 1978 report that provided suggestions for a new parole model (Parole and Community Services Division, 1978a). The authors suggested a functionalist organization would be better adept at providing services, as parolees would be more willing to seek assistance from agents who are not supervising them. Assuming this view was correct, a functional organization still did not address the lack of resources or training available to service-oriented parole agents. Although some of the documents from this time period discussed using community programs and the Parolee Out Patient Clinic to assist parolees (Sutton, 1986; Department of Corrections, 1990; L'Ecluse, 1993), none discussed how the disconnect between policy and reality was to be reconciled. While the provision of services and a social-work approach were supported on the books, little was done to enforce those provisions, but the provision of providing supervision was supported at all levels.

An ethnographic study of a California parole office (Lynch, 2000) confirmed this shift. Lynch found that while the official language of the penal code stated that parole agents were to strive for the ideal of mixing assisting parolees with protecting the public, the tools and resources available to achieve the rehabilitative aims were lacking. The agents with whom she spoke claimed they were adequately trained on issues such as sanctioning parolees, but information on resources and programs available to parolees was learned on the job. What resources were available through the parole system were inadequate (Lynch, 2000).

Another major change was the rehabilitative process became more reliant on determining parolees' risk to society rather than their deficiencies. The new parole model called for a "comprehensive assessment of the risk each adult offender represents to the community" (Parole and Community Services Division, 1978b, p. i). Parolees were to undergo frequent comprehensive assessments based on diagnostic and predictive techniques (i.e., risk assessment tools). These assessments were to determine the parolee's risk to community and need for services (Parole and Community Services Division, 1978b). In this way, the notion of services and rehabilitation were reframed as a way of decreasing risk, similar to the way rehabilitation was reframed in England (Robinson, 2008), and signaled a shift towards the new penology approach to corrections (Feely & Simon, 1992).

The shift to functional specialization, as opposed to generalization, under the new parole model was based on the desire to better attack an individual's risks and needs. As parole agents were now working as teams to assist a parolee, they were supposedly better able to determine "what works, for whom, and when" (Parole and Community Services Division, 1978b). The level of supervision on which one was placed now depended on the risk posed by the parolee and the services needed. Those posing the greatest threat to the community were placed on higher levels of supervision, those posing the least threat to the community were placed on minimum supervision, and everyone else was placed on medium supervision. Within these levels, parolees were placed on "supervision emphasizing controls" or "supervision emphasizing services" caseloads (Parole and Community Services Division, 1978b), presumably determined by the comprehensive assessments. This was in stark contrast to the prior practice of placing everyone on maximum supervision and reducing services and supervision based on the parolee's rehabilitative progress. The use of programs based on "what works, for whom, and when" also eliminated the uniformity by which programs were provided, especially as it was believed that certain parolees were less likely to benefit from programs than others (Parole and Community Services Division, 1978b). These distinctions embraced the idea that some people will always be a risk to society, some people could reintegrate into society with some help, and some people would be able to reintegrate on their own.

A third major change in the rehabilitative process was the way in which parolees were discharged. Under the indeterminate sentencing structure, parolees were discharged when it was believed they no longer needed the assistance of the parole system and their rehabilitation was nearly complete. Under the determinate sentencing structure, this was no longer the case. The Board of Prison Terms[13] released very few individuals eligible for discretionary release from prison. A study conducted for then-Governor Deukmejian found no prisoner sentenced to life with the possibility of parole was released from prison from 1965 to 1990 (San Francisco Chronicle, 1990, April 13). The lack of releases continued under Governor Davis, who consistently overturned release decisions made by the parole board (Associated Press, 1999, October 3; San Jose Mercury News, 1999, October 17). The lack of releases meant those sentenced under the original indeterminate sentencing structure were never deemed even partially rehabilitated.

Those sentenced under the determinate sentencing structure were required to be released, regardless of their rehabilitative progress or risk to the community. These parolees were discharged upon completion of a legislatively determined set of time: three years for non-lifers, five years for lifers (State of California, 1976; Department of Corrections, 1977; Parole Policy and Procedures Committee, 1977). While there was the possibility of early discharge, it was only available if an individual remained continuously on parole for at least one year for non-lifers and three years for lifers and was dependent on the discretion of the parole agent. As returns for technical violations, returns for new crimes, and periods of absconsion stopped the parole clock, it was not clear how often an early discharge was possible. Such discharge was subject to review by the Board of Prison Terms and included factors such as commitment offense and institutional behavior as criteria for denying discharge (Parole Policy and Procedures Committee, 1977; Board of Prison Terms, 1988). When one was eligible for early release, one's past may preclude and even overshadow present behavior, which made obtaining an early release quite difficult. Because the parole clock stopped upon revocation, the length of time spent on parole was likely longer than the prescribed maximum. It was difficult to know when, or even if, the parole part of the rehabilitative process ever ended.

Change for the Better

Although the process after the passage of SB 42 and SB 1057 still implied a move away from criminal behavior and addressing the reasons behind the criminal behavior, the language was much more blatant in this regard. Whereas prior manuals and documents discussed the need to determine an inmate's willingness to exercise self-control and sincerity for improvement (Adult Authority, 1972), manuals created after 1977 focused on the need to determine one's risk to society, particularly for those still required to go before a parole board before being released.

The positive factors that were considered by the parole board included those that showed an individual was less likely to commit a crime. While some of the suitability criteria overlapped with prior criteria (e.g., ability to lead a crime-free life), others were new. These new positive factors included the "Achievement of significant skills which substantially reduce the likelihood that new crimes will be committed," "Significant improvement in self-control," and "Acceptance of new responsibilities indicating an increased ability to lead a crime free life" [Department of Corrections, 1977, Ch. 3, Art. 5, §2284(2)]. Although the factors included items such as academic achievement and participation in psychiatric programs, they seem to be geared solely towards determining whether or not one would commit another crime rather than a holistic improvement of the self. The only time the phrase "change for the better" was used was in describing the factor that indicated one was unsuitable for release: "A persistent pattern of criminal behavior and a failure to demonstrate evidence of a substantial change for the better" [Department of Corrections, 1977, Ch. 3, Art. 7, §2316(c)]. Once again, this criterion linked change for the better with the ability to end criminal behavior. Furthermore, the Certificate of Rehabilitation was described to parolees as a "certificate signed by the Governor stating that you have become a law-abiding citizen" (Department of Corrections, 1990, p. 6), signifying rehabilitation was solely about criminal behavior and nothing else. New factors also focused on the reasons behind the criminal behavior. One criterion stated [Department of Corrections, 1977, Ch. 3, Art. 7, §2284(2)(N)], "Changes in circumstances such as the personal, economic, or social circumstances which were a factor in the crime have been eliminated or substantially changed or the circumstances of environment into which the prisoner is to be released has changed." This criterion was in line with Petersilia's definition of rehabilitation (Shaughnessy, 2007).

Once on parole, the special conditions were also aimed at removing the causes of criminal behavior. This included requirements the parolees attend psychiatric treatment, abstain from alcohol, and avail themselves to anti-narcotic testing (Department of Corrections, 1977). Additional special conditions would be imposed if "the behavior to be controlled [was] sufficiently documented in the parolee's case history to explain the need for imposing a special condition" [Department of Corrections, 1977, Ch. 5, Art. 1, §2513(e)]. Combined, these factors and special conditions acknowledge societal and mental stressors could have led to criminal behavior, echoing the medical model's notion the individual was not inherently bad and could change to meet societal norms.

This link back to prior moments in the parole system suggested that while the rehabilitative process was altered, the view that offenders could somehow be made better or improved had not. This was particularly important for California's parole system, as it provided a rationale for why parole should be continued—that is, the supervision provided by parole agents and achieved through conditions of parole were uniquely situated to ensure offenders moved away from criminal behavior and factors that caused the behavior in the first place. The need to address these factors and change offenders embraced the new penology (Feely & Simon, 1992) and was reframed as a way of managing risks posed by groups rather than assisting individuals. The special conditions, once framed as a rehabilitative tool, were now framed as a way of encouraging supervision, as the agents were now looking for compliance for its own sake rather than as a way of ensuring improvement. This shift is highlighted when comparing Lester's (1952) discussion that supervision was not to be used to determine revocation with the 1998 Parole Revocation Guidelines (Board of Prison Terms, 1988) that specifically pointed to factors such as mental health and the presence of alcohol or drug use when determining revocations.

Return to Former Self

The idea of returning to a former self following SB 42 and SB 1057 implied a restoration of full civil rights, an idea unchanged from rehabilitation in the 1940s through the early 1970s. By 1975, almost all civil rights were restored upon release from prison. Some rights, however, were not returned until release from parole or later. The conditions of parole throughout this time period reminded a parolee: "You waive extradition to the State of California from any State or Territory of the United States, or from the District of Columbia. You will not contest any effort to return you to the State of California" and "You and your residence and any property under your control may be searched without a warrant at any time by any agent of the Department of Corrections or any law enforcement officer" (Department of Corrections, 1977, Ch. 5, Art. 1, §2511; State of California, 2001). Neither the right to fight extraditions nor protection from search and seizure were restored until after release from parole. If the new parole system did indeed reinstate "life on the installment plan," however, it was unclear when these rights were ever restored.

The rights to vote, to hold office, or to act as a trustee were still not returned until a returning individual received a pardon. The switch to determinate sentencing created an interesting problem for those applying for a Certificate of Rehabilitation who were sentenced prior to July 1, 1977. In *Daudert v. People* (1979, 94 Cal. App. 3d 580 [156 Cal.Rptr. 640]), the attorney general argued the period of rehabilitation should be computed based on the maximum sentence length at the time when the applicant was sentenced. The California Appellate Court disagreed and found that the period of rehabilitation should be calculated based on maximum sentence term in place at the time one applied for the certificate. This ruling allowed discharged individuals applying for a certificate after the passage of the Uniform Sentencing Law to apply sooner than if the law had not passed. The ruling was amended in *Sovereign v. People* (1983, 144 Cal. App. 3d 143 [192 Cal.Rptr. 469]) such that the period of rehabilitation was calculated based on the laws in place when the petitioner completed his term (i.e., discharged from parole). A case from 1998, however, suggested that obtaining a certificate was not easy. The decision in *People v. Lockwood* (1998, 66 Cal. App. 4th 222 [77 Cal. Rptr. 2d. 769]) found the trial court had sole discretion to deny or grant a certificate, meaning the requirements could vary from court to court. Given that parolees often served "life on the installment plan" and faced uncertainty in terms of requirements necessary for the trial court to grant a certificate, it was difficult to know when or even if released prisoners were fully returned to their former self.

Assistance or Right to Opportunity?

On the surface, the parole system maintained its purpose of helping parolees transition back to the community (Veit, 1986; Legislative Analyst's Office, 1991). Parole agents were to provide the parolee with services such as educational and vocational training, substance abuse treatment, and psychiatric care (Legislative Analyst's Office, 1998). Increased supervision supposedly allowed parole agents to intervene before illegal activity occurred or before the illegal activity escalated (Department of Corrections, 1981; Veit, 1981). Assistance was provided through casework, which included cash assistance or finding temporary residence; development of contracts with local community resources that were to provide help with employment, residence, substance abuse, and other services; and the Parole Outpatient Clinic (POC), the in-house psychiatric program developed in the 1950s (Legislative Analyst's Office, 1998). In some cases, assistance such as mandatory psychiatric treatment was forced upon the parolee as a special condition (State of California, 1976; Parole Policy and Procedures Committee, 1977; Board of Prison Terms, 1988).[14] At the same time, there was a growing acceptance that some individuals would "perform well in the community, regardless of the nature and scope of supervision and assistance they receive" while others "will require a return to an institution, no matter what system of supervision is available" (Parole and Community Services Division, 1978a, p. 5). For the middle group, it was often unknown whether parole's influence would result in "a marked improvement in readjustment to community life" or "represent only a reduction or delay in renewed criminal or delinquent activities" (Parole and Community Services Division, 1978a, p. 5).

As predicted by the Department of Finance (1976, September 16), SB 42 resulted in a "significantly larger number of offenders mandated to serve time in state prison under California's determinate sentencing law . . . more prison inmates inevitably and eventually lead to more offenders released . . . to parole" (Legislative Analyst's Office, 1998, p. 7). The quality of supervision diminished as the increased population led to higher caseloads and decreased contacts with parolees (Legislative Analyst's Office, 1998). These changes led to greater reliance on community-based alternatives for programming and intermediate sanctions (Unknown, 1990; Legislative Analyst's Office, 1991), thus relieving agents of some of their service responsibilities. It was argued community corrections would save money by reducing costs associated with time spent in prison for revocations. There was concern, however, that there were not enough programs, particularly for those with drug or alcohol addiction or who were homeless, mentally ill, or illiterate (Legislative Analyst's Office, 1998). The increased parolee population resulted in a higher demand for a limited number of resources and services (Unknown, 1990). Funding for such programs also decreased, which resulted in greater competition for program slots, waiting lists, and reluctance amongst community program directors to accept parolees.[15] Combined, these issues led to a greater reliance on prisons to hold parole violators (Unknown, 1990), contradicting the promise of reducing costs.

Perhaps in response to the uncertainty of parole supervision's impact on the parolee and limited access to services, there was a shift in who was responsible for rehabilitation. Assistance was available should parolees desire the help, but it was up to them to take advantage of these opportunities and decide whether or not they met the goals specified in the release plans. This was to be achieved by developing an environment that encouraged accountability and responsibility (California Department of Corrections, 1979). This shift was relayed through the parole handbook, which stated, "How well you do on parole will be your responsibility" (Department of Corrections, 1990, p. 1). The handbook also reminded parolees to ask their agents for assistance and provided parolees with information on how they may find their own employment and housing. This official language carried over into the everyday work of the parole agents, as Lynch (2000) found they viewed the parolees' attitudes and behavioral choices as the main factor in achieving change. While agents were to provide and in some cases force assistance when necessary, they were also supposed to help parolees choose to take advantage of those programs.

The increased responsibility of parolees and movement away from state intervention was in line with national trends in that crime control was now placed on the individuals rather than the government (Garland, 1996; Rose, 2000; Hannah-Moffat, 2001). For California, correctional authorities began to argue parolees were in charge of their own success and reform, reducing the role of parole agents in the rehabilitative process. This does not mean that the parole system—a state agency—was completely removed from the process. Rather, the role of parole echoed Garland's (1996) notion of "governance-at-a-distance" in that its reach had increased but was no longer viewed as solely responsible for the governance of prisoners and parolees (see also Hannah-Moffat, 2001). Reducing the role in rehabilitation and maintaining the power to supervise framed the parole system as a means of ensuring public protection through supervision and the appearance of maintaining the service aspects. This framing provided paroling authorities the power to rationalize the continuance and funding of the parole system, enabling the parole system to remain politically relevant.

In many ways, the contention between supervision and services also echoed the ways in which street-level actors created and implemented policies on the ground. As Lipsky (1980, p. xii) argued, front-line agents encountered a dilemma in that they were "wanting their organizational life to be more consistent with their own preferences and commitments" and that a lack of resources resulted in picking and choosing whom to assist. In addressing these dilemmas and lack of resources, the front-line actors created the policies they can actually carry out. For the parole agents, the dilemma became whether to stick to their combined function of providing services and supervising parolees as they did prior to the passage of SB 42 and SB 1057 or shift to solely focusing on the supervisory role and throw away their social work aspects as mandated by law. This dilemma was addressed by reframing who was responsible for what. Responsibilizing the parolees enabled the agents to relieve themselves of the burden of dealing with a lack of resources and allowed them to focus more on supervision, meeting the legislative requirements of their role. The agents were now providing a watchful and suspicious gaze over the parolees and were waiting for them to trip up, rather than being medical professionals adept at treating parolees and helping them get better. This gaze was also turned on to the agents, as several policies were considered or put into place that expanded and supervised how an agent was viewed as effective (e.g., consideration of longer working hours, requirement to arrest parolees themselves rather than waiting for police assistance, etc.). Rehabilitation, though it existed, was treated with an air of skepticism and the parole agents were now judged for how well they attended to their supervisory activities rather than their service activities.

Support and Criticisms of Emphasis on Supervision

Many parole agents supported the push towards greater supervision. One agent even felt increased supervision and returns to custody were the mark of a job well done, stating, "Agents were so enthusiastic and good at their jobs, that in 1988 we returned almost 80 percent of all California parolees to prison at least once" and that such arrests protected the community (Scherb, 1993, p. 41). He also argued public safety was de-emphasized when the parole system showed signs of shifting back to social work following budget cuts.

These sentiments were further supported in a press packet created for agents (Unknown, 1993). Included was a list of facts indicating parole "is the only law enforcement agency designated to monitor and supervise these parolees in an attempt to deter them from returning to their criminal lifestyles and creating more victims" (Unknown, 1993, p. 1). Once again, parole agents were referred to as law enforcement, not social workers. The role of parole agents as law enforcement was legislatively solidified with the passage of AB 3603 in 1992, which encouraged agents to respond to any criminal action, not just the criminal action of parolees (Loy, 1994). The press packet also listed 13 aspects of the parole agents' job, 11 of which discussed their supervisory functions and only two of which discussed service-oriented functions. Finally, the press packet noted, "Parole is a privilege, and his freedom can be revoked at any time. This fact alone makes parole a great motivation for many parolees" (Unknown, 1993, p. 3). This final statement not only equated the threat of re-arrest as a means of controlling parolee behavior, but also brings in language used when the indeterminate sentence was in place. Under the indeterminate sentence, parole was indeed a privilege that could be revoked at any moment, but under determinate sentencing, parole release was supposed to be a statutory fact.

Although the parole system moved towards a greater emphasis on supervision, a desire to maintain casework was apparent. In memos to individuals at the administrative level of parole and corrections, two line agents noted their frustration at a lack of consistency in both creation and enactment of policy. One agent indicated supervisors at various levels provided inconsistent support for services such as cash assistance and bus passes, which led "parolees [to] feel alienation, intimidation, rejection, and agents [to] feel embarrassment when the rules change" (Gatlin, 1989, p. 3). Following changes to training and the passage of AB 3603, another agent asked (Loy, 1994, p. 1), "Should we throw away casework and take up the gun and become members of our local Police Departments?" The Legislative Analyst's Office (1998, p. 17) also found that many agents were concerned "that some parolees who had failed one drug test, but who had otherwise behaved well on parole, secured employment, and established stable family relationships, were being returned to prison by the BPT [Bureau of Parole Terms]," suggesting dissatisfaction with the push towards greater arrests and revocations. Finally, through an ethnographic study of a California parole office, Lynch (1998) found that, in practice, parole agents functioned as more than "risk managers" even though they often lacked the necessary tools.

Rising caseloads, decreased access to programs, and role conflict among agents prompted the Legislative Analyst's Office (1998) to suggest a new parole model. This model would have three supervision levels. Low-risk parolees would not be required to meet with agents, but would still be required to follow conditions of parole and be subject to search and seizure requirements.[16] Medium-risk parolees would be required to meet with agents, but would do so at day-reporting centers where they would work with a team of agents to access services. High-risk parolees would receive the most intense level of supervision and be required to attend the Psychiatric Outpatient Clinic. In this way, parole agents would be able to supervise those who pose the most risk to the community and assist those who pose some risk, but were in need of greater services. This recommendation signaled a shift back towards the use of services along with supervision to achieve public protection and suggested openness to the return to rehabilitation that occurred in the 2000s.[17]

These changes were proposed in the midst of a changing correctional landscape. Additional changes, often passed through voter propositions, included building dozens of new prisons, the establishment of victim's rights as a focus of the criminal justice system, and passage of the "Three

Strikes" law (Barker, 2009). The switch to determinate sentences and the corresponding expansion of the correctional system, the increased focus on surveillance, and the cycling in and out of prison because of parole revocations created a crisis within California's correctional system. The system was now woefully overcrowded, which led to multiple lawsuits, increased correctional spending, and one of the highest recidivism rates in the nation. These issues led to numerous calls for revamping the correctional system. As the next chapter shows, the growing criticisms and calls for reform led to a reorganization of the Department of Corrections and re-emphasis on rehabilitation.

Notes

1 In both letters, the names were removed to protect the identity of the prisoners.
2 For an alternate explanation of the rise in prison violence, see Simon, 2012.
3 This raised the question, however, as to the amount of power judges actually have in determining sentences. Since prosecutors determine the charges and thus possible conviction offense against an individual, one could argue that sentencing was really determined by the prosecutor and the judge formalized this choice. Scholars later found that changes in sentencing laws did, indeed, increase the role of prosecutorial discretion and that the legislators shifted much of the responsibility for sentencing to prosecutors (e.g., Griset, 1991; Misner, 1996).
4 These changes seem to be a continuation of the changes begun in the 1960s under Governor Reagan (Barker, 2009).
5 The amount of good time available increased throughout the process of passing the bill. Initially, good time credit was to allow for a 25 percent reduction (Unknown, 1975, May 14), was raised to a one-third reduction (Legislative Analyst's Office, 1976), and was finally set at 50 percent (Kenady, 1976).
6 This criticism seems to be justified given the gradual increase in sentence lengths over the last 30 years (Griset, 1991) and the support from legislators for propositions such as Three Strikes.
7 Although this practice raised questions about whether one can be held in prison without being convicted of a new crime, and presumably not having committed a technical violation, the documents do not address this issue. Recent scholarship, however, has been critical of California's "back-end sentencing" of parolees (Lin, Grattet, & Petersilia, 2010; Mayeux, 2011).
8 This argument was based on the idea that the conditions of parole were designed to address the factors that led one to criminal behavior. As such, a technical violation was a sign that the same troubling factors would once again lead to criminal behavior.
9 A manual published in response to SB 1057 was not found.
10 Interestingly, in a preliminary I study conducted in 2008, at least two parole agents told me they would prefer to have two agents per caseload. The division of power, according to them, should be designed so that one person does the fieldwork and interpersonal work and another kept up with the paperwork.
11 At least one study argues, however, that while the rhetoric moved away from rehabilitation, the actual practices and funding for programs within prisons changed very little (Phelps, 2011).

12 This is likely not the first time existing structures and language are reframed to meet new correctional goals, nor is it likely to be the last. For example, Maurutto and Hannah-Moffat (2006) trace how the Level of Supervision Inventory, originally developed in the 1970s in response to shifts in penological focus, shifted to become the Level of Services Inventory today with little meaningful change to the tool itself.

13 This board, which was previously called the Community Release Board, was responsible for revocation hearings and parole hearings for those serving life with the possibility of parole.

14 That said, all parolees were to some degree forced to participate in "services," as they were legally mandated to be placed on parole.

15 As recent scholarship reflects, these community resources are still unable to meet their high demand (Hipp, Jannetta, Shah, & Turner, 2011).

16 While not immediately implemented as proposed, this form of low-risk supervision was eventually realized with the passage of Non-Revocable Parole in 2009.

17 On the other hand, no files indicated whether or not such a change actually occurred, but other studies of parole systems (e.g., Petersilia, 2003) indicate that a similar organization of levels was eventually implemented.

Chapter 4

Re-Emergence of Rehabilitation

2000 to 2005

[T]he purpose of corrections should be to correct.
~Governor Schwarzenneger, 2005

After decades of emphasizing punishment within the correctional system and shifting towards law enforcement within the parole system, California was faced with massive overcrowding, the highest recidivism rate in the nation with over 60 percent returning to prison each year, and a general belief that the correctional system was defunct (Warren, 2005, March 27). In light of this, newly elected Governor Schwarzenegger made reforming the correctional system one of his top priorities. In 2005, California formally reorganized and renamed the Department of Corrections to the Department of Corrections *and Rehabilitation*, created the Division of Adult Parole Operations, and changed the department's mission: "*To improve public safety through evidence-based crime prevention and recidivism reduction strategies*" (CDCR Expert Panel, 2007, p. 6, emphasis in original).

This shift back towards rehabilitation seemed to fall in line with a larger linguistic shift away from "tough on crime" and towards "smart on crime" that was also occurring in the early 2000s. As Altheide and Coyle (2006) argued, recent criminal justice policies and reforms such as California's generally followed the call by social scientists and reformers to minimize the emphasis on prison sentences and increase support for early release from prison. As these ideas were in direct contrast to the "tough on crime" mentality of the 1990s, politicians and other government leaders needed to avoid appearing "soft on crime." The newer reforms were framed as being "smart on crime," particularly as they focused on cost-saving measures. Doing so helped ensure these changes would "resonate with 'tough on crime' actors, principles, and practice" (Altheide & Coyle, 2006, p. 291).

The similarities between these new policies and the ones prior to the 1970s are striking. Both eras called for evidence-based practices and for a focus on treatments and programming (Simon, 1993; CDCR Expert Panel, 2005; Fairfax, 2011). For California, the 2005 reorganization was the capstone to several changes already in the works. Questions remain as to whether this shift was coming to fruition or whether it was a change in name only.

Reforming Parole

Years before Schwarzenegger focused on reorganizing the correctional system, several state policy organizations pushed for a revamping of the system generally and parole specifically and a court settlement required specific changes within the parole system. The parole system began reorganizing its policies and practices with the development of a new parole model in the early part of the decade. This new model was intended to re-elevate the role of social work within the everyday practices of parole agents. The new model also seemed to be a pre-emptive means of addressing many of the criticisms raised by the Little Hoover Commission in 2003. Although the commission noted that the parole system was an utter failure, it believed the parole system served a valuable purpose within the correctional system, but needed several changes to be viable (Little Hoover Commission, 2003). Some of these changes were implemented following the settlement of *Valdivia v. Schwarzenegger*. It was not until 2005, however, when the governor released his Reorganization Plan, that the legislature began to address the issues raised by the commission.

Growing Criticism of the Parole System and Attempts at Reform

In an attempt to address the focus on surveillance to the exclusion of social work that developed in the parole system in the later part of the twentieth century, a new parole model was developed in 2001 (Corrections Independent Review Panel, 2004) and implemented statewide by 2004 (Legislative Analyst's Office, 2005). The new parole model hoped to shift the practices of parole towards a more service-oriented model while protecting its law enforcement capabilities in an attempt to increase parole success and protect public safety (Woodford, 2004). The new model consisted of six key components: pre-release planning; Parole and Corrections Team (PACT) orientation; use of a violation matrix; electronic monitoring; the Substance Abuse Treatment Control Unit (SATCU); and a Halfway Back program (Corrections Independent Review Panel, 2004). The new parole model encompassed an expansion of existing (pre-release planning; SATCU; halfway houses) and development of new (PACT meetings; violation matrix) practices and programs.

The pre-release planning portion of the new model required a continuation of evaluating all inmates using a risk-needs assessment prior to release onto parole. In this way, agents determined which services and programs would be beneficial to individuals upon release and predicted the likelihood that they would reoffend, thus indicating the level of supervision required. A risk-needs assessment would now be utilized periodically while the individual was on parole to determine any changes needed in the level of services or supervision provided (Corrections Independent Review Panel, 2004; Legislative Analyst's Office, 2005). Andrews, Bonta, & Wormith (2006) argued the use of such assessments to develop a continuum of care and periodic reviews were elements of a fourth generation of risk-needs assessments; however, this form of assessment was also reflective of the practice of developing and revising release plans during the 1940s to 1960s. While the instruments might be new, the theoretical framing of them was not. What was new was how the assessment tools further entrenched the relationship between rehabilitation and supervision. The risk-needs assessments were not only used to determine the risk level posed by groups of people, but also the treatment necessary to control that risk. Thus, the risk-needs assessment became a diagnostic tool that formally framed supervision as a means of achieving treatment. It also reframed rehabilitation as a tool for judging the amount of risk posed and the amount of supervision needed (see also Maurutto & Hannah-Moffat, 2006).

This pre-release planning was followed by mandatory attendance at the newly established Parole and Corrections Team (PACT) parolee orientation. While PACT meetings originally began in a small number of units, they were expanded to all parole districts following the 2003–2004 Budget Act (Legislative Analyst's Office, 2005). The PACT meetings were designed to connect parolees just released from prison[1] with service providers in the area. At the meeting I observed, parolees were not allowed to leave without completing their parole plan and obtaining the contact information of at least five (out of roughly 15) organizations/providers that would be beneficial to completing parole. The parolees had to turn the forms into their agents when they left and the agents were to use the forms to discuss what the parolees felt was important in ensuring they completed parole successfully. As discussed below, however, the agents felt it was up to the parolees to actually take advantage of these services and that, in many cases, the parolees did not follow through on contacting the service providers.

The remaining aspects of the new parole model were designed to provide guidelines and alternatives to revocations for dealing with parole violations. The implementation of electronic monitoring, the halfway back program that provided residential treatment, and the SATCU program that provided a 30-day in-custody drug treatment program offered alternative sanctions for those who committed a technical violation by providing an increase in supervision and, in some cases, services (Corrections Independent Review Panel, 2004). In this way, rehabilitation was once again framed as a form of punishment (Robinson, 2008).

The Parole Violation Decision-Making Instrument (PVDMI) was created to implement a structured system of determining how best to respond to a parole violation (Corrections Independent Review Panel, 2004). This violation matrix provided a grid by which the parole agent would determine a parolee's "punishment" for violating a condition of parole based on specified criteria and resembled the sentencing matrixes many states use upon conviction. Ideally, the matrix was to increase uniformity and decrease discretion among parole agents when determining a response to violations and ensure alternatives were utilized to reduce returns to prison and reduce prison populations. The matrix also further entrenched the use of actuarial tools and risk management methods into the parole system (for a critique of this entrenchment, see Harcourt, 2007). Based on the interviews with parole agents, reaction to the matrix was mixed. While one unit supervisor interviewed found the matrix useful and helped justify decisions made by the agents, another agent hated the matrix and felt it reduced the individuals on parole to nothing more than numbers.

Implementation of the new parole model was slow. The violation matrix was not implemented until November 2008, when a pilot project was conducted in four counties (Murphy & Turner, 2010) and was not implemented statewide until a 2009 law mandated its use (see Chapter 5). While the 2003–2004 Budget Act expanded funding for the Parole and Corrections Team to all parole districts in the state, PACT meetings in at least one area did not begin until 2006 (Bock, 2009, October 23). Many of the agents interviewed noted that funding for programs was lacking and it severely limited the ability of agents to take advantage of the community programs and alternative sanctions available. Still, the new parole model was a signal that the parole system was attempting to refocus on its rehabilitative aspects, a move that was soon embraced by the correctional system as a whole.

Two years later, in 2003, the Little Hoover Commission released its report on whether or not California should maintain the parole system. The basic, and harshest, criticism was that the "parole system is a billion-dollar failure" (Little Hoover Commission, 2003, p. i). The commission found four problems: 1) inmates were not prepared for release; 2) available programs in the community were not being utilized; 3) the majority of parole violators were returned to prison; and 4) revocation was often used in place of prosecution for a new crime. The commission argued these issues combined to create a system in which the vast majority of parolees failed and only "21 percent of parolees complete their parole term without being returned to prison for some period of time or absconding" (p. ix). It was unclear whether the inability to reintegrate parolees meant that it was also failing at protecting the public or if the high return rates were viewed as a public safety success story.

To combat these issues, the Little Hoover Commission made five recommendations. First, the correctional system needed to "improve the performance of the correctional system by changing laws, budgets, and programs to increase success among parolees" (Little Hoover Commission, 2003, p. 38), including using risk-needs assessments to determine how to utilize prison programs, address revocations, and determine services while on parole. Second, the state needed to increase programs available in prisons to better prepare inmates for release and make changes to good time credits to incentivize program participation. Third, it called for an elimination of unnecessary legal barriers to reintegration and changes to parole so that services and supervision were front-loaded and individualized as they were prior to the 1970s. They also recommended reducing conditions of parole or earned discharge for those making progress and restorative justice programs as conditions of parole and in lieu of violation sanctions. Fourth, it called for use of a violation decision-making matrix that utilized alternative sanctions for violations and separate housing for parolees who were returned to prison. Finally, the Little Hoover Commission (2003) recommended charging new crimes through the court system rather than through the revocation process.

The new parole model seemed to be pre-emptive strike, as the six components directly address the four major issues raised by the Little Hoover Commission (pre-release planning addressed problem #1, PACT meetings addressed problem #2, and the remaining components addressed problems #3 and #4) or mimicked its recommendations. This attempt at "fixing" problems followed similar attempts at "fixing" prisons. As Foucault argues (1975/1977), when prisons were criticized as failing, the answer was to fix and maintain the prison rather than get rid of them altogether. Similarly, the answer to a failing parole system here was to revamp and continue the parole system, rather than get rid of it. While reforms were made, they seemed to either be extending or formalizing existing practices. As will be discussed below, these reforms—coupled with the reorganization and switch back to rehabilitation—did not undo surveillance and punishment as desired. Rather, the reforms made them stronger.

None of the policy changes implemented through the new parole model or proposed by the Little Hoover Commission addressed how the determinate sentencing structure was impacting parole, an issue raised by then-Oakland Mayor Jerry Brown. During the hearings, Brown testified that he made a "big mistake" signing the law implementing the determinate sentencing structure when he was governor of California (see Chapter 3).

As the San Francisco Chronicle (Zamora, 2003, February 28, p. Online) reported, Brown stated, "We never should have gotten rid of indeterminate sentencing—we lost the ability to rehabilitate offenders." He noted existing laws meant the current system lacked the mechanisms to motivate prisoners into rehabilitation. Brown also stated he supported overhauling the system so that an indeterminate sentencing structure was reinstated for many crimes. This about-face seemed to be the result of the realities of crime levels Brown faced as a mayor; realities he did not face as governor (DeFao, 2003, February 18).

The new parole model ended in 2007. As another report by the Little Hoover Commission (2007) found, programs under the model were underutilized because of strict eligibility requirements. Limited funding and a statewide hiring freeze also prevented the parole system from contracting with community organizations and local jails for programming or hiring individuals to provide programming internally. Finally, the Crime Victims United organization criticized the model as a danger to public safety, creating political opposition to the changes implemented.

Settlement of Valdivia v. Schwarzenegger *(Formerly Davis)*

In 1994, Jerry Valdivia and several other parolees entered a class-action lawsuit against then-Governor Gray Davis and other members of the State of California (*Valdivia v. Davis*, 206 F.Supp.2d 1068 [2002]). The parolees argued the existing parole revocation process violated the due process clause of the Fourteenth Amendment as the process took too long, ranging anywhere from one to three months, and did not allow parolees to challenge the evidence against them, present their own evidence, or question the witness(es) prior to the revocation hearing. In 2002, the United States District Court of Eastern California ruled in favor of the parolees (*Valdivia v. Davis*, 206 F.Supp.2d 1068 [2002]) and required the state develop a plan to address the issues raised (Legislative Analyst's Office, 2005). In November 2003, on Governor Schwarzenegger's first day in office, a settlement agreement was signed. The settlement plan included five major changes, including an agreement to increase the use of intermediate sanctions for nonviolent and non-serious parole violators in lieu of prison time (Legislative Analyst's Office, 2005).

Following approval of the settlement by the Federal District Court, the Department of Corrections faced criticism from parole agents and victim advocates alike. As the San Francisco Chronicle reported (2005, April 10), members of the California Corrections and Parole Officers Association (CCPOA)[2] argued the diversion programs were not working. Specifically, agents criticized the possible diversion programs as not matching the crimes supposedly committed and not being well thought out. As one agent said in a statement to the Associated Press (2004, March 15), "It's just stupidity." Another agent argued the use of drug treatment programs would not work for everyone, as some areas simply did not have the necessary programs (Associated Press, 2004, March 15). The advocacy group Crime Victims United in California also ran several television ads criticizing the program (San Francisco Chronicle, 2005, April 10). The SF Chronicle also noted that "A more fundamental problem is that most inmates were not getting any serious rehabilitative services while in prison—and do not have the financial and other support they need to stay out of trouble once released" (San Francisco Chronicle, 2005, April 14, p. Online), echoing criticism raised by the Little Hoover Commission and suggesting that existing policies and programs could not support the goals of the newly established diversion programs. In response to such criticism, rather than attempt to make the programs more viable, Governor Schwarzenegger and his administration abruptly ended the diversion programs in April 2005.

The end to the programs provided insight into the ability of changes to withstand political pressure. First, it indicated that government officials were willing to scrap a policy rather than attempt to revamp it, even when doing so could violate a court settlement. Second, it indicated the power of organizations to end the use of state funding for rehabilitative programs, even though a poll by the National Council on Crime and Delinquency (Krisberg, Craine, & Marchionna, 2004) found that 63 percent of Californians favored funding such programs in prisons and on parole, rather than punishment only. Third, it indicated the ability of new policies to be successful was largely dependent on factors outside of the policy, including support from the implementing agency and citizens as well as the ability of existing policies and programs to support the goal of the new policy. Thus, while the governor was attempting to create a cultural change towards rehabilitation, political pressure was maintaining a culture of control.

Reforming Corrections

While implementation of the Valdivia settlement was being hashed out, criticisms of the parole system were growing and the prison system faced several issues, including massive overcrowding and a pending lawsuit regarding healthcare in adult facilities [*Plata v. Schwarzenegger*, docket no. 3:01-cv-01351-TEH (N.D. Cal.)]. Yet, the push to officially reform the Department of Corrections did not come from department officials. This was not entirely surprising. By declaring "the purpose of prisons is to punish," the Determinate Sentencing Law created a culture of punishment and control through risk management techniques (see Chapter 3) that did "not rehabilitate offenders" (Terry Thorton, then DOC spokesperson, quoted in Zamora, 2002, December 23, p. Online). The declaration also ensured any changes made to the culture of prisons, and by extension the organization as a whole, must also come from the legislature.

As criticism of the *Valdivia* settlement suggested, attempts at reducing the parole system's reliance on prisons as a means of punishing parole violators and shifting towards more rehabilitative programs was not possible without a shift in the larger organizational culture. The push for reform came from Governor Schwarzenegger, who was quoted by the *Los Angeles Times* as saying that corrections "should correct" (Warren, 2005, February 13, p. Online). While the development of a new organizational structure did not occur until 2005, Schwarzenegger was creating the route to change early in his first term.

The first sign that change was coming occurred in February 2004. Schwarzenegger appointed Jean Woodford as the director of the California Department of Corrections, noting "[her] extensive background in corrections and proven ability to lead will be instrumental in bringing about the necessary changes in California's prison system" (Office of the Governor, 2004, February 19, p. Online). Less than a month later, Schwarzenegger set out to determine what changes needed to be made. In March 2004, he appointed former Governor Deukemjian to lead an Independent Review Panel (later named the Corrections Independent Review Panel) comprised of current and retired employees of the Office of Inspector General, Department of Corrections, Board of Prison Terms, California Highway Patrol, and California Youth Authority that "will produce a series of near and long-term action steps to increase accountability, make better use of scarce resources, and reduce risks to employees, inmates and the public" (Office of the Governor, 2004, March 5, p. Online). At this point, the language still focused on risks and management, not rehabilitation.

After reviewing documents and interviewing multiple leaders and workers within the Department of Corrections, the Corrections Independent Review Panel (CIRP) released a roughly 250-page report of recommended changes in June 2004. The report claimed the correctional system was failing at all levels and these failures resulted in multiple lawsuits, a threat to place the "state's prisons under federal receivership," and inmates who "cycle in and out of institutions with little effort made to provide education and rehabilitation services to keep them from re-offending" (Corrections Independent Review Panel, 2004, p. i). The report called for a "sustained investment" in such services and a "shift in attitude toward non-violent offenders" that would allow for the use of community level alternatives to incarceration. The report also noted that providing such services would not only reduce the state's high recidivism rates, but also protect the public and be cost effective.

The CIRP report echoed the Little Hoover Commission's (2003) report when it highlighted the limited number of rehabilitative services available within prisons and made the case that such services should be increased. It defended this recommendation, saying, "This is not about coddling criminals—this is about protecting the public by ensuring that offenders do not commit a second crime" (Corrections Independent Review Panel, 2004, p. ii). This language, as well as the language addressing rising costs, reflects the move away from "tough on crime" framing of crime policy and towards a "smart on crime" framing (Altheide & Coyle, 2006).

Before these changes could occur, the panel argued the Department of Corrections was in need of wholesale reform that had to begin with the organizational structure. The panel called for a "flattening" of the correctional system's organization and for the prison institutions and parole operations to work together to prepare inmates for release from the moment they entered the prison, similar to the continuum of care in place from the 1940s to mid-1970s. The report called for the development of an independent Civilian Corrections Commission. The purpose of the commission was to bring transparency to the department by providing a public voice to the department's activities. The commission would report directly to the governor and be responsible for overseeing the newly created Department of Correctional Services, appointing an inspector general, and giving directives to the Department Secretary. While the existing organization was a decentralized structure, in which each institution (run under either the Department of Corrections or the California Youth Authority) was responsible for itself and the parole division (Board of Prison Terms) operated separately from the institutions, the proposed secretary of Correctional Services would provide a centralization of powers and be in charge of all aspects of the correctional system. This centralization would also include the development of eight system-wide offices, such as an Office of Research and Planning and Office of Information, and two directors: director of Youth Operations and director of Adult Operations.

The panel also recommended changes specifically aimed at reducing the state prison population. These recommendations focused on "the length of time inmates serve in prison; the training and treatment they receive during incarceration to decrease the likelihood that they will return; and the services they receive during parole to help remain crime-free and successfully integrate into society" (Correctional Independent Review Panel, 2004, p. 121). In terms of the length of time served in prison, the panel members argued for elimination of a time-credit system and the introduction of a "presumptive sentencing" model post-incarceration. Individuals would still be sentenced to a determinate sentence as specified by the penal code, but good time credit would no longer be used. Instead, the judge would determine a presumptive sentence that was shorter than the assigned term and presumed good behavior, "so that the presumptive term becomes the actual time served *provided that* good behavior is maintained" (Corrections Independent Review Panel, 2004, p. 129, emphasis in original). Good behavior was defined as developing and achieving a set of goals/requirements (i.e., program plan) prior to release from prison. The plan would be constantly re-evaluated while the inmate served his time and completion of requirements would be verified prior to release. If the inmate had not completed his requirements, he would not be released until all requirements were met or the maximum term (original determinate sentence) was served, whichever came first (Corrections Independent Review Panel, 2004). Implementing this "presumptive sentencing" system would create a hybrid between indeterminate and determinate sentencing structures. While the individual would still be sentenced under the determinate sentencing structure, release would be dependent on the appearance of rehabilitation (assuming, of course, that the goals/requirements established in the program plan were designed to rehabilitate the individual), much like those released under the indeterminate sentencing structure. Individuals released under the presumptive sentencing structure were also dependent on the review of a third party, similar to the way in which individuals under the indeterminate sentencing structure were subject to third-party review by a parole board. The panel's recommendations do not provide any indication on how discretion played a role in the review of an inmate's plans or if the reviewing party would be able to change the plan such that inmates would never earn early release.

The second major change recommended by the panel was an increase in the training and treatment inmates received while in prison. The report noted that massive overcrowding, inadequate staffing, and in-prison violence currently impeded one's ability to take advantage of programs while serving time. It also argued that increased programming opportunities decreased the risk of in-prison violence by eliminating idleness amongst inmates. Programming decreased the prison population by better preparing inmates for release and decreasing the likelihood of recidivating. Thus, the panel recommended increasing both staff levels and space available for in-prison programs. This recommendation echoed the system in place (at least on paper) under the indeterminate sentencing structure, which also relied on in-prison programming opportunities to maintain control of inmates and provide avenues for rehabilitation. The panel was not specific, however, on how such programs were to be implemented given the existing overcrowding in prisons.

These first two recommendations focused on what could be done prior to release that would increase the chances of successful reintegration and decrease the likelihood of being sent back to prison. As almost all of California's prisoners were released on to parole, these recommendations would hopefully also increase the likelihood of a successful release from parole. The final set of recommendations focused on structural changes to the parole system. One of these recommendations followed directly from the changes made to the time spent in prison. The panel (2004) questioned the practice of releasing all inmates onto parole and recommended early discharge from parole for low-risk individuals. Arguably, if inmates participated in programs while in prison, they would be better prepared for release and thus less likely to violate their parole. In this manner, one who has been adequately prepared for release could be discharged from parole without any concerns to public safety.

For those who were not discharged early, the panel recommended several other changes. One recommendation was an expanded use of risk-needs assessments that were administered on each inmate upon release and updated periodically, echoing the recommendations of the Little Hoover Committee. In this way, the parole agent could adjust levels of supervision and services as necessary. The panel also recommended changing eligibility rules for drug treatment programs, as they found that those most in need of such programs were often barred from participation, and increasing alternative intermediate sanctions to eliminate the high rates of re-imprisonment for those who violate a condition of parole. The recommendation of constant re-evaluation of treatment plans suggested a belief that the needs of a released individual changed over time and seemed to echo the re-evaluation of plans developed in the 1940s to the mid-1970s, particularly as the goal of re-evaluation in both eras was to ensure the programs sufficiently addressed parolees' risks and needs at different moments in time.

The panel also argued that a coordination of services was necessary in order for the recommended changes to achieve the desired impacts. Specifically, the report (2004, p. 121) claimed:

> Underlying the panel's recommendations is the fundamental principle that the main goal is to protect public safety, but that public safety is best served by a system that not only locks up criminals, but also helps inmates prepare for release and improves opportunities for parolees to stay out of prison. For these efforts to succeed, the custody and parole systems must work in concert, beginning with the first day inmates enter prison and continuing until parolees are released from supervision.

Thus, the panel argued that a coordination of services would not only ensure that their recommendations would result in a reduction of prison population, but would also ensure the system met its stated goal of public protection. The language used in the report was similar to the language used by the Adult Authority (1945, p. 2) when it stated, "protection of society is the aim and purpose of the penal system. It does not believe that punishment alone is truly protective. Only when prisoners are rehabilitated as well as punished, does the penal system solve its problem." Like the arguments made under the medical model, the panel argued that focusing on the rehabilitation of offenders does not require a shift in the system's goals, but simply a shift in the day-to-day practices of achieving its goal. The panel noted that the reorganization would help achieve this goal by centralizing both the prison and parole systems under the Department of Adult Operations, allowing for a common focus: ensuring the preparedness of inmates for release and discharge into society (Corrections Independent Review Panel, 2004). This recommendation called for a re-establishment of a continuum of treatment that began in prison and continued onto parole, a continuum that was the basis of the indeterminate sentencing structure and was removed as a result of overcrowding and lack of funding for in-prison programs following the shift to determinate sentencing.

While the panel noted the organization and recommended changes would result in a greater opportunity for public safety, it also stated these changes would cost less. The reorganization would save the department an estimated $20 billion[3] by consolidating administrative and executive functions and eliminating "overlapping and duplicative functions" (Corrections Independent Review Panel, 2004, p. 15). The implementation of a presumptive sentencing scheme was said to "generate significant savings as inmates become better prepared for reintegration into society" (p. 133), even though the panel stated it was not possible to estimate the actual fiscal impact. Finally, the panel argued that increasing programming opportunities in prison, discharging low-risk parolees early, and using intermediate sanctions would save money by improving an individuals' likelihood of successfully completing parole.

The Governor's Reorganization Plan

Months after the panel made its recommendations, Schwarzenegger presented his plan for reorganizing the Department of Corrections. Prior to releasing the Governor's Reorganization Proposal 2 (later named the Governor's Reorganization Proposal 1 when the original Proposal 1 was dropped), the governor hinted he would be following some of the same philosophy proposed in the Little Hoover Commission and CIRP reports. While on a fact-finding mission at Mule Creek State Prison, Schwarzenegger laid out his thoughts on the Department of Corrections (Office of the Governor, 2004, August 16, p. Online):

> My vision of California's prison system is one where violent, dangerous offenders are kept behind bars, so our families stay safe. But I also see a system committed to rehabilitating our prisoners so they can be successful when they are released and a system managed with the highest degree of professionalism.

This was the first time while in office the governor formally indicated his desire to include rehabilitation as an aspect of the correctional system. It was also the first indication that Schwarzenegger would attempt to create a system that recognized that not all individuals convicted of a crime were a part of the dangerous class, thus aiming to alter the culture of the Department of Corrections so that not all individuals were automatically subject to punishment and control. It also hinted at a system in which rehabilitation was used as a means of socially controlling and normalizing inmate behavior of nonviolent offenders, much the way punishment was supposed to do for violent offenders.

On January 6, 2005, he submitted his proposal to the Little Hoover Commission for review. The choice of using a Governor's Reorganization Plan, as opposed to reform through the legislative process, was an interesting one. The reorganization process was similar to an executive order in that a legislative veto was required to prevent the plans from passing, but approval was not necessary for the plans to go into effect. That said, the plans must be submitted to both the Little Hoover Commission and the legislature for review and the legislature has the option of altering the plans. If the legislature chose to take action, it could pass legislation to veto or amend the plan. If the legislature chose not to take any action, the plan passed as written (Office of the Governor, 2005, January 6). In this way, the governor would be able to move the Department of Corrections towards a culture of rehabilitation while potentially avoiding political factions within the legislature and the community that were opposed to such a shift.

The governor's plan built much of the reorganization on the Corrections Independent Review Panel report. In his proposal, the governor noted that while the system has grown since the 1970s, the organizational structure and operations remained the same, resulting in individual institutions being run independently of each other. Following the recommendation of the CIRP report, the Governor's Reorganization Plan established a "Secretary for the newly established Department of Corrections and Rehabilitation [who] will have authority over all activities in the Department" (Schwarzenegger, 2005, p. 1). The plan also established a series of system-wide offices, including research and information technology housed in the Office of the Secretary. The Governor's Reorganization Plan also flattened the organization with the intent of reducing duplication and operational costs (Schwarzenegger, 2005).

Unlike the Corrections Independent Review Panel recommendations, however, the governor's plan separated the parole operations from institutional operations, resulting in three main divisions: Adult Operations, Youth Operations, and Parole Operations. Both Divisions of Adult and Youth Operations would focus on issues within the correctional institutions while the Division of Parole Operations would focus on the day-to-day issues of parole supervision for both youths and adults. These three divisions would report to a chief deputy Secretary. Joseph Gunn, Executive Director of the Corrections Independent Review Panel, criticized the separation of these three divisions, arguing that doing so "diminishes the opportunity to develop the coordinated, seamless transition of inmates back into society. Since no one has the overall responsibility at the operational level, no one is accountable" (Gunn, 2005, January 27, p. 1).

Furthermore, the day-to-day operation of parole supervision would be entirely separated from decisions made regarding release of those sentenced to life with the possibility of parole and parole revocations. The Board of Parole Hearings (BPH) would be created to address these issues. It was unclear why these functions were separated from the Division of Parole Operations or the impact such separation would have on the revocation process. Finally, it was also unclear if the new board would change the criterion of release for life-termers, a criterion that appears to focus solely on the original offense regardless of in-prison behavior after sentencing (Feige, 2005, February 1).[4]

These changes were curious if the goal was to reinforce rehabilitation within the parole system. Arguably, the day-to-day actions were directly linked to the decisions made by the BPH in order for a continuum of services to exist. Those running the day-to-day operations would potentially have a better sense of what services were needed immediately following release for those facing a life sentence and would be better able to determine which services and programs would complement the programs in which someone participated while in prison. They would also likely be better equipped to determine how a revocation would impact a parolee's access to services and whether such services would be eliminated if returned to prison. De-linking the day-to-day operators of parole from those in charge of release and revocation decisions seemed to create the potential for a delay or even interruption of the desired continuum of services without regard to how such de-linking from services could impact an individual's ability to rehabilitate or the department's ability to provide for rehabilitation.

Another difference between the CIRP recommendations and the governor's plan is the latter did not include the Civilian Corrections Commission to oversee the operations of the department as a whole. Rather, the governor created a Division of Community Partnerships that would "establish, maintain and expand cooperative agreements with the local law enforcement and community-based organizations and other entities that can aid in the rehabilitation and reintegration of inmates, wards, and parolees" (Schwarzenegger, 2005, p. 16). The decision to not include such a commission was blasted by the panel, particularly by the panel's director. Gunn argued that changing the culture of the department would be difficult without an independent, politically free group directing the reform (Warren, 2005, April 1).

The governor's plan created a chief deputy secretary who would also be responsible for the Division of Education, Vocation, and Offender Programs, and the Division of Correctional Health Care Services (Schwarzenegger, 2005). This seemed to be a large departure from the CIRP's recommended organizational structure in that issues such as programs and healthcare were assumed to be the responsibility of those running day-to-day operations of the institutions and parole systems, not a separate entity. Rod Hickman, then secretary of Youth and Adult Correctional Agency, argued that separating out these functions elevated rehabilitation and treatment services so they were equal to the custodial functions, which would ultimately "enhance service delivery and reduce recidivism" (Hickman, 2005, January 14, p. 3). Hickman's argument suggested that in order for rehabilitation to take hold, an organizational shift was necessary such that the offices responsible for rehabilitation were viewed as equal, rather than subordinate, to the offices responsible for control. It also signaled that rehabilitation was equally capable of controlling individuals as punishment and custody.

That said, the separation of offices raised questions as to how the programs developed and healthcare issues raised would be integrated into the daily operations of prisons and parole, questions that were never answered in the Governor's Reorganization Plan or in subsequent discussions of the legislation that amended the plan. Indeed, the governor's plan did little to address the three specific recommendations of the Corrections Independent Review Panel on how to reduce the prison population other than claiming that the reorganization was necessary to achieve a reduction in costs and "making communities safer by doing more to ensure that inmates and youth wards leave custody better prepared to function in society" (Schwarzenegger, 2005, p. 17).[5] Exactly what "doing more" consisted of was not discussed.

The Little Hoover Commission's Review of GRP 2

After reviewing the Governor's Reorganization Plan, the Little Hoover Commission recommended the legislature allow the plan to go into effect with the caveat that such a suggestion was based heavily on Secretary Hickman's assurance that further reforms were forthcoming, acknowledging that the governor's plan was a reorganization only and did not provide any concrete changes to the daily operations of prisons and parole. The Little Hoover Commission also noted that while there was concern that the juvenile justice system would begin to resemble or be forgotten amidst the problems facing the adult system, not passing the reorganization would not guarantee a better juvenile justice system and would only delay necessary changes to the adult system (Little Hoover Commission, 2005).

The Little Hoover Commission (2005) praised the reorganization's emphasis on evidence-based practices and elevation of rehabilitation.

The commission noted the creation of the Office of Policy, Planning, and Research signaled an important first step to ensuring that evidence-based practices would be utilized, the department was up-to-date on what worked to reduce recidivism, and the department constantly assessed the programs implemented and utilized their measured outcomes to determine effectiveness. The commission also noted that the name change "signals an important, renewed focus on preparing offenders for return to the community" (Little Hoover Commission, 2005, p. 9).

On the other hand, the commission stated the reorganization plan did not address parole reforms and the implementation of evidence-based reentry programs was not scheduled to occur until 2007. The commission argued that both of these issues raised concerns as to how well the reorganization plan would work. The commission also raised concerns about the separation of program and operation functions. Similar to the concerns raised by the Corrections Independent Review Panel, the Little Hoover Commission (2005, p. 15) argued that such a separation made "accountability for offender outcomes more difficult. . . . Separating custody and parole functions could thwart the goal of a coordinated, seamless transition of inmates back to the community." Although Secretary Hickman assured the commission that the organizational chart did not adequately show the management structure he envisioned (one that was supposedly implemented both vertically and horizontally), it was not clear how the concerns raised by both the Little Hoover Commission and the Corrections Independent Review Panel would be addressed.

The commission noted that the proposed reorganization and subsequent reform would likely be rather costly to the state in terms of initial costs, but could not draw any conclusions in terms of how the changes would impact the overall corrections budget in the future. It argued the state must be willing to make up-front investments in new technology, programs, and services both within prisons and in the communities in order to achieve the goal of rehabilitation. While the commission did not provide an estimate of such costs, it did note the governor's 2005–2006 budget included "a $95 million unallocated reduction in the CDC that the secretary indicated would result in a 28 percent reduction in programming" (Little Hoover Commission, 2005, p. 17). Such cuts, as the commission pointed out, seemed counter-intuitive to the reforms proposed by the Governor's Reorganization Plan, particularly in terms of raising the role of rehabilitation so that it was equal to the role of custody.

Finally, the Little Hoover Commission recommended additional changes before the Legislature allowed the reorganization to take effect. The commission suggested that parole reforms ought to be a top priority following the reorganization. The commission argued the best way to ensure prisons were able to adequately prepare individuals for release was to reduce the prison population to a more manageable size so that programs may be adequately implemented. Because the parole system returned roughly 70 percent of parolees per year to prison (approximately 60 percent for technical violations and 10 percent for a new crime), which in turn impacted the size of the prison population, reforming the parole system would help maintain a lower prison population (Little Hoover Commission, 2005). This presented a catch-22, however, in that adequate program implementation was (supposedly) necessary to prepare inmates for release, but the parole reforms recommended in an earlier report (Little Hoover Commission, 2003) would only impact those already released who, presumably, were not prepared for release because programs have not yet been adequately implemented. Thus, without knowing the specific parole reforms to be implemented, it was unclear how the cycle of releasing-returning-releasing individuals who were not receiving programs in prisons would be eliminated.

The second suggestion potentially helped this issue. The commission recommended the secretary reevaluate which aspects of the Correctional system would be cut under the $95 million budget reduction. The commission noted that it may be possible to make cuts from custody functions rather than inmate programs by reallocating resources from ineffective efforts to new policies, such as implementing graduated sanctions for parole violators and reducing the length of time served under revocation sentences. If such changes were implemented, the Little Hoover Commission argued, it was possible to not only save the in-prison programs, but also begin to reduce the prison population (Little Hoover Commission, 2005).

SB 737: Legislative Changes to the Governor's Reorganization Plan

Following the recommendation of the Little Hoover Commission, Senator Gloria Romero (D-Los Angeles) introduced SB 737, which would amend and legislatively enact the Governor's Reorganization Plan. The governor's basic organizational structure was maintained with one change: the operations of institutions were separated into adult and youth operations. Rather than a chief deputy secretary of Operations and another for Program Services, SB 737 created three chief deputy secretaries: Adult Operations, covering the Divisions of Adult Institutions and Adult Parole Operation; Correctional and Rehabilitative Services, covering the Divisions of Community Partnerships, Education, Vocations, and Offender Programs, and Correctional Health Care Services; and Juvenile Justice, covering the Divisions of Juvenile Facilities, Juvenile Programs, and Juvenile Parole Operations. This change arguably reinstated the ability to create a coordinated system from prisons onto parole and continued to separate out programs and services in an attempt to elevate their status as comparable to custodial functions.

Additional changes were made in the areas of juvenile justice and confirmations (not discussed here), as well as the parole board. In terms of the parole board, SB 737 created a "firewall" for the Board of Parole Hearings. This firewall would ensure that members responsible for juvenile hearings were not also responsible for adult hearings and vice versa. Changes were also made to reinstate language that required a diverse background among parole board hearing officers and restored language regarding hearing backlogs (Senate TV, 2005).

Following the second draft of the bill, Kevin McCarthy, assembly Republican leader, submitted to the assembly Republican members a list of proposed amendments. As McCarthy (2005, p. 1) argued, the amendments would "blunt some of the more objectionable features of the Reorganization Plan." The major objections focused on the change towards rehabilitation. Briefing materials attached to McCarthy's letter argued the change in the department's name implied a shift in the department's function away from the statutory mandate that the purpose of prisons was to punish. The briefing materials reminded the reader that rehabilitation was rejected as an organizational philosophy and that "[t]here are still major concerns about the efficacy for the rehabilitation programs and their ability to transform most criminals" (McCarthy, 2005, p. 5).[6] Concerns were also raised regarding the possibility of "lawsuits by prisoners demanding more programs and reinforce inmates' sense of victimization" (McCarthy, 2005, p. 2).

The author of the attachment also argued that the firewall provisions were not strong enough. Many who criticized the consolidation of these commissioners focused on the potential impact of lifer and parole revocation hearings on the Youth Authority, arguing that such a consolidation would move this authority to a more correctional aim. The Republican concern seemed to be that this authority would move the lifer and revocation hearings to a more rehabilitation-oriented aim (McCarthy, 2005). It appears that while the Republican members seem to support rehabilitation for youths, McCarthy at the very least did not support it for adults, believed that the commissioners focused on adult hearings should not consider rehabilitation in its decisions, and used this argument in a briefing to other Republican Assembly members to describe the "not so good" portions of the Governor's Reorganization Plan.

The focus of the amendments was to restate the statutory mandate that the purpose of imprisonment was to punish. McCarthy noted that such amendments would reaffirm current policies and "allow Republicans to show that they have not supported any fundamental shift in correctional philosophy and undercut claims that the name change reflects a fundamental shift" (McCarthy, 2005, p. 9). Such a statement would also allow Republicans to maintain their "tough on crime" appearance to their constituents and supporters without needing to pass an entirely new bill or reframe their stance as "smart on crime."

McCarthy feared that Democrats would reject his suggested amendments; however, this does not appear to have occurred. A document showing amendments added to the April 6 version of the bill (Unknown, 2005, April 5), included two of the amendments McCarthy presented to his fellow Republicans (both of which ended up in the final bill):

> Amendment 4. On page 23, between lines 25 and 26 insert:
>
> Nothing in the act enacted by Senate Bill 737 of the 2005–2006 Regular Session shall be construed to alter the primary objective of adult incarceration under the reorganized Department of Corrections and Rehabilitation, which remains public safety as articulated in the legislative findings and declarations set forth in Section 1170.
>
> Amendment 11. On page 58, between lines 27 and 28, insert:
>
> SEC. 101. (a) It is the intent of the Legislature that nothing in this act shall compromise public safety or cause public safety to become subordinate to economic or other interests.
> (b) It is the intent of the Legislature that any expansion of rehabilitation programs by this act shall not change the public safety objective, nor shall the creation of new education, rehabilitation, or parole programs or alternatives pursuant to this act be construed to create new entitlements.
> (c) It is the intent of the Legislature that this act is not designed to create new programs that are alternatives to incarceration. Any additional programs should be evidence-based, result-oriented and subject to periodic review.

Both of these amendments appeared to cover the Republicans' main concerns that the name change reflects a fundamental shift in the purpose of incarceration and that the call for more programming would lead to lawsuits. It was interesting that neither the original text of SB 737 nor these amendments addressed the impact of the name change, and the presumable shift in the department's mission, on the parole system. Arguably, this was because one of the objectives of the parole system has always been to assist parolees as they reintegrate into society, eliminate criminal activity, and other aspects related to rehabilitation, even when this was not reflected in its practices or in the overarching philosophy of the correctional system.

Two additional proposed amendments focused on the use of evidence-based programs. The first would require such programs to be evaluated by an independent evaluator, thereby ensuring confidence in positive evaluations, but also raising costs.[7] The second would require funding for faith-based programs, but did not include any indication they must be evidence based. While McCarthy's letter noted an opposition to rehabilitative programs, there seems to be an attempt at compromise on this front. Ultimately, neither of these amendments appeared in subsequent versions of the bill.

Another issue raised, particularly following the fourth (and final) version of the bill, was the financial impact of both the Governor's Reorganization Plan and SB 737. The Corrections Independent Review Panel (2005) estimated a possible savings of up to $20 million. An analyst for the Assembly Committee on Appropriations supported this figure, claiming the reorganization would save $20 million over three years (Long, 2005, April 20a). He also noted, however, that both the governor's plan and SB 737 would increase costs by millions of dollars, including an initial $400,000 on physical changes such as consolidation of offices and computer systems (Long, 2005, April 20b). The Legislative Analyst's Office also noted, "Whatever minimal level of administrative savings is achieved from the [Governor's Reorganization Plan] would be likely more than offset by the upfront costs of the reorganization" (quoted in Long, 2005, April 20a). Once again, no estimates were made as to the cost/benefits of implementing programs and services for inmates and parolees. Without this information, it appeared the reorganization would result in no net fiscal impact, thus eliminating the benefits espoused by the Corrections Independent Review Panel and one of the governor's justifications for the necessity of the reorganization. Regardless of these issues, and issues raised regarding the actual impact of the reorganization (discussed below), SB 737 was signed into law on May 10, 2005. Both the Governor's Reorganization Plan and SB 737 went into effect on July 1, 2005.

Impact on Parole

At the time of the interviews, almost five years after the reorganization was implemented, the reviews amongst parole agents were mixed. While some agents were generally happy there was a renewed emphasis on rehabilitation and believed the department was slowly trying to make changes (Andy, Ellie, Dug), several stated that the change was in name only and the policies following the reorganization did not show a renewed focus on rehabilitation or dramatic alteration in day-to-day practices. Helen stated:

> It was reorganization, but it was mainly title changes. It was agency changes, name changes. The Youth Authority: Department of Juvenile Justice. Parole is now Department of Adult Parole Operations. Those kinds of things. It was, like, yeah, name changes, but where was the rehabilitation?

This view was echoed by James who recognized that cultural changes took time, but also said, "I don't see that change coming from the central office down to the field." In a similar vein, Mike argued, "I think you should start with the inside, develop it and then your name will develop by itself, by the reaction people get from you." As these agents argued, the internal culture did not reflect the re-emphasis on rehabilitation and the re-emphasis should have occurred first so as to provide more weight to the name change.

The reorganization has also done little to address the limitations placed on the parole agent's ability to provide assistance to those who want it. In some cases, agents continued to be limited by the time they had to spend on each case, as the reorganization did not address agent caseloads. Dug said there were times when family members wished to speak with him, but he was unable to because of time constraints:

> I would see in the fiancé's eyes or the mother's eyes, "I need to talk to you, ——." But you know what? I can't stay 'cause I have fifteen other home calls to make, plus I gotta arrest five people, plus I gotta go back and do five reports plus I have to do a discharge review, plus I gotta help somebody else.

The agents' large caseloads prevented them from being able to adequately serve the parolees and their families, undermining the shift to rehabilitation.

The biggest issue seemed to be the number of programs and services available that were able to work with parolees, suggesting the increased funding for programs that was to come with the reorganization did not occur. As Russell noted, while they put rehabilitation back in, they "left the resources out." Some agents noted that the extent to which they were able to provide assistance still varied based on their location. Carl stated some cities and counties had numerous programs available while others had few, if any:

> You know, San Diego is a great, great place for resources. If you're a parolee in San Diego, you have a lot better chance 'cause you have a lot more resources. Orange County parolees? A lot of resources. Riverside? Not so much. . . . Los Angeles? Lots of resources.

Carl also noted that even if resources were available, gang affiliation might prevent a parolee from being able to travel to or attend a particular program, another issue not addressed by the reorganization. At the same time, these complaints about resources were nothing new. As Lipsky (1980) and Silver (1967) find, front-line actors often faced a lack of resources, or a perceived lack of resources. It is likely parole agents would always feel they were lacking in resources or that their level of resources was not as adequate as what was available in other locations. In this instance, the agents noted that the lack of programs often had to do with a lack of money or budgetary limitations for the parole department (though any agency would argue for more funding to perform their job properly). As Mike stated, many programs refused to accept parolees because the department was unable to pay the programs. In other cases, agents were unable to place parolees in programs because the programs were often unfunded or too full (Mike; Carl), a claim supported by Hipp, Jannetta, Shah, and Turner (2011).

Mike was particularly critical of this lack of funding, as he felt the money spent on reorganizing the department was ill spent:

> Well they spent millions of dollars on that R, 'cause they had to change all the documents and everything else. I'd rather have them spend those millions of dollars in programs and schools and everything else, and doing the things that are necessary if you really want to be rehabilitative.

His critique echoed that posed by the Legislative Analyst's Office (Long, 2005, April 20a) when one of its analysts noted the money saved because of the reorganization would be spent on actually carrying out the reorganization.

What is Rehabilitation?

The changes to the prison and parole systems in California in the early part of the twenty-first century attempted to elevate rehabilitation to the same standard as custodial and control functions. In doing so, however, rehabilitation once again became a tool by which the state imposed punishment and supervision over those under its control. The use of rehabilitation as a form of punishment was once again framed in such a way as to equate this use of rehabilitation as a means of achieving public safety and thus the betterment of society. Furthermore, rehabilitation was still viewed as a means of achieving an end to criminal behavior and integration into society, but the process by which these goals were achieved changed.

Robinson (2008) argued that the current version of rehabilitation in the United Kingdom and Wales was a tool for the improvement of society, risk management, and as a form of punishment. California's parole system also framed rehabilitation in this way. Several policies implemented both before and after the reorganization focused on the use of rehabilitation as a form of risk management and punishment, but were framed as a means of improving society. Services and supervision were also reframed so that they were now tools of each other and created a feedback loop in which more supervision and more services were always necessary.

For example, the new parole model included an expansion of the Parole and Corrections Team (PACT) meetings to a statewide level. The PACT meetings were designed to provide a centralized means of connecting parolees to local rehabilitation programs. Yet, failure to attend these meetings was considered a violation of parole (Pitchford, 2000, August 28). Rather than assisting the parolees, the PACT meetings became another means by which a policy aimed at rehabilitation was used as a means of controlling and punishing parolees.

The new parole model, the Little Hoover Commission, and the Corrections Independent Review Panel all called for the expanded use of risk-needs assessments such that treatment plans could be periodically updated. On the surface, this appears to be a good way by which to judge the progress made by parolees, provide better ways of assisting them, and ensure their risk level had not elevated. It also appeared to be a means of reframing and using risk assessment tools as part of the diagnosis of rehabilitative needs. On the other hand, it was unclear what these updated treatment plans would do, how failure to comply would be handled, or at what point a treatment plan would be deemed "completed." For parolees making progress, an updated treatment plan could result in the establishment of more goals or the addressing of more needs (i.e., supervision illuminating the need for more treatment), rather than early discharge. For those not making progress, failure to follow the treatment plan could result in a return to custody for a violation of a condition of parole (i.e., treatment illuminating the need for more supervision). Either way, the treatment plan could be used to punish parolees, even when they were "making good."

The merging of supervision as a rehabilitative tool and rehabilitation as a supervisory tool created a feedback loop, such that as the need for rehabilitation increased, the need for supervision also increased, which resulted in an increased need for rehabilitation, and so on and so forth, ad nauseam. This continued need for rehabilitation and supervision could lead to a situation where a parolee was never deemed eligible for early discharge and was never deemed fully rehabilitated. As Werth (2012) found, parolees see the constant requirements of the parole system and lack of meaningful supports as setting them up for failure. This failure, however, seemed to also be a means of justifying the extension of control into the community.

The new parole model (Corrections Independent Review Panel, 2004), the Little Hoover Commission (2003), and the Corrections Independent Review Panel (2004) also called for greater reliance on intermediate sanctions for parole violators and use of the Parole Violation Decision-Making Instrument (PVDMI). As discussed above, PVDMI implemented a system by which agents would determine how to handle a technical violation (Corrections Independent Review Panel, 2004; Murphy & Turner, 2010). The matrix allowed for the consideration of the severity of the violation and the risk posed by the parolee in order to determine whether to return the parolee to prison or some other form of response. In doing so, PVDMI solidified the use of treatment programs as a formal means of punishment as a violation of parole could result in mandatory and coerced attendance in order to avoid more prison time. Treatment programs became a way to manage the risk posed by parolees, as ideally the program would address the reason behind the technical violation and reduce the parolee's risk level.

Yet, the use of rehabilitation as a risk management tool and form of punishment was framed as a tool for the betterment of society. As discussed earlier, the shift to rehabilitation was not the end goal. Rather, rehabilitation was once again framed as the means by which to reduce the prison population, lower the prison budget, and achieve public safety by reducing recidivism and thus crime. Reducing the prison population would provide a safer working environment for correctional officers. Lowering the prison budget would enable state administrators to eliminate a large deficit and allocate funding to other areas. Reducing recidivism and crime would reduce the likelihood one would become a victim and thus improve public safety. The shift back to rehabilitation would supposedly improve multiple aspects of California's society.

Rehabilitation as an Ongoing Event

Rehabilitation was still framed as a means of helping parolees transition into society following a period of incarceration. The agents interviewed echoed this view of rehabilitation, even as they expressed frustration with a lack of policies and cultural changes by which to achieve this rehabilitation. The agents suggested rehabilitation continued to be an ongoing event, but this process was to be made available to parolees rather than something required by the state in order to earn discharge (see also Goodman, 2010). The agents also argued that the end goals still included a change for the better and return to former self. This process was not without its problems and the problems expressed by the agents may have helped perpetuate the belief that parolees were responsible for their change and a shift in the view of rehabilitation to now include a right to the opportunity, rather than a state-imposed "cure," to successfully go through the rehabilitative process.

It should be noted that this change in the rehabilitative process was not necessarily the result of the reorganization of the Department of Corrections. As discussed below, the agents showed a mixed response to whether or not the reorganization actually impacted the policies and procedures of the parole system. Rather, the following discussion of the changes to the process is based on the agents' personal view of rehabilitation at the time of the interview and highlights the ways in which the parole system is, in many ways, independent of the larger correctional organization. While none of the agents stated that their view of the process or desired outcomes changed because of the reorganization or that it necessarily changed over time, their comments do suggest a shift in how the agents viewed the rehabilitative process compared to prior time periods. Their comments also suggest that their view of the process contains some similarities to prior time periods and suggests ways of changing the process to be more reflective of how rehabilitation was carried out prior to the 1970s.

The Process

The Little Hoover Commission (2003), in an analysis of whether or not California should maintain the parole system, argued that the parole system should move "felons from their deserved punishment to responsible community members" (p. iii–iv), thereby reinforcing the purpose of parole as the system in which the process of reintegration occurs.[8] One parole agent agreed that it was possible for agents to assist felons as they move from prisons to the community. He stated, however, that agents needed to recognize that the process of parole was different for each parolee and often involved "baby steps."[9]

Rita: How would you define rehabilitation?

James: It's baby steps. It's recognizing that they're moving at a certain pace in their lives at a certain time, and it depends on what their behavior patterns have been in the past. . . . So, rehabilitation looks a little bit different depending on the individual and their life experiences and where God placed them to start. So, again, as a parole agent, we have to recognize those things, and we have to understand that not everybody starts at the same starting point, and not everybody moves at the same pace. And are they working hard to get to that direction, in a positive direction, and even though they may not be moving at the same pace we'd like them to move at, are they moving in that direction? And if they are, then we've got to support that and encourage them and do what we can to assist them and their support system. (James, parole agent with over 22 years of experience)

James echoed the prior use of treatment plans and re-evaluation of treatment plans to ensure the parole process was adequately addressing an individual's need and not serving parolees in a one-size-fits-all model, suggesting a desire to move away from the management of risks posed by groups and back towards the management of risks posed by individuals. As James suggested, not all agents held this belief and this lack of belief could hinder the agents' ability to assist parolees. What was particularly interesting about this comment was that the new parole model, implemented in 2001, was supposed to have increased the use of risk management and release planning to include a periodic review and adjustment of the treatment plan, but James's statement highlighted the failure of these efforts.

Similarly, the Little Hoover Commission (2003) noted that the existing parole process was a billion-dollar failure and changes were necessary. The parole system needed to be reorganized so that services and supervision were front-loaded, which echoed recommendations of several scholars (e.g., Travis, 2002, 2005; Petersilia, 2003; Grattet, Petersilia, & Lin, 2008) and was similar to the methods adopted during the 1940s to 1970s. Also similar to the prior time period, the commission argued that time in prisons should be used to prepare for release by providing the means to "learn basic skills, kick drug habits, and plan for their release" (Little Hoover Commission, 2003, p. iii). The commission's recommendation of creating a continuum of care also suggested a desire to re-establish prisons within the rehabilitative process. This need to expand the rehabilitative process to once again include prisons was supported by the agents and at least one agent (Andy, parole agent with two years of experience) noted that a major problem with the corrections system is that "[w]e think rehabilitation is once they leave prison."

Three of the agents argued the expansion of the process could only be accomplished by shifting back to an indeterminate sentencing structure, even if in an altered state. For example, Randall, a retired parole agent with almost 30 years of experience, argued that under the indeterminate sentencing structure, "people had to show that they had some responsibility, that they had learned, learned some skills that could be transferable to, to society." Although Randall acknowledged there was always the risk that some individuals would fake it (a concern also raised under the medical model), he felt many prisoners did not understand the concept of punishment and rewards and the indeterminate sentencing structure helped prisoners learn that concept by requiring they show progress in order to be released.

Andy also believed the sentencing structure should be shifted back to an indeterminate structure for two reasons. First, he argued,

> the board [should be] more involved in that process at the institution, and make that part of an incentive program. . . . That [programs] should be an incentive for them to be on parole. If they're doing

> things, again we come up with rehabilitation at the institutional level, and they're plugging into programs, and they can go to the board and say, "Hey, you know, I got my GED. I did this, this, and this." Those are things the board would be more involved in.

Andy seemed to be arguing that a release board, which was a key component of the indeterminate sentencing structure and the medical model, should once again be in place to determine whether someone was prepared for release based on one's participation in various programs. This was similar to the Little Hoover Commission's (2003) recommendation to incentivize program participation. Second, he argued that an indeterminate sentencing structure would allow judges the leeway to decide who should and should not be placed in prison to begin with, arguably determining who needed to be a part of the rehabilitative process and who did not. Presumably, this would enable the prison and parole systems to focus on those most in need of assistance and most in need of the rehabilitative process.[10] Similarly, James argued that an indeterminate system would put the "teeth back into parole" in that it would allow parole to hold parolees accountable for their actions or send them back to prison to complete their term, as was the case during the medical model.

An attempt to prove one has rehabilitated and receive a Certificate of Rehabilitation was also hampered. As the Little Hoover Commission (2003) noted, neither parolees nor parole agents were familiar with the process by which to obtain the certificate. Several court cases also suggested the process could take years for some defendants. *People v. Lockwood* (1998, 66 Cal. App. 4th 222 [77 Cal. Rptr. 2d. 769]) found the trial court had sole discretion to deny or grant a certificate. *People v. Ansell* (2001, 25 Cal. 4th 868, 875 [108 Cal. Rptr. 2d 145; 24 P.3d 1174]) argued the standards for "determining whether rehabilitation has occurred are high." As the facts of *People v. Failla* (2006, 45 Cal. Rptr. 3d 585 [140 Cal. App. 4th 1514] suggested, denial of a certificate could be based on the trial court's determination of criminal behavior even when such supposed behavior did not result in a conviction. Combined, these cases suggested that obtaining a Certificate of Rehabilitation was relatively elusive and almost as uncertain as obtaining release through a parole board. Additionally, if a press release from Governor Schwarzenegger's office (Office of the Governor, 2004, December 22) was any indication, obtaining a pardon, and thereby getting all rights of citizenship restored, took decades, with some pardons occurring 20 to 30 years or more after discharge from parole. Thus, questions remained as to when the rehabilitative process finally ended, as it was not clear if it happened upon discharge or upon receipt of the elusive Certificate of Rehabilitation and pardon.

Change or Return, but Not Both

The goals of the rehabilitative process seem to have changed little from those expressed in official documents over the past 60 years. All of the agents interviewed argued a successful case was a person who no longer committed crimes and stayed out of prison. The agents also argued a successful case had a job, cared for one's family, and was an otherwise "productive member of society" (Randall) or "functional citizen" (Andy). When asked what was meant by a "productive citizen," Carl, a retired parole agent with over 20 years of experience, provided the following explanation:

> I mean somebody who does not commit crime, gets a job, goes to work and has a family and supports themselves, pays taxes, and contributes to what we as normal citizens contribute to and is not a burden. They're not on welfare. They're not on unemployment. They're not locked up.

A "successful" or "rehabilitated" individual, then, achieved some level of normalcy within society. All of the agents noted their successful cases were those who achieved the goals described by Carl by the time the parolees were discharged. That said, all of the agents indicated that they had also lost track of many of their successful cases, so it was still possible the parolees' changed behaviors did not prevent further criminal behavior or were not maintained after discharge. As with previous understandings of a completed rehabilitation process, the only goal that seems to be measurable over time was a parolee's continued criminal conduct, or lack of officially defined criminal conduct, and it was unclear if the definition of success or "productive citizen" required all or some of the aspects described by Carl. The lack of data on successful cases also seemed to indicate the only official data available to the parole system was data on who failed, rather than who succeeded, in both leaving parole and staying crime free. The lack of such successful data likely explains why the paroling authorities framed failures as a success for the parole system, as it provided a means of justifying the work of parole even when it was unable to achieve the desired outcome (i.e., rehabilitation).

Although the notion of rehabilitation as an ongoing event typically required a change for the better and a return to a former state (Raynor & Robinson, 2005), one theorist disagreed. Lewis (2005) argued the rehabilitative process could be a change for the better *or* return to a former self. This distinction seems to be supported by the agents, with many (Dug, Jessie, Helen, Russell) believing it was only possible to achieve one or the other, not both. For some, rehabilitation meant a change. As Gill, a retired parole agent with over 40 years of experience, explained:

> Change in how you view yourself, your life. Changing who you associate with. Change in what you want to achieve, if anything, in life.

> Just kind of a hard look at yourself in terms of who you are, what you've done with your life, and can you change if you want to.

Or, as another agent stated, rehabilitation and parole are about redeeming lives (James); changing lives so that they were able to move away from their past.

Mike, a parole agent with three years of experience, adopted the language of physical therapy to describe a change away from the criminal behavior. He offered the following description:

> Rehabilitation is actually redeveloping new skills to make these [parolees] successful and if it's rehabilitation that I'm rehabilitated from an injury, I got back, and I'm back on my feet. I'm rehabilitated from crime; you're not going to repeat that crime; you have the skills to go ahead and become a productive member of society.

Although Mike equated criminal behavior to an injury, he also implied that, unlike rehabilitation through physical therapy, moving away from crime was an improvement for the better without returning to a former state.

Many agents believed change for the better was the only achievable goal within the parole/rehabilitative process and that it was not desirable for parolees to return to a former self. Part of this may be related to the belief that "We don't get successes. We get all the failures" (Woody, a regional parole administrator). Woody stated parole agents were responsible for helping parolees figure out how to live with other people because other social institutions failed to ensure parolees were properly adjusted to the norms of society. The other agents who shared this belief seemed to argue that it was not about going back to the right direction, but putting the person on the right track for the first time. Helen, a parole agent with 11 years of experience, argued that part of a parole agent's job was "to provide services for life skills and those kinds of things; to teach the adults that missed how to become responsible adults." Some of these skills included learning how to search for a job, develop a resume, or dress for an interview (Mike).

Conversely, one agent suggested that while some parolees never lived within the confines of societal norms, other parolees did follow societal norms with the exception of the criminal behavior. Because of these differences, rehabilitation may not apply to every parolee equally. Parole agent James provided the following explanation:

> [H]abilitation is somebody who's never joined us in society. They've never been living a really positive crime-free life, a healthy lifestyle, and those folks, there's no "re" to it. They're not returning to anything that's positive. So, that's habilitation—when those people are finally

> in a direction. Of course, rehabilitation is somebody who started out positive. It might be that Newport Beach guy that I explained who had all his resources, did all his things, and then made some stupid choices and got caught. That person can return to something positive, and they have the skills and experience to get there much faster than that person who has never been there and all of their experiences have been about crime or unacceptable social behavior.

In other words, while many parolees already had skills, resources, and social support that would enable them to reintegrate into society (return to former self), other parolees lacked some or all of these supports and needed assistance obtaining them so they could be a part of society for the first time (change for the better). Hence, it seems the understanding of the process at the time of the interviews has altered to view the end goals as either a change for the better or a return to a former self, not both, as was the expectation under prior time periods. It was unclear what role the return of legal rights plays for those changing for the better. That said, it was also unclear if a return to former self was truly possible given the difficulty of regaining all legal rights.

Assistance, Not Intervention

One of the biggest changes from prior periods was a shift in the role parole agents played in the process. During the 1940s to 1970s, agents were viewed as local therapists who could "cure" parolees. Today, agents do not "cure" anyone. Rather, they serve as "a broker of services" (Gill). Carl offered the following analogy that he tells his parolees:

> Look it, I'm an expert out here. I've lived my whole life here on the streets. I know how to get things done. If I went to prison, I would come to you, the inmate, and I'd ask you to school me and tell me what to do because you have to tell me how to walk, who to talk to, who to be around, how to handle a situation, 'cause you're the expert in there. Out here, I'm the expert; so listen to me. Stick with me and let me try to get you through these steps that you need to do and how you need to do 'em to be successful. Because my expertise is out here and your expertise is in prison.

This analogy was similar to Walter Gordon (1946) and the Inmate Committee for Higher Education (1974)'s description of the transition from prison to the community as moving between two different cultures. Carl extended this analogy and argued the parole agent served as the translator or tour guide who helps the parolee make the move successfully while also surveilling everyday life on the outside.

The assistance focused on helping parolees determine their needs and assisting them find the services to meet those needs. The parole agent worked with a parolee to determine a parole plan, or prescription (James), that outlined the needs and goals of the parolee. From there, it was the agent's job to plug parolees into services and put "tools in their toolbox" (Andy). Agents searched for and helped parolees obtain access to services in the community. These resources and services include in-house programs such as cash assistance, the Parole Outpatient Clinic (in-house counseling service first developed in the 1950s), and the literacy lab (in-house program that teaches basic literacy skills), and private programs such as drug treatment and sober living facilities. The addressing of needs was used as a way of reducing or eliminating the factors that led to criminal behavior and managing the risk posed by the parolee, though it is not framed that way (see also, Hannah-Moffat, 1999).

It was up to the parolee, however, to take advantage of the opportunities offered (Carl):

> So, rehabilitation is making those opportunities [drug program, job training, employment, residence, etc.] available. Now, if a man doesn't take advantage of all of that, that's his problem. . . . But you, society, parole agents, Department of Corrections, we have, has the system set-up where if he wants to take advantage of that rehabilitation, it's there. We can help him get into those, get the rehabilitation he wants for himself.

The responsibilization that began in the 1970s to 1990s was now complete. Parole agents were completely detached and rehabilitation was the sole responsibility of the parolees. What happened after the agent made the recommendation was up to the parolee. The very nature of parole, however, implied a supervised change with consequences for not meeting the standards set by the agent. While parolees were responsible for their change, there was also little leeway in terms of meeting agent requirements. In other words, the parolees did not really have a choice of not following up, even if they were not satisfied with the assistance provided.

This responsibilization may stem from a belief that parolees lack the motivation to change, limiting what agents could accomplish. Mike compared the parole agent-parolee relationship with that of a teacher-student relationship (using this project as the example):

> But you know, a lot of it is on the oversight of the parole agent, but everything depends on that parolee. I mean . . . [y]ou can say you want to do a great paper and everything else. Your teacher says, "Oh, yeah, I want you to do a really good job." But if you don't go out there, do the interviews, do the paper, do the research, and you

> just go off and say, "Yeah, you know, I'll type it the last day, three hours before the class starts." You know? . . . and they always say you can have the best teacher, you can have the most motivating teacher, but if the person also is not self-motivated. I mean, you can bring this person, you know, you could have a typewriter, the computer, all the research, drive him to the place; if they don't want to do it, they're not going to do it.

Many agents claimed they often "handed" parolees multiple opportunities—jobs, residence, drug treatment—and the parolees would not use the opportunities provided. The agents said sometimes parolees quit or lose a job because they did not want (or did not know how) to work a 9–5 schedule or would leave a drug treatment program for, what seemed to the agent, no reason at all. As at least one study suggested (Werth, 2012), however, the parolees' desire not to partake in a program or job could be because the parolee had other goals or employment prospects in mind and found the parole requirements were hindering their everyday lives.

The agents were unable to pinpoint why some parolees were motivated and others were not, or why some chose to take advantage of the opportunities provided by the parole agent and others did not, suggesting once again that success was fleeting while failure was measurable. As Jessie, an agent of 10 years, stated of her successful cases, "something just clicked." Dug noted that sometimes the parolees simply got tired of repeatedly going in and out of prisons. If it was the case that some parolees were a part of society prior to prison and some were not (habilitation versus rehabilitation), as James argued, parolees who wished to re-establish a life similar to the one they had prior to going to prison may have more motivation to take advantage of the assistance provided by parole agents than others.

As the parole agents generally believed that "We can't change other people" (Jessie), they often picked and chose whom to help (see also Lipsky, 1980). As Helen argued:

> I don't wanna feel like my time is wasted. I would rather give to those that want to change, and I can tell. The ones that don't want to change, I'm not gonna invest much time, but I'm out there when they are ready; then we can move forward with the efforts.

With parolees now solely responsible for their own rehabilitation, failures that occurred on parole, whether for a technical violation or a new crime, was also the sole responsibility of the parolee. Whereas failures in the past were viewed as part of the process (and possibly a sign that parole was doing its job by ensuring those needing additional assistance received it), failures were now viewed as an inability of individuals to rehabilitate themselves. In turn, the parole system argued failures were a success, as they highlighted the agents' ability to detect and remove individuals who pose a risk to public safety.

Criticisms of the Move Back to Rehabilitation

Reorganization or Reform?

The renewed focus on rehabilitation had support from individuals throughout the state, including then Inspector General Matthew Cate (2005), Director of the Prison Law Office Donald Spector (2005), and Ventura County Chief Probation Officer Calvin Remington (2005). The supporters not only applauded the elevation of rehabilitation to the same level as security operations, but also supported the change in the mission of the organization to support rehabilitation, calling it a "dramatic and welcome change" (Spector, 2005, p. 2).

Rehabilitation did not appear to be the goal in and of itself. Rather, the goal was still public protection:

> Nothing in the act enacted by Senate Bill 737 of the 2005–2006 Regular Session shall be construed to alter the primary objective of adult incarceration under the reorganized Department of Corrections and Rehabilitation, which remains public safety as articulated in the legislative findings and declarations set forth in Section 1170. (Senate Bill 737, Ch.1, Sec. 32)

This section is a throwback to the 1940s to mid-1970s, where rehabilitation was the means by which to achieve the goal of public safety. While the bill did little to change the role of parole within the correctional system, the reorganization had the potential to reinstate programs and policies that not only supported the intent of parole, but also provided options for those working directly with parolees, including funding for community-based rehabilitation programs and intermediate sanctions for parole violators.

Questions remained as to the true impact the reorganization would have on increasing funding and support for rehabilitation services and evidence-based programs. As Schwarzenegger said, "The proposed reorganization is a vital first step. . . . Changing the organization will not in itself change the way it operates. What it will do is set the basis for reform" (Schwarzenegger, 2005, p. 8). A common theme throughout discussions of the Governor's Reorganization Plan centered on reorganization before reform:

> While the restructuring alone will not produce the necessary reforms, it will serve as the foundation for [among other things] making communities safer by doing more to ensure that inmates and youth wards

> leave custody better prepared to function in society. (Corrections Independent Review Panel, 2004, p. 1)

> Organizational structure alone cannot solve any of the specific challenges you identified. (Hickman, 2005, p. 3; then Secretary of the Department of Corrections)

While SB 737 was drafted to address the concerns raised by the governor's plan, the issue of the impact of the reorganization was not addressed.

> Criticism of GRP 1 centered on three major fronts: a reduction in Senate confirmation authority; a perceived diminution of state juvenile issues; and whether an organizational restructuring with no substantive policy changes provides substantive progress for departments beset by litigation, cost overruns and controversy. SB 737 amply addresses confirmation authority and juvenile justice issues. (Long, 2005, April 20b, p. 5)

> It's reorganization, not reform. (Gloria Romero, author of SB 737, in a hearing before the Senate Public Safety Committee; Senate TV, 2005)

At the very basic level, the shift to rehabilitation—at least at the outset—seemed to be more of a desired outcome, rather than an implementation of new policies and procedures. As the above quotes demonstrate, the reorganization was not designed to go beyond a moving around of boxes and people and skepticism remained as to whether the shifts would lead to actual reform.

On the other hand, many argued that, without the reorganization, reforms would not be possible. The Little Hoover Commission (2005, p. 19) stated, "the internal structure of the agency has long been recognized as the source of many of the problems and a barrier to timely and effective solutions." Still, skepticism remained. The Little Hoover Commission (2005) also recognized that reorganization does little to change the culture of a place. This skepticism was further bolstered following the appointment of the secretary and staff of the newly created Department of Corrections and Rehabilitation, many of whom held parallel positions prior to the reorganization. The language of SB 737 specifically stated that any contracts or staff in place prior to the reorganization would be maintained following the reorganization (Senate Bill 737, § 12838.9–12838.12). If the reorganization did not result in any new policies and the individuals in charge of the organization did not change, it was unclear what reforms, if any, would be made, regardless of assurances that such reforms were coming.

These critiques hinted at larger issues within California's attempt to re-emphasize rehabilitation. The reorganization seemed to be a shifting of boxes within the organizational structure rather than actual reformation of policies or procedures. Several parole agents argued that while lip service was given to rehabilitation, it was unclear that the culture within the correctional system generally and parole specifically has altered to reflect this new goal. These criticisms are echoed in the years following the reorganization. The reorganization did not bring about the necessary changes the governor claimed it would. As several organizations and court cases make clear, the correctional system was still in need of major reforms. As the next chapter shows, two legislative changes attempted to implement these reforms, but did so in a way that altered who was eligible for the state's version of the rehabilitative process.

Notes

1 According to the agent running the PACT meeting I observed, parolees are required to attend the next available PACT meeting following his/her release. PACT meetings are offered every two weeks to ensure parolees are able to attend a meeting soon after their release.

2 CCPOA is the union for prison guards and parole agents. For more information, see Joshua Page's (2011) *The Toughest Beat.*

3 Note, however, that this estimate is a "potential savings." The Corrections Independent Review Panel does not appear to have run any actual cost-savings analysis of its own and seems to have relied on cost-savings estimates from the other reports it reviewed. This lack of cost-benefits analysis became an issue in the later discussions on whether or not to allow the reorganization to occur.

4 In the early part of the 2000s, Governor Gray Davis stated he would not allow anyone with a murder conviction to be released on to parole (San Francisco Chronicle, 2000, August 20). Although his decisions were challenged in court, the California Supreme Court argued that Davis's reversal of parole decisions did not result in a blanket policy to veto parole release of convicted murders (Kravets, 2002, December 17). Decisions not to release inmates based solely on the original offense were further upheld by the California Supreme Court in February 2005 (*In re Danneburg* [34 Cal 4th 1061, 2005]). Although the decision came out after the Governor's Reorganization Plan was submitted to the Little Hoover Commission and legislature (and Schwarzenegger has been more supportive of release for convicted murderers than Davis [San Francisco Chronicle, 2003, December 1]), neither group mentions the criterion used to determine release for individuals serving life with the possibility of parole. It was unclear whether such criterion would be addressed within the organization or legislatively.

5 It was possible that the Governor's Reorganization Plan could not address at least one of the recommendations. As the current sentencing structure and use of good time was legislatively created, new legislation was likely needed to make the recommended change to a presumptive sentencing scheme.

6 This comment seems to ignore the multiple research studies that indicate the types of programs known to reduce recidivism. For a review, see Aos, Phillips, Barnoski, and Lieb 2001 and Aos and Drake, 2013.

7 In 2005, academics at the University of California, Irvine negotiated with the State of California to develop the Center for Evidence-Based Corrections, which became an independent evaluator contracted to conduct various research projects.
8 Given that this same report declared the parole system a failure, this statement by the Little Hoover Commission seems to be both a restatement of the purpose of parole and also an attempt to provide a rationale for maintaining it.
9 This particular agent argued that the baby-steps concept was similar to that presented in the movie *What about Bob?*
10 Determining who those individuals are and how they would be separated out is, of course, up for debate. This was a major concern of those arguing for the determinate sentencing structure and a big reason why people lost faith in the release system under indeterminate sentencing.

Chapter 5

Correcting Corrections

2005 to Present

California recycles rather than rehabilitates.
~State Senator Jackie Speier, 2006

The reorganization and re-emphasis of rehabilitation were praised as a much-needed first step in solving California's many correctional woes. They did not, however, stave off what many considered to be a growing crisis. California had a growing correctional budget and still had one of the highest recidivism rates in the nation. The Little Hoover Commission (2007, p. i) argued, "California's correctional system is in a tailspin that threatens public safety and raises the risk of fiscal disaster." The calls for additional reform came shortly after the 2005 reorganization went into effect. Two key reports were released in 2007. The first, released in January, laid out a stark picture of the challenges faced by the state. The second, released in June, discussed weaknesses in the correctional systems' recidivism reduction efforts and recommended several changes. Combined, the reports laid the groundwork for significant changes to both prisons and parole, but only if the recommendations were adopted.

At the same time, California's prison was facing a constitutional crisis. In October 2006, then-Governor Schwarzenegger proclaimed a state of emergency in California prisons. In doing so, he focused on the severe overcrowding found in 29 of the state's 33 prisons. This overcrowding, he argued, "caused harm to people and property, leads to inmate unrest and misconduct, reduces or eliminates programs, and increases recidivism" (Schwarzenegger, 2006, p. Online). It also increased the risk of violence and transmission of infectious diseases (Schwarzenegger, 2006). The state was also battling two court cases that argued the overcrowding resulted in unconstitutional health and mental health care. The prison system was placed under federal receivership to address healthcare and a special master to address mental health care. These problems came to a head in 2009 when a three-judge panel ruled the state must reduce its prison population to regain constitutional compliance.

In the years following the 2005 reorganization, California implemented several laws aimed at reform. These laws were an attempt to support the reorganization and bring the system into constitutional compliance. Two of these laws led to dramatic changes in which individuals were held and who was eligible for parole, changes that also altered who was eligible for the state's version of the rehabilitative process.

Calls for Further Reform

In January 2007, the Little Hoover Commission released another report on the state of California corrections. It declared the failing correctional system was "the largest and most immediate crisis facing policy-makers" and argued that "governors and lawmakers fearful of appearing soft on crime have failed to muster the political will to address the looming crisis" (Little Hoover Commission, 2007, p. i). The commission blamed decades of "tough on crime" policies for the systems numerous problems and noted multiple failed attempts at changing the culture following the reorganization. As former CDCR Secretary Hickman said in his testimony to the Little Hoover Commission, "Corrections is still years away from sustainable change and the environment needed to truly reform corrections is still overly influenced by special interests wedded to the status quo" (Hickman, 2006, October 26, p. 1). Part of the challenge, he argued, was an organizational leadership that was "unwilling, unable or afraid" (Hickman, 2006, p. 2) to make the necessary changes. A second challenge, he said, was efforts by outside groups to hinder changes that would "diminish their political and policy influence" (Hickman, 2006, October 26, p. 3). Similarly, Simon (2012, p. 24) argued, "nothing more than tinkering at the edges of mass incarceration is likely to occur until the false assumptions supporting it are publicly disproved." The inability to create such change led to the resignation of two CDCR secretaries in 2006.

To address the failures, the commission (2007) made three recommendations. First, it recommended immediately implementing prior reform recommendations made over the years. These reforms included calls to re-invent parole and expand programming in prisons. It also recommended establishing an inter-agency task force that coordinates partnerships between the CDCR and any other governmental organization that can assist with in-prison and reentry programs. These reforms suggested the Little Hoover Commission recognized the correctional system could not address rehabilitation alone and hinted at the need to also consider social rehabilitation if the process was to be successful. If the state refused to implement these changes, the commission recommended creating an independent board responsible for making the necessary changes. Second, the Little Hoover Commission recommended establishing a sentencing commission. This commission would be charged with reviewing current sentences and making adjustments as needed. The commission would be independent and represent California's diverse population.

Finally, the commission recommended implementing evidence-based programs to reduce overcrowding. The move to determinate sentencing and the declaration of prisons as punishment led to a decrease of in-prison programs and a prison system at 200 percent design capacity that created an unsafe environment that "obstructs the efficient delivery of services" (Little Hoover Commission, 2007, p. 19). These changes meant only a small percentage of inmates were able to complete programming to prepare for release. While the Governor's Reorganization Plan emphasized in-prison programs, the commission echoed agent Russell when it stated, "most observers agree that little has been done in the two years since the reorganization to support the 'R' in CDCR" (Little Hoover Commission, 2007, p. 25). The commission also argued that recidivism-reducing programming would remain a lower priority to custody if the population was not reduced, but such a reduction was not possible without raising the priority of programming.

To fix this contradiction, the commission recommended reducing the prison population by increasing in-prison programming and incentivizing participation. It recommended linking good time credit to completing programs and developing employment and housing plans after release. The commission also argued for expanding judicial discretion to address overcrowding. It recommended judges use risk assessment tools to divert low-level offenders from state prison into community supervision through local probation. The judge would be responsible for determining goals the offender must achieve and overseeing progress.

The commission also found that prison overcrowding was linked to the parole system. The commission reiterated its finding that parole was a billion-dollar failure. It pointed to the inability to properly fund the new parole model and implement parolee risk assessments as driving the continued failure. Reiterating their findings from 2003, the Little Hoover Commission also argued parole in its current form made little sense after the shift to determinate sentencing. The shift from discretionary release to mandatory release meant individuals were "released from prison when they have served their time—ready or not" (Little Hoover Commission, 2007, p. 22). The commission further argued the release of all individuals onto parole meant agents were unable to supervise the most dangerous parolees and led to a higher number of returns for technical violations. It concluded this cycling in and out of prison contributed to the high prison population. To address these concerns, the commission recommended eliminating parole, implementing post-release supervision for those deemed most at risk, and waiving supervision for nonviolent, low-risk individuals. For those under supervision, it recommended using a violation matrix to determine responses to violations and earned discharge for those who met their goals. The commission also recommended shifting supervision to local communities, similar to how parole functioned when it was first created, expanding state support for local organizations, and helping counties develop reentry courts. Finally, the commission recommended trying new crimes committed while under supervision through the court system.

Several of the Little Hoover Commission's findings were repeated in June 2007 when the CDCR Expert Panel on Adult Offender Reentry and Recidivism Reduction Programs released its report. The panel was formed after the reorganization to evaluate existing in-prison programming and recommend changes. Similar to the Little Hoover Commission, the Expert Panel argued the passage of SB 42 led to "a thirty-year cycle of increasingly stringent 'tough on crime' laws" that "resulted in more and more people being sentenced to state prison terms for longer periods of time" (CDCR Expert Panel, 2007, p. viii). While the reorganization attempted to shift course, the panel found two barriers to this attempted move to rehabilitation: dangerously overcrowded prisons and treating all offenders the same regardless of program participation. Addressing these two issues was the necessary first step if the system was to re-emphasize rehabilitation.

Like the Little Hoover Commission, the Expert Panel argued overcrowded prisons led to a reduction in programming space in prisons and parole offices and a shutdown of in-prison programs because of repeated security lockdowns. Second, "California's correctional culture is oriented more towards control and punishment, rather than rehabilitation" (CDCR Expert Panel, 2007, p. viii). This culture led to a lack of incentives to participate in programming. Echoing the Little Hoover Commission, the Expert Panel recommended incentivizing rehabilitation program completion, good behavior in prison, and completion of parole requirements. Unlike the Little Hoover Commission, the panel argued the positive reinforcements could also include benefits such as expanded visitation rights or vouchers for the prison canteen.

Once overcrowding and rehabilitation incentivization were addressed, the correctional system would be able to improve how it functioned. To this end, the panel made several recommendations. It recommended using risk/needs assessments for all offenders in prisons and on parole to determine the appropriate rehabilitation programs based on one's criminogenic needs. To better address these needs, the panel recommended delivering a core set of programs available in prisons and the community. These programs would target the seven criminogenic needs that drive male offending[1] and be evaluated to determine the effectiveness and areas of improvement of each program. The panel also recommended developing case management plans for each individual in prison and on parole. The plan was to be monitored to ensure progress was made on the rehabilitative goals. It was not clear if this plan created a continuum of care similar to plans during the medical model or if the prison and parole plans were separate entities.

To maintain rehabilitative progress after release, the panel recommended developing formal relationships with community members such as family members and social service agencies. It also recommended developing informal social controls to protect against reoffending. Parole and community-based programs should be modified to address these needs and assist with reintegration, which would reduce the parolees' risk to society. Finally, the panel recommended using structured sanctions based on an individual's risk level to respond to violations.

In making these recommendations, the Expert Panel hoped to "guide California in creating a rehabilitation *system*" (CDCR Expert Panel, 2007, p. vii; emphasis in original):

> The word *system* is emphasized to underscore the fact that the external environment plays an important role in determining the outcomes of rehabilitation programs. In other words, the activities that occur in the cellblocks, institutional common areas, parole offices, and communities either diminish or enhance the changes offenders make as a result of their rehabilitation programs.

By focusing on the system and linking rehabilitation through corrections with external factors, the Expert Panel also seemed to be suggesting that rehabilitation could not be accomplished through corrections alone. On the other hand, the Expert Panel fell short of calling for other institutions to be involved in the process as the Little Hoover Commission did. The panel argued implementing these changes had several positive outcomes. First, they would reduce the prison and parole populations. Second, they would save between $561 and $684 million a year. Finally, they would "establish a credible and accountable correctional system" (CDCR Expert Panel, 2007, p. xv).

Attempts at Reform

The reports released in 2007 painted a troubling picture of the state's ability to run its correctional system. Similar concerns were raised by two class-action lawsuits claiming California's prison overcrowding amounted to cruel and unusual punishment. These concerns were addressed in three ways. First, the decision reached in *Brown v. Plata* required the state reduce its prison population. Second, the legislature passed SBx3 18 in 2009 as a first attempt to reduce the prison population. Finally, the legislature passed AB 109 and 117 in 2011 in direct response *Brown v. Plata*.

In the end, these legal decisions and legislations led to changes in not only who was housed in state facilities, but also who was released on to state supervision.

Brown v. Plata

While California was reconsidering its correctional system, two court cases were working their way through the judicial system. The first, eventually known as *Coleman v. Brown* (docket no. 2:90-cv-00520-LKK-JFM [E.D. Cal.]), began as a class-action lawsuit filed in April 1990. The lawsuit argued the California adult prison system violated inmates' Eighth Amendment rights by failing to deliver adequate mental health care. In June 1994, California was found in violation and a special master was ordered in September 1995. The special master was to oversee changes necessary to bring the prison system into compliance. The second case, ultimately known as *Brown v. Plata* (docket no. 3:01-cv-01351-THE [N.D. Cal.]), began as a class-action lawsuit in April 2001. This lawsuit argued the adult prison system violated inmates' Eighth Amendment rights by failing to provide adequate healthcare. Both cases argued the lack of care led to numerous preventable deaths, exacerbated illnesses, and improper diagnosis and care.

Shortly after California passed SB 737 and the reorganization went into effect, the saga regarding the prison healthcare system reached a critical moment. On October 3, 2005, US District Judge Thelton Henderson established a federal receivership to address the growing health crisis. In the decision, he argued, "By all accounts, the California prison medical care system is broken beyond repair" (*Plata v. Schwarzenegger*, 2005 WL 2932253, p. 1). This decision was the latest in a series of decisions dating back to 2002. While the class-action lawsuit was filed in August 2001, the court worked to provide the state time to make changes. As Henderson discussed, the state not only failed to deliver these changes, but structural changes made these changes difficult. Judge Henderson pointed to the development of "operational silos" (*Plata v. Schwarzenegger*, 2005 WL 2932253, p. 5), poor funding for healthcare, a plethora of issues within the medical delivery system, and a lack of leadership to make changes. All of these problems amounted to what Henderson described as gross negligence within the prison healthcare system and a "prison culture that devalues the lives of its wards" (*Plata v. Schwarzenegger*, 2005 WL 2932253, p. 22). He was not confident the reorganization was a sufficient response. Judge Henderson noted a receivership was a last resort, but one he felt was necessary after the state "ultimately failed to achieve even a semblance of compliance" (*Plata v. Schwarzenegger*, 2005 WL 2932253, p. 27).

The first receiver was appointed in February 2006 and the federal court and State of California approved a plan in June 2008. Following the governor's emergency proclamation in state prisons, the plaintiffs in *Plata* and *Coleman* filed separate motions to "convene a three-judge court to limit the prison population" (*Coleman v. Schwarzenegger/Plata v. Schwarzenegger*, 2009 WL 2430820, p. 44). As both *Plata* and *Coleman* addressed the care of inmates, resulted in federal oversight to implement changes, and argued overcrowding was the primary cause for the constitutional violations, the cases were consolidated and decided by one three-judge panel. In February 2009, the judges released a tentative ruling indicating they would mandate a reduction in the prison population. They pointed to overcrowding as the primary cause preventing adequate changes in both healthcare and mental health systems, but noted it was not the only cause (*Coleman v. Schwarzenegger/Plata v. Schwarzenegger*, 2009 WL 330960).

In the final ruling (*Coleman v. Schwarzenegger/Plata v. Schwarzenegger*, 2009 WL 330960), the three-judge court argued several factors led to declaring overcrowding as the primary cause of the constitutional violations. The court argued the continuous population increase reversed any progress made by the receiver and special master. The court also argued the overcrowding was a result of "political decisions made over three decades, including the shift to inflexible determinate sentencing and the passage of harsh mandatory minimum and three-strikes laws, as well as the state's counterproductive parole system (*Coleman v. Schwarzenegger/Plata v. Schwarzenegger*, 2009 WL 330960, p. 181). The court gave the state 45 days to submit a plan to reduce the prison population to 137.5 percent of the design capacity, from a high of almost 200 percent, within two years of the court's order becoming effective. The court also noted such a plan should not be difficult to produce as the court released a tentative ruling almost six months earlier to allow time to plan (*Coleman v. Schwarzenegger/Plata v. Schwarzenegger*, 2009 WL 330960).

Schwarzenegger's administration submitted a plan in a timely manner, but the court rejected it. The plan included several provisions that were rejected by the assembly during discussions of SBx3 18 (Yi and Egelko, 2009, September 19). By October, the state had yet to resubmit a new plan and the court demanded a plan within 21 days or the state would face a court-ordered plan. The state submitted a new plan in November 2009 (*Coleman v. Schwarzenegger/Plata v. Schwarzenegger*, 922 F. Supp. 2d 882 [2009]) that was approved in December 2009 (*Coleman v. Schwarzenegger/Plata v. Schwarzenegger*, 2010 WL 99000). This new plan (*Coleman v. Schwarzenegger/Plata v. Schwarzenegger*, 922 F. Supp. 2d 882 [2009]) utilized a mix of existing legislation, existing administrative efforts, and new measures to reach 137.5 percent of capacity in two years. Existing legislation included funding for community programs to supervise felony probationers and the provisions passed in SBx3 18 that would release some prisoners early and prevent others from returning. The use of existing administrative changes included expanding the out-of-state transfer program, increasing reliance on community corrections facilities, transferring inmates and parolees to federal jurisdiction for deportation, and expanding use of GPS monitoring in place of parole revocation. Finally, the plan called for increasing the design capacity through implementation of AB 900 (*Coleman v. Schwarzenegger/Plata v. Schwarzenegger*, 922 F. Supp. 2d 882 [2009]).[2]

Although California was complying with the decision, it also filed an appeal with the Supreme Court of the United States. The three-judge panel's order was stayed until the Supreme Court's decision was released. In the meantime, California passed two bills aimed at pre-emptively reducing the prison population.

2009: Passage of SBx3 18

In December 2008, Governor Schwarzenegger declared a fiscal emergency and called a special session of the legislature (Unknown, 2009, August 28). Senator Ducheny (D-District 40) introduced SBx3 18 on January 5, 2009. The bill originally addressed the Budget Act of 2008 (Unknown, 2009 June 28). It was amended on August 31, 2009 to address "statutory changes necessary to implement the changes to the 2009–2010 Budget Act" (Stephenshaw, 2009, p. 1), which cut funding for the Department of Corrections and Rehabilitation by $1.2 billion (Csizmar & Osterli, 2009).

The purpose of the bill was to reduce costs by reducing the number of individuals in prison and on parole. Given the bill was debated shortly after the three-judge panel released its decision in *Brown v. Plata*, it had the added bonus of addressing overcrowding. Earlier drafts of the bill included alternative custody methods for older inmates and the Little Hoover Commission's (2007) recommendation of establishing a sentencing commission to review existing law. Neither of these recommendations was in the final bill. Addressing overcrowding and the budget cut were accomplished in four ways. First, it provided funding to county officials to expand and implement evidence-based programs for felony probationers in the hopes that successful program completion would reduce the number of probationers being sent to state prisons. Second, it increased the amount of good time credit earned and eligibility for such credit. This change followed the Little Hoover Commission's (2007) recommendation to link good time credit with program completion. Inmates successfully completing a program could earn up to six weeks of credit. A day of credit was also earned for each day of good behavior or each day spent in jail awaiting transfer to a state prison. Finally, good time was extended to those waiting assignment to a conservation camp (Gmeinder, 2009).

Third, it included several changes to parole. It called for the creation of a Parole Reentry Accountability Program, which followed the Little Hoover Commission's (2007) recommendation to develop a reentry court system and "authorize a grid of community-based sanctions" (Little Hoover Commission, 2007, p. 31). The reentry courts were to address parole violations committed by those with a history of substance abuse or mental illness. Rather than returning to prisons, agents would recommend these individuals to reentry courts. There, the judge would work with a team of individuals—including a parole agent, defense attorney, prosecutor, and case managers (Administrative Office of the Courts, 2012)—to determine new conditions for the parolee and a reentry program. While individuals remained on parole, they were monitored and assisted through the court and successful completion often resulted in recommendation for early discharge from parole. The courts would become a part of the California court system and reduce the number of individuals under parole supervision through the Division of Adult Parole Operations. SBx3 18 also mandated the implementation of the Parole Violation Decision-Making Instrument (PVDMI), which was to have been implemented under the 2001 parole model. PVDMI would mimic sentencing guidelines for parole violations and "bring uniformity to parole staff determinations of sanctions to be used for parole violations and emphasize the use of responses based on the severity of the violation and the risk level of the parolee" (Turner, Braithwaite, Kearney, Murphy, & Haerle, 2012, p. 273).[3]

The final and perhaps biggest change to parole was implementation of Non-Revocable Parole (NRP). This change was a modification of the Little Hoover Commission's (2007) recommendation of eliminating parole and establishing post-release supervision for specified individuals. NRP created a hybrid system by creating a banked caseload for parolees "classified as non-serious, non-violent, and non-sex offense offenders, with no prior serious or violent convictions, and who are assessed as low and moderate risk as determined by a validated risk assessment tool" (Gmeinder, 2009, p. 3). Under NRP, designated parolees no longer had to report to an agent, but they also did not have access to parole-based services. They also did not have to follow traditional conditions of parole save one. They were required to allow searches by agents and police officers until their parole term was completed. The goal was to reduce caseloads so agents could focus on the highest risk parolees and those most in need of services, while maintaining the ability to investigate parolees suspected of committing a new crime.

Those in support of the changes focused on the need to save money and improve the system. As reported in one analysis (Csizmar & Osterli, 2009), NRP and changes in sentencing credits would save an estimated $220 million. According to the same analysis, supporters of changes to the sentencing credits argued the changes would act as a way to "manage inmate behavior" (Csizmar & Osterli, 2009, p. 3), as inmates would not want their credits revoked for bad behavior. Supporters also argued the changes regarding credits for programming would help inmates learn to be productive citizens, which in turn would reduce recidivism (Csizmar & Osterli, 2009). Finally, supporters argued changes to parole would allow the system to function better and reentry courts would provide additional help to those parolees in need.

Opposition to the changes focused on the need for the bill itself. Those opposed argued the changes needed to be made administratively, rather than through law, so adjustments could be made more easily. The biggest argument was the savings and response to the three-judge panel could be made without releasing any inmates. One analysis argued, "We have a per inmate spending problem, not a too many inmates problem" (Olson & Cooper, 2009, p. 8). The proposed solution was to use funding allocated through AB 900 to construct more cells and prisons, which would address the overcrowding problem and cut funding on "extravagant spending on per inmate healthcare" (Blakeslee, 2009, p. 1) and bloated bureaucracy (Csizmar & Osterli, 2009). In a letter to then-Governor Schwarzenegger urging a veto, Assembly Minority Leader Sam Blakeslee (2009) cited healthcare costs in other jurisdictions to argue in favor of cutting healthcare costs in California. Given the state was under orders to reduce its prison population because of its constitutionally inadequate healthcare system, it was unclear how this cut would address requirements of the three-judge panel decision.

Those opposed also argued the sentencing credits amounted to early release and parole changes weakened the effectiveness of parole, which were a threat to public safety. Opponents of the sentencing credits argued some credits created an entitlement in which inmates earned a "credit for breathing" (Csizmar & Osterli, 2009). They also argued the credits for program completion were too high. In terms of changes to parole, those opposed argued revocations were a necessary tool and reducing the ability of agents to revoke parolees would tie their hands. In terms of NRP, one analysis (Olson & Cooper, 2009) cited Al Capone as an example of someone who was "nonviolent" and could be released on a banked parole caseload. Presumably, the argument was that those labeled "nonviolent" may appear so on paper, but were not in reality, and placing them on NRP would endanger the public. This argument seemed to be a direct refutation of the three-judge panel's review of literature that found incarceration does not necessarily reduce crime rates and inmates could be released without endangering public safety (*Coleman v. Schwarzenegger/Plata v. Schwarzenegger*, 2009 WL 330960). Finally, those opposed argued the changes were a "soft on crime" approach. Several authors claimed "tough on crime" laws worked and the current bill weakened criminal laws (Blakeslee, 2009; Csizmar & Osterli, 2009; Olson & Cooper, 2009). As Simon (2012) argued and the three-judge panel (*Coleman v. Schwarzenegger/Plata v. Schwarzenegger*, 2009 WL

330960) confirmed, however, California's "tough on crime" approach led to the constitutional violations present in the prison system.

Ultimately, Governor Schwarzenegger signed the bill into law on October 10, 2009. Many of the provisions of this bill were then cited in the state's November 2009 plan submitted to the three-judge panel for approval (*Coleman v. Schwarzenegger/Plata v. Schwarzenegger*, 922 F. Supp. 2d 882 [2009]). The state response estimated the use of programs for felony probationers, good time credits, Non-Revocable Parole, PVDMI, and reentry courts would reduce the average daily prison population by at least 9,827 individuals, approximately one-fourth of the estimated 40,000 needed to meet the court's requirement of reducing the population to 137.5 percent of design capacity. The law went into effect on January 10, 2010.

Impact on Parole

In response to the passage of SBx3 18, the Division of Adult Parole Operations (DAPO) convened the Parole Reform Task Force (TPRTF) to "comprehensively reexamine parole policies and practices" (The Parole Reform Task Force, 2010, p. 1). In January 2010, TPRTF released a new parole plan entitled, *California Parole Supervision and Reintegration Model* (CPSRM). The plan included eight systemic changes.

First, the plan called for implementation of a pre-release plan developed prior to release that addressed potential parolees' criminogenic needs. Second, DAPO would utilize these plans to develop a case plan that would guide how the parole agent intervened and interacted with parolees. The case plan was to adopt the risk, needs, and responsivity model of rehabilitation. It was unclear what role parolees played in developing the pre-release and case management plans. The report indicated inmates would receive a copy of the plan prior to release, but there was no indication they had input in creating the plan. The report also cited research that "engagement of the offender in his/her own Case Plan" led to positive results (The Parole Reform Task Force, 2010, p. 19), but none of the implementation issues discussed covered how parolees were engaged in the development of case plans. The third change called for utilizing case conferences with parolees to review progress and adjust the case management plan and supervision level as needed (The Parole Reform Task Force, 2010). Through the use of in-depth interviewing techniques, parole agents were to collaborate with parolees on determining monthly goals that

> were a tool for the parolee to receive the "dosage" (i.e. number of hours) required to impact their criminogenic risk factors, and were also a mechanism for the parolee to *be part of* their supervision rather than supervision being something that *happened to them.* (Braithwaite, Tatar, & Turner, 2012, p. 1; emphasis in original)

Yet, it was not clear if the collaboration included the parolees' desired goals that did not link to a risk factor.

Fourth, supervision would be aligned with risk level rather than a one-size-fits-all model. This change called for services to be front-loaded since "time immediately following release from prison is a particularly high-risk time for offenders" (The Parole Reform Task Force, 2010, p. 25), echoing the medical model. This change would also create five levels of supervision, ranging from the highest level for those first released and certain types of offenders deemed high risk to the lowest level for low-risk individuals. As a parolee's risk level changed and specific goals were met, they would be moved through the supervision levels. The fifth change called for equitable caseloads so that no agent had more than 40 parolees in the highest supervision level, though the plan did not specify a maximum caseload for other supervision categories. One study found caseloads dropped from 70:1 to 48:1 (Braithwaite, Tatar, & Turner, 2012), but it was not clear if this meant the majority of caseloads were high supervision or if they followed the formula set out by the TPRTF to determine the maximum percent of parolees with specified risk scores per caseload.

Sixth, the plan called for expanded use of evidence-based programs and argued programming "is critical to the ultimate success of this plan" (The Parole Reform Task Force, 2010, p. 34). Seventh, DAPO was to establish a means of determining rewards and incentives for progress on the case management plan. These rewards ranged from verbal recognitions and certificates to adjustments to parole conditions or early discharge to community celebrations. Finally, the plan called for implementing a Discharge Review Committee to conduct periodic reviews of parolees and determine early discharge eligibility.

The effectiveness of CPSRM is questionable. One study (Turner, Braithwaite, Tatar, Omori, & Kearney, 2011) found the new model did not significantly impact how agents viewed the balance of their social work and law enforcement roles. Another study (Braithwaite, Tatar, & Turner, 2012) suggested implementation of CPSRM did not significantly change parolees' satisfaction with their supervision. This was largely due to generally high levels of satisfaction among both CPSRM parolees and the control group. Finally, a third study (Braithwaite, Turner, & Hess, 2013) found no significant impact on recidivism, though there was a slight decrease in arrests and convictions for drug offenses.

2011: Passage of the Realignment

While California was awaiting the Supreme Court's decision, the state legislature developed a plan to reduce the prison population. AB 109, the Public Safety Realignment Act, passed in April 2011, a full month before the Supreme Court released its decision. This plan appeared to be a pre-emptive strike in case the Court upheld the three-judge ruling, as it ultimately did. Once implemented, The Public Safety Realignment Act represented a major shift in California's sentencing and supervision practices.

First introduced in January 2011 as a budget enactment bill, AB 109 was amended in March 2011 to become the Realignment Act. The bill created the means by which "certain low-level offenders, adult parolees, and juvenile offenders [moved] from state to local jurisdiction" (Unknown, 2011, March 17, p. 1). First, certain felonies (not specified) for which one was to be imprisoned would now be housed in county jails instead of state prisons. Felony convictions where the offender had a prior serious or violent felony, the current conviction was a serious or violent felony, or required registration as a sex offender would still be housed in state prison. To ease local jail populations, the bill allowed local facilities to shift some individuals to home detention with electronic monitoring. The bill also established a local Community Corrections Partnership, which required a committee to submit a plan to county supervisors on how best to implement the Realignment, including recommendations on utilizing evidence-based programs and sanctions. Finally, the bill allowed counties to contract with the CDCR for beds in state prisons when local facilities were at capacity and implemented an earned credits system within local jails similar to that available to those housed in state facilities.

Perhaps the largest changes made were within the parole system. AB 109 eliminated NRP and implemented a new system. For those sentenced prior to implementation of AB 109, parole functioned the same. For those sentenced after implementation, however, parole depended on their risk level. Under AB 109, the parole system only supervised those "whose current conviction is for a serious or violent offense, those who are third strikers, and those who are High Risk Sex Offenders" (Unknown, 2011, March 17, p. 3). All other offenders were shifted to post-release supervision by local agencies. The county board of supervisors would determine which agency would supervise these returning citizens and supervision was to be "consistent with evidence-based practices demonstrated to reduce recidivism" (Unknown, 2011, March 17, p. 3). While AB 109 set the terms and conditions that applied to all individuals under post-release supervision, local authorities were empowered with the ability to set additional terms and conditions, including programming, incentives, and sanctions, as necessary. Each individual was to serve three years on post-release supervision with the possibility of early discharge if approved by the supervising agency and the court. Early discharge could be considered as early as six months of supervision assuming the individual did not have any violations (Unknown, 2011, March 17). In creating this system, the legislature adopted another hybrid version of the Little

Hoover Commission's (2007) recommendations. The bill did not eliminate parole entirely, but the authors did recognize the state system could not be responsible for supervising all released individuals.

The revocation process was also altered (Unknown, 2011, March 17). Following implementation of AB 109, those supervised by state parole who violated a condition would still undergo review by the Board of Parole Hearings. Those under local jurisdiction would undergo review by local courts. Local courts were also charged with the ability to "modify terms and conditions, add additional terms and conditions, and terminate supervision for those under its jurisdiction based on violations" (Unknown, 2011, March 17, p. 4). Finally, except for those serving a life sentence, revocations for any parolee or those under post-release supervision would be served in county jails. Revocations could be up to 12 months long, though the bill encouraged courts to use "flash incarcerations" as an immediate punishment for violating a condition of supervision/parole.

Concerns were raised that the Realignment would shift the burden of overpopulation from state prisons to local jails and probation offices. This concern was echoed in a letter to the California State Legislature from Linda Penner, president of Chief Probation Officers of California. In the letter, Penner noted local jails and adult probation caseloads already exceeded capacity and raised concerns those held in local jails or supervised by county probation would be displaced (Penner, 2011, March 17). That said, Penner supported the bill. AB 109 was signed into law in April 2011 with an effective date of July 1, 2011.

AB 117, however, altered this date. AB 117, first introduced a mere seven days after AB 109 was signed into law, provided funding for implementation of AB 109, moved the implementation date to October 1, 2011, moved the implementation of local courts assuming jurisdiction to July 1, 2013, and amended several provisions of AB 109. One amendment altered the make-up of the Community Correction Partnership committee. AB 117 now required the local chief probation officer to serve as chair and required the committee to include "a chief of police; the sheriff; the district attorney; the public defender; the presiding judge" or designee; and a county department head from either the "department of social services, mental health, or alcohol and substance abuse programs" (Unknown, 2011, June 28, p. 2). In making these changes, the social services heads played a smaller role in the committee, while criminal justice practitioners now made up the majority of the committee. The new make-up heavily favored state interests and limited the number of designees serving the offenders' interests.

AB 117 also altered who was to be housed in local jails after conviction. These amendments specified felonies that were exempt from local incarceration and included several convictions related to firearms as well as other felonies such as injuries to a child, "inflicting great bodily injury to a police officer," and felonies related to arson and weapons of mass destruction (Unknown, 2011, June 28, p. 4). Sentencing was also altered to provide judges with the ability to sentence some individuals to county jail or a combination of county jail and mandatory probation.

Several changes were also made to the new post-release supervision plan (Unknown, 2011, June 28). First, AB 109 was amended so that individuals released from prison who had mandatory treatment by the Department of Mental Health as a condition of supervision were to remain under state jurisdiction. Those who did not have such a condition, but did have mental health problems, were supervised under post-release supervision. In these cases, counties could contract with CDCR to provide day treatment and crisis care services to these individuals. Second, AB 109 was amended so the review process of those under local supervision included the individual's risk assessment and clarified possible intermediate sanctions. Changes to the court's role in revocation hearings included allowing local courts to appoint hearing officers who were responsible for revocation hearings and determine whether violations occurred. AB 117 also delayed the court assuming jurisdiction over revocations and terms of custody until 2013. Further, AB 117 amended the restrictions by which a violation could be punished by "flash incarcerations" by increasing the maximum consecutive days from seven to 10 and eliminating a restriction on the number of aggregate days. Finally, AB 117 clarified the release process to "expressly provide that a person who has been on post-release supervision continuously for one year with no violations shall be discharged from supervision within 30 days" (Unknown, 2011, June 28, p. 7). This appears to be the first time state legislation specified a guarantee to release from post-incarceration supervision.

Brown v. Plata *Settled*

In May 2011, in a 5-4 decision, the Supreme Court upheld the lower court's decision and upheld the prison population reduction requirement (*Brown v. Plata*, 131 S. Ct. 1910 [2011]). In response, the three-judge panel filed a new order lifting the stay of their prior order and requiring the state to reduce its prison population to 137.5 percent of design capacity by June 2013. The state submitted an updated plan to reduce the prison population, which now included the Realignment as a major component, to the three-judge panel. California submitted monthly updates on the progress of the reductions and explanations for missed benchmarks.

On January 7, 2013, Governor Jerry Brown submitted a request to lift the federal court order capping the prison population and remove oversight of the prison mental health care system. In its filing to the court,

California initially argued it had met its requirement to implement a constitutionally compliant medical and mental health care system. The state amended its motion to argue that due to the large reduction in the prison population already achieved, overcrowding was no longer the primary cause of unconstitutional medical and mental health care (*Coleman v. Brown/Plata v. Brown, ECF 2590*). The following day, the governor also released a proclamation ending the prison overcrowding emergency proclamation issued by former Governor Schwarzenegger (Brown, 2013).

The three-judge court, however, denied the request for modification of orders. In its decision (*Coleman v. Brown/Plata v. Brown*, ECF 2590, p. 12), the court noted, "Realignment was not sufficient on its own to achieve the 137.5 percent benchmark by June 2013 or to meet the ultimate population cap at any time thereafter, in the absence of additional actions by the defendant." The decision also discussed several reports by the state in which they indicated it would not be possible to meet the required benchmarks on time. As such, the court found the state failed to adequately justify how the overcrowding was no longer an issue when it had yet to meet the 137.5 percent benchmark set by the court or show the circumstances changed sufficiently to warrant a benchmark higher than 137.5 percent. The court also argued the state failed to demonstrate that overcrowding was no longer the primary cause of unconstitutional medical and mental health care systems. Finally, the court argued that even if the state had demonstrated overcrowding was no longer an issue, they failed to demonstrate how they would maintain a constitutionally compliant prison population (*Coleman v. Brown/Plata v. Brown*, ECF 2590).

The state appealed to the Supreme Court, but it appears the Supreme Court denied this appeal. In February 2014, the three-judge court (*Coleman v. Brown/Plata v. Brown*, ECF 2766/2767) approved the state's request for an extension in meeting the requirement to reduce the prison population to 137.5 percent of design capacity. The state now had until February 28, 2016 to comply with this benchmark and develop a plan for maintaining the reduced prison population. In its decision, the court also implemented a compliance officer "for the purpose of bringing defendants into compliance with any missed benchmarks by ordering inmate releases" (*Coleman v. Brown/Plata v. Brown*, ECF 2766/2767, p. 4). The most recent report submitted to the three-judge court in September 2016 suggested the state met its 137.5 percent benchmark, but was still under court supervision (*Coleman v. Brown/Plata v. Brown*, Defendants' September 2016 Status Report in Response to February 10, 2014 Order).

Impact on Rehabilitation

The changes made following the reorganization and in response to federal court mandates altered the way in which individuals were sentenced and the parole system functioned. In some ways, these changes link back to the purpose of parole when it was originally created in 1893. The language in both SBx3 18 and AB 109/117 indicated the use of in-prison programming and changes to the parole system were linked to reducing prison overcrowding, one of the stated purposes of parole at its inception. Implementation of post-release supervision also shifted supervision to local organizations, much as it was when parole began to expand in the early 1900s. These changes also maintained rehabilitation as a form of punishment. The full implementation of PVDMI and reentry courts in particular potentially expanded the use of rehabilitation as punishment. The shift first to Non-Revocable Parole and then the Realignment established a system by which parole and access to its rehabilitative opportunities were reserved for those posing the most risk. Rehabilitation once again became a risk management tool in and of itself and was further framed as an indirect tool of supervision. The passage of NRP also created a situation in which released prisoners wanting access to programs offered through or in conjunction with parole supervision were punished for not being enough of a risk to the public. Although NRP was repealed, it is unclear if the Realignment was a better solution. Given the already high caseloads of local supervisors (Penner, 2011, March 17) and high demand of local services (Hipp, Jannetta, Shah, & Turner, 2011), it was likely those deemed middle or low risk were unable to access the services desired. Whether on parole or post-release supervision, treatment programs were used to increase punishment of returning citizens at all levels.

These changes, however, continued a practice already in place. The remaining changes altered the process itself. Both the Little Hoover Commission and the CDCR Expert Panel called for reducing the prison population while developing a continuum of services and treatment beginning in prisons and continuing onto parole. While the legislature passed several bills aimed at reducing the prison population, the continuum of services did not seem to materialize. Rather, the legislative changes led to a shift in who was eligible for the state's version of the rehabilitative process and raised questions as to the relationship between rehabilitation at the state and local levels.

Changes to the Rehabilitation Process

As one of the goals of the reorganization was to raise the priority of rehabilitation to the same level as custody and supervision, both the Little Hoover Commission and the CDCR Expert Panel called for more access to and incentives for participating in in-prison programing. In doing so, both organizations called for putting prisons back into the rehabilitative process. The legislature responded to this call in 2009. SBx3 18 changed the good time credit system to allow inmates to obtain credit for participating in certain rehabilitative programs, thus incentivizing participation and not just completion. Given the impact of overcrowding on program availability, however, the extent to which prisons became a part of the process is unclear. SBx3 18 also led to changes in the parole system. The parole plan developed in response to SBx3 18 attempted to bring rehabilitation to the forefront of parole practices. This was to be accomplished through the creation of a pre-release plan, front-loading services and supervision, and utilizing new interviewing techniques. The pre-release plan and front-loading of services harkened back to the parole model of the 1940s to early 1970s while the interviewing techniques drew from modern understandings of therapeutic change.

The biggest change, however, came in terms of who was eligible for the process. Under SBx3 18 and the implementation of Non-Revocable Parole, certain individuals were no longer eligible for the second half of the rehabilitation process. While everyone was still placed on parole, services and agent contact were reserved for the most at-risk, and arguably most in need, parolees. This enabled low-risk offenders to live in the community without being bogged down by the conditions of parole. On the surface, NRP addressed the criticisms raised by the Little Hoover Commission that not all returning citizens needed supervision and that higher caseloads limited parole agents' ability to work individually with parolees. As one agent noted in an interview (Russell), however, parolees on NRP were unable to access programs and services through parole, even if they wanted such access.

Eligibility was changed again with implementation of the Realignment, which eliminated Non-Revocable Parole and impacted access to the process as a whole. Shifting sentencing so some individuals were held in local facilities and released on to local supervision meant some individuals were completely removed from the state's version of the rehabilitative process. Those individuals held in state prisons but released on to local supervision had access to the first half of the state's process. In some ways, the process for those placed on post-release supervision may have expanded. These individuals were to have access to a variety of programs offered through the local court system, including local reentry courts. It was possible the local version of rehabilitation process was similar to the state's, but there was little discussion of how to ensure this was the case or if such similarities were desirable.

Following implementation of the Realignment, the end of the process became even more unclear. If the TPRTF plan was still utilized, discharge from parole was potentially a moving target. Parolees could move across the levels of supervision in either direction, though the hope was they would move towards less services and supervision and towards discharge. In cases where parolees made sufficient progress, early discharge was a possibility. For those who were not eligible for early discharge, however, neither the plan nor the Realignment legislation made it clear if discharge after three years was guaranteed regardless of level of supervision or how returns to custody impacted the parole clock. The end of post-release supervision was also unclear as supervision varied from county to county. The only clear indication to the end of post-release supervision was a presumptive eligibility for early discharge after six months of violation-free supervision and guaranteed discharge after one year of violation-free supervision. For those who were not eligible for early discharge, it was again unclear whether release after three years occurred regardless of progress made or how returns to custody impacted the supervision clock. Unfortunately, none of the legislative documents discussed whether release from parole or post-release supervision was a sufficient end to the rehabilitative process or if it continued in the community until a Certificate of Rehabilitation or pardon was obtained.

Still a Change, but What Else?

While eligibility for the rehabilitative process changed dramatically, the end goal of change for the better seemed to remain the same. As indicated by the TPRTF plan, parolees were to show they had adjusted to life on the outside, established a home and employment, and adopted pro-social behaviors and activities to move to lower levels of supervision. Discharge from both parole and post-release supervision ideally occurred when a change in the individual's behavior indicated movement away from criminal activity and a change for the better. Though, again, it was not clear such changes were required for release at the end of the mandatory three-year supervision period. The only clear factor indicating eligibility for early discharge was for those on post-release supervision and focused on a lack of violations. Presumably, no violations indicated the returning citizens had changed their ways, but it was not clear if that was the case or if they simply avoided detection. It was also not clear what other factors local courts and reentry courts used when determining early discharge.

It was unclear if return to former self remained a goal of the rehabilitative process or not. None of the reports or legislative documents discussed the return of rights following release from supervision. It was also not clear if, as the agents interviewed indicated, the return to former self was only desirable for some individuals. Presumably, this goal remained on the books but became less achievable, as it did following the reorganization.

Assistance for Some, Maybe

Following passage of Non-Revocable Parole (NRP) and the Realignment, the state's role in providing assistance in the rehabilitative process also changed dramatically. The shift to NRP created a system in which only some individuals were eligible for assistance. Many agents argued the inability to provided services for some parolees was "not the best idea" (Helen). For example, Russell mentioned two parolees who were addicted to heroin and wanted access to drug treatment programs. As they were both placed on NRP, however, the state would not pay for state programs available through parole, so he was unable to enroll them. Being placed on NRP also prevented the agent from charging the parolees with a violation and sending them to prison for an in-prison drug detoxification program. While NRP was aimed at helping parole agents play a larger role in the rehabilitative process, it also tied their hands when it came to helping those who desired access to the programs or to those they were most concerned about.

While the Realignment eliminated NRP and reestablished supervision for all, it did not change how state assistance was distributed. Only those deemed most at risk remained eligible for assistance from the state either in prison or on parole. All others received assistance from local prisons, supervision, and courts. What assistance at the state level looked like was unclear. Credits for program participation in prisons and jails were dependent on the inmates' decisions. This potentially fully responsibilized individuals for the in-custody portion of the process. On the other hand, the pre-release plan developed for those remaining on parole suggested a shift back to some combination of assistance and responsibilization both in prisons and on parole. What assistance looked like on local supervision was also unclear, again because such decisions were up to each locale independently. As far as the state was concerned, however, assistance for those individuals was no longer their concern unless local officials requested support. Given that failures at the local level potentially impacted the state's prison population and rehabilitative process, it was unclear why greater coordination between the state and local levels was not sought following the Realignment.

These changes show California grappled with improving its correctional system and implementing a renewed focus on rehabilitation. As the story of rehabilitation continues, it will be interesting to see how well California achieves its goal or if this latest attempt is a moment, not a movement. Yet, the story of rehabilitation thus far suggests a need to consider the past to better understand the future. Thus, the concluding chapter discusses the connections across time. It also discusses the implications of these connections for rehabilitation and parole.

Notes

1 No information was provided on how, or even if, the programs would be adjusted to meet the needs of female offenders.

2 AB 900, signed into law in March 2007, was a prison construction bill. The bill allocated millions of dollars for prison construction projects and expansion of

rehabilitation programs for prisoners and parolees. Implementation of the plan was slow (Taylor, 2009).

3 The use of such tools is not without concern. As a recent ProPublica investigation found, risk assessments used when determining sentences were not reliable at predicting violent crime and replicated racial biases. Specifically, the investigation found black defendants were twice as likely as white defendants to be labeled as future criminals and white defendants were "mislabeled as low risk more often than black defendants" (Agwin, Larson, Mattu, & Kirchner, 2016, p. Online). Given these findings, it is not clear if risk assessments such as PVDMI are reliable or simply perpetuating racial biases.

Conclusion

History doesn't repeat itself, but it does rhyme.

~Mark Twain

As with all histories, the story of rehabilitation in California corrections generally and parole specifically does not end here, nor are the eras described distinct moments in time. In tracing the meaning of rehabilitation as a legislative goal, what emerges is a story with a rough beginning, a muddled middle, and no clear ending. What is clear is a definition of rehabilitation found in the legislative and policy documents that is broader than typically thought. Embedded in this definition are remnants of prior definitions and alterations made through legislative changes. Fully understanding the meaning of rehabilitation has broader implications for our understanding of parole and corrections.

Impact of Major Legislative Changes

Tracing the meaning of rehabilitation as a legislative goal requires tracing the history of correctional philosophies. Echoing Hutchinson's (2006) braided penology, the correctional philosophy determined whether punishment or rehabilitation took prominence. When looking at the analysis of legislative changes as a whole, four patterns emerge: rehabilitation is for achieving public safety; rehabilitation might require some version of indeterminate sentencing; reorganization might be needed for rehabilitation to succeed; and changes in purpose do not seem to change organizational practices.

First, rehabilitation is never a goal for its own sake. Rather, it is a means of achieving public safety. The way in which rehabilitation is framed as achieving this goal shifts over time (see also Robinson, 2008). During the medical model of the 1940s to 1970s, rehabilitation was framed as a form of welfarism. The purpose of rehabilitation was to improve the inmates' lives by curing them of their social ills and deficiencies. Curing these individuals, prison and parole authorities argued, would eliminate criminal behavior, thereby reducing harm and increasing public safety. In the 1970s to 1990s, rehabilitation was a way of managing risks. Treatment programs were no longer solely based on individual need. Rather, they were used to address common risk factors and participation was determined by the factors an individual possessed. Successful participation eliminated these risk factors, thereby reducing harm and improving public safety. Under the current version, rehabilitation is still used to manage risks, but the risk reduction was for the improvement of society. Risk management still led to a reduction of harms and improvement of public safety. The programs also enabled individuals to become "productive members of society" by getting them into employment, paying taxes, and paying child support, among other responsibilities, which arguably improved society as a whole. Rehabilitation was also key to reducing prison populations, which would save money, allow prison funds to be allocated to other social services, and bring the prison system into constitutional compliance, all of which also improved society as a whole.

Second, the changes suggest that rehabilitation and determinate sentencing are incompatible. Both time periods in which rehabilitation took prominence are linked to conversations about sentencing reform. The change to indeterminate sentencing in 1917 was the precursor to declaring rehabilitation as the purpose of correctional custody. Today, the goal of rehabilitation is being used to argue for a shift in sentencing. Several reports (CDCR Expert Panel, 2007; Little Hoover Commission, 2007) argued that rehabilitation should be linked to good time credits in prison and early discharge from parole. They also called for larger sentencing reform so only those who are truly the most risk are subjected to correctional custody and rehabilitation. Several parole agents even directly called for a return to indeterminate sentencing. Combined, these calls suggest rehabilitation needs a more malleable sentencing structure to be successful.

Third, the changes suggest rehabilitation is not possible without reorganization, but punishment is always possible regardless of the organization. Although the 1917 Indeterminate Sentencing Law implemented rehabilitation as a correctional goal, it was not until after the 1944 departmental reorganization that rehabilitation truly took hold in California corrections. When the California legislature declared the purpose of prisons was punishment, however, there was little discussion of the need to reorganize the department. What reorganization occurred was about streamlining the department rather than a necessary requirement for the new philosophy to take hold. Yet, in 2005 Schwarzenegger argued reorganization was a necessary first step to achieving both reform and rehabilitation, suggesting an organizational design created for rehabilitation and supported punishment was no longer effective. This suggests rehabilitation may need more than just a reorganization to succeed; it may require a rethinking of systems and structures.

Finally, the legislative changes also show that while the purpose of the correctional system changed, the everyday realities changed very little. As Hagan, Hewitt, and Alwin (1979, p. 509) argued, an advantage of loosely coupled systems is that "the organization is able to maintain and often increase its institutional legitimacy without dramatically changing its day-to-day practices. The more such organizations change, the more for many practical purposes, they stay the same." For California corrections, the organization was reframed to support the correctional philosophy, thus maintaining the legitimacy of both prisons and parole. During periods of rehabilitative prominence, prisons and parole are framed as necessary so that offenders receive targeted programs and services. When punishment was prominent, prisons and parole were framed as necessary to control and surveil offenders. Yet, analysis of the parole manuals show little changed in terms of parole policies. Several parole agents also noted their day-to-day operations changed little after the recent reorganization. What does seem to have changed, however, is access to resources and funding to support the day-to-day activities.

When suggestions were made to alter the system, they were dismissed. For example, several individuals argued prisons failed at institutional care during the medical model because the atmosphere was artificial and they were not originally designed for treatment. Rather than rethink the purpose and use of prisons, legislators and correctional officials cited this concern to criticize the effectiveness of and ability to achieve rehabilitation. The move to determinate sentencing attempted to eliminate parole with proponents of its elimination arguing it did not fit in a determinate scheme and no longer served a purpose without rehabilitation. It was brought back to life by the parole agents union, which argued parole was necessary for public safety. More recent calls to rethink sentencing are dismissed as "soft on crime" and dangerous for society. At the same time, both Non-Revocable Parole and the Realignment argued low-risk offenders did not need to be supervised in the community or in the state correctional system. If this argument is true, it raises questions as to the need to place low-risk individuals in prisons (or local jails after the Realignment) in the first place, which raises questions as to the true purpose of prisons. For low-risk individuals, at least, these policies suggest a prison sentence is for punishment, not rehabilitation.

Given what appears to be an inability for reorganization to achieve change, the legislative history suggests that truly embracing rehabilitation may require a rethinking of the correctional system as a whole, including its philosophy, systems, and structures. A key question that must be grappled with is whether the correctional system is the appropriate site for offender rehabilitation. If the answer is no, then academics, practitioners, and legislators should focus on possible alternatives. Some of these considerations are already occurring. The implementation of reentry courts, the acknowledgement that not all individuals need post-release supervision, and shifting some responsibility for rehabilitation to local organizations all suggest that our current reliance on corrections is being rethought. The question remains as to whether this hybrid system will be effective or if more dramatic changes are needed.

Defining Rehabilitation

As this book argues, rehabilitation as a legislative goal is both a form of punishment and an ongoing event. Unlike Robinson's (2008) finding that only the most recent version of rehabilitation in the United Kingdom and Wales is a type of punishment, the legislative history in California suggests rehabilitation served as a type of punishment as early as the 1940s. Beginning with the medical model, rehabilitation justified the isolation of individuals in prisons. The idea of prisons providing institutional care created a situation where the response to crime was forced participation in treatment away from the community. Punishment for being convicted was prison-based rehabilitation. Even in moments when prisons were for punishment, access to in-prison programs was an additional justification for incarceration. A lack of rehabilitation justified keeping individuals in prison for longer time periods. This is particularly evident during the 1940s to mid-1970s when some level of rehabilitation was necessary for the parole board to grant release. After the passage of determinate sentencing, requiring participation in rehabilitation programs to earn good time credit created a situation where those who participated in such programs were rewarded with an earlier release than those who did not. Since the 1940s, those who did not rehabilitate in some way were punished with longer prison terms.

After release from prison, rehabilitation was a means of punishing those who failed to meet certain standards. Throughout the history of parole in California, failure to comply with the conditions of parole was met with some form of sanction. In many cases, these sanctions included an increase in program requirements, especially drug treatment and mental health treatment programs, or movement to community correctional facilities designed to partially remove parolees from the community while requiring a certain level of programming in order to remain out of prison. As some of the agents stated, the sanction could also include a return to prison for the sole purpose of gaining access to an in-prison treatment program, especially when programs in the community were lacking. In this way, rehabilitation expanded and extended control over individuals into the community and punished parolees for failing to meet standards higher than those for non-supervised persons. More recent legislation codified rehabilitation as punishment with the mandated use of PVDMI and intermediate sanctions. In an ironic twist, the temporary implementation of Non-Revocable Parole and implementation of the Realignment altered who was able to access services offered through parole. Those placed on summary parole through NRP or discharged to post-release supervision after the Realignment could not use state-based programming as they were deemed too low risk even if they wanted assistance. In other words, denying access to rehabilitation on the state level still punished some returning citizens. While those placed on local supervision potentially had access to additional programs through the local courts and the reentry courts, those programs were available precisely because the courts determined they were a necessary condition of supervision.

Rehabilitation was not framed as punishment, however. Instead, it was framed as benefitting the parolee or reducing risks. Rehabilitation as punishment in the 1940s to 1970s was framed as the application of more "medicine" needed to help cure the offender. The move away from the medical model led to rehabilitation as punishment being framed as addressing risk factors, thus ensuring offenders were no longer a threat to society. Intermediate sanctions of program participation also benefitted the offender by addressing their criminogenic needs and keeping them in their communities.

Rehabilitation was also viewed as an ongoing event and combined several theories of rehabilitation (see Raynor & Robinson, 2005). As an ongoing event, rehabilitation becomes something the convicted person strives to achieve on a daily basis rather than a label acquired by meeting certain accomplishments. One is not rehabilitat*ed*, but rehabilitat*ing*. The ongoing nature of rehabilitation provides a rationale for the continued use of punishing regimes. If rehabilitation was an accomplishment, then the need to punish, assist, supervise, treat, or otherwise control convicted individuals ends when they meet the stated requirements. The ongoing nature of rehabilitation ensures that rehabilitation takes years, if not decades, to complete, thus requiring continued control until the process is over (assuming such an end is possible). Similarly, the ongoing nature of rehabilitation provides the rationale for focusing on risk management and control within correctional systems. Arguably, certain groups of people take longer to work through the rehabilitative process than others. Those taking the longest time, then, also pose the most risk to public safety because they have not yet reached a point where they are no longer a threat. As such, it becomes necessary to control, and even manage, these individuals so as to reduce the risk posed by the groups of individuals still working through the rehabilitative process. As individuals became more responsibilized for their rehabilitative process, rehabilitation as an ongoing event allows state actors to deflect blame when parolees failed. Such failures are viewed not as a failure of policies and practices in place, but as a failure of parolees to take advantage of the opportunities provided to them. State actors are able to maintain their institutional legitimacy and power while detaching themselves from the everyday realities of those they govern.

The basic aspects of rehabilitation remained the same across time. First, rehabilitation was viewed as a process. Second, the process was completed when one changed for the better and/or returned to a former self. A change for the better was viewed as no longer participating in criminal behavior, whether that was by no longer committing crimes or eliminating the factors that led to the criminal behavior (i.e., correctional rehabilitation). A return to a former self was viewed as returning to society, becoming a part of society such that the individual's former status as a prisoner or parolee is unknown, and regaining full rights of citizenship (i.e., legal rehabilitation). Unlike other views of legal rehabilitation, however, the restoration of all citizenship rights did not occur until returning individuals proved they were correctionally rehabilitated. Finally, the state was involved in some way.

This is as far as the similarities go, however. The process changed depending on the prominence of rehabilitation or punishment. During the 1940s through mid-1970s, the process began in prisons, transferred to parole, and continued even after release from parole. Release onto parole did not require complete rehabilitation, but a sign the individual had begun the rehabilitative process and no longer needed to be confined. Release off parole also did not require complete rehabilitation, but a sign that one would continue one's rehabilitation on one's own. Presumably the process ended when one earned a Certificate of Rehabilitation or pardon and full legal rights were restored.

Following passage of the Uniform Sentencing Law, prisons were no longer legislatively viewed as part of the process and inmates were not required to participate in rehabilitative programs.[1] Rehabilitative progress no longer determined release on to and off parole. Law mandated it. Completion of the process, and restoration of full legal rights, still depended on earning a Certificate of Rehabilitation and pardon.

Although the process did not officially change after the 2005 reorganization, several reports (Little Hoover Commission, 2003; CDCR Expert Panel, 2007; Little Hoover Commission, 2007) and the agents interviewed argued that rehabilitation should begin in prisons and release onto parole should not be as rigid as current sentencing guidelines mandate. These same reports also recommended implementing program plans that began in prison and continued on parole, creating a continuum of care. While legislation after the reorganization attempted to place prisons back into the process, the continuum of care does not seem to have materialized. The Little Hoover Commission (2003) called for and the new parole model implemented a reorganization of the parole system so that services and supervision were front-loaded, similar to the parole organization under the medical model. The process seems to end with the achievement of a Certificate of Rehabilitation or pardon. As the Little Hoover Commission (2003) noted, however, agents and parolees are not familiar with the Certificate of Rehabilitation and recent court cases indicated the trial court has large discretion in granting or denying the certificate, suggesting the process never truly ends.

Changes also occurred to the desired end goals, particularly in the time periods where rehabilitation was supposed to play a prominent role. Although the parole-related documents from the 1940s to the 1990s indicated both a change for the better and a return to a former self were desirable, the agents interviewed seemed to indicate it was not possible to achieve both today. They argued that most of the individuals they work with were never a part of societal norms, so it was not possible to return to such a position. For those who were a part of societal norms, the criminal behavior was the only divergence, so it was not necessary to change for the better.

The legislative and parole-related documents indicate a return of legal rights was also desirable. As the Little Hoover Commission (2003) found, however, parole agents were unfamiliar with the process for obtaining a Certificate of Rehabilitation. Pardons took years if not decades to achieve. While most legal rights were returned upon release from prison, returning citizens were still barred from holding office, voting, or acting as a trustee until a pardon was obtained. As such, a return to former self that includes full legal rights seems impossible to achieve, suggesting the process never truly ends.

Finally, there was a change in the belief as to the extent to which the state can be involved in the rehabilitation process. Under the medical model, the state had to intervene to achieve rehabilitation and the correctional system was the only remaining agency that had the power to achieve such results, especially as other agencies failed. Prisons were the sites of institutional care with treatment lasting just long enough for inmates to move past the acute phase of their illness. Parole agents were viewed as expert therapists skilled in treating parolees. It was their responsibility to ensure parolees continued to improve or were returned to prison for additional treatment. In many ways, parolees were painted as passive recipients of medication that would solve their ailments so long as they followed the treatment plan.

The shift to the control model changed that. After passage of the Uniform Sentencing Law, the correctional system as a whole was viewed as incapable of producing change. Prisons were sites for punishment and nothing more. Parole agents were no longer able to "give" parolees treatment; parolees had to seek it out. The responsibility for achieving rehabilitation shifted to the parolee, though agents still provided some intervention when necessary.

This idea carried into the current call for rehabilitation. Today, inmates and parolees are fully responsibilized. Prisons can be sites for rehabilitation, but only if the inmate chooses to participate in appropriate programs and only if such programs are available. Parole agents no longer believe they can change anyone. Instead, they provide parolees with opportunities and it is up to the parolees to take advantage of those opportunities. The Realignment complicates this responsibilization. Returning citizens released on to post-release supervision who want opportunities may find they are not available. Local programs are often inaccessible, especially for those most in need (Hipp, Jannetta, Shah, & Turner, 2011), and they may not qualify for state-funded programs if they are not under state control. Legislative changes may be creating a situation where no one is responsible for rehabilitation because it is so inaccessible.

These changes indicate that the current call to rehabilitation is a conglomeration of prior notions of rehabilitation. The idea that rehabilitation should begin in prisons resonates back to the process under the medical model. Individuals being responsible for their own rehabilitation and state actors only being able to assist, rather than force, rehabilitation continue a belief prominent in the later part of the twentieth century. Some scholars are even calling for a return to some version of the idea that offenders must be cured. For example, during the 2016 Aspen Ideas Festival, Marc Levin (director at Center for Effective Justice at the Texas Public Policy Foundation) said, "We need to diagnose someone as soon as they're arrested, and figure out what would reduce their criminogenic needs" (Appelbaum, 2016, June 27, p. Online). This argument hints at the possibility of the framing of the need for rehabilitation coming full circle.

As this book highlights, the current version has multiple limitations that raise questions as to the ability to truly achieve rehabilitation. With regards to correctional rehabilitation, there are some limitations as to the ability to truly eliminate the reasons behind criminal behavior. As the radical criminologists argued, individual treatment is ineffective without first implementing structural changes to society (Rotman, 1990). They argued that without these changes, returning individuals would return to unchanged conditions—the same conditions that propelled them into crime in the first place. While the prison and parole systems included multiple treatment programs and conditions aimed at eliminating the criminal behavior and the current call for rehabilitation is shifting more responsibility to local organizations, state correctional funds still do not address fundamental social-structural conditions that drive criminal behavior. While those could be addressed in other bills, none of the legislative documents or court-mandated plans discussed these changes or their impact on offender rehabilitation. Given studies that find released offenders live in socially disorganized communities (e.g., Visher & Farrell, 2005; Shah, 2007), it is unclear how a focus on rehabilitation through correctional systems can be successful without making the necessary societal and structural changes.

Limitations also exist as to the extent in which legal rehabilitation can be achieved. As Raynor and Robinson (2005, p. 11) note, legal rehabilitation calls for a "restoration of the state of citizenship." Although there is a path to restore full citizenship rights and removal of the conviction from one's official record, this process can take decades and is not guaranteed. In the meantime, the criminal conviction impedes a parolee's ability to obtain adequate employment (Pager, 2003; Quillian & Pager, 2005; Love, 2006; Uggen, Thompson, & Manza, 2006; Western, 2006), stable housing (Helfgott, 1997; California Department of Corrections, 1997; Nelson, Deess, & Allen, 1999; Travis, 2005; California Secretary of State, 2006; Joint Center for Housing Studies, 2007; Legal Action Center, n.d.;), or higher education (Jacobs, 2000; Mauer, 2010), among other barriers.

Given the plethora of legal and non-legal barriers facing returning citizens, it is no surprise that parolees would have difficulty reintegrating into society. While the rehabilitative process is supposed to help returning individuals become "full citizens" and "productive members of society," it is not designed to help these individuals move past structural barriers. Unlike other countries (e.g., England), California does not have a means of legally sealing a criminal conviction besides the governor's pardon.[2] Without such a means, it is unclear how convicted persons are expected to successfully reintegrate into society such that their past is unknown, thus achieving at least a partial return to former self, even with the most diligent of support from the correctional system.

How long this version of rehabilitation remains in place, and what comes next for the correctional system, is unclear. What is clear is that, if past is prologue, the rehabilitative process will continue to change. And it will remain an open question of how much the correctional system can accomplish on its own and without changes in daily policies and practices.

Impact on Parole

What is evident through this analysis is that the changing role and meaning of rehabilitation in California corrections had an interesting impact on parole. It did not appear to change day-to-day policies and practices. What did change was the role of parole in the process, how failures were viewed, and the relationship between supervision and services.

When parole was first created, it was a convenient means of addressing prison overcrowding. As the correctional system embraced the medical model and rehabilitation as its guiding philosophy, the parole system became an integral part of the correctional system and the rehabilitation process. Without it, returning citizens would be fighting the last throes of their illness without the appropriate oversight. Release onto parole was needed if parolees had any hope of successfully completing their rehabilitation. As the system moved towards a punishment philosophy, parole maintained rehabilitation as a goal, though perhaps at a lower priority. Prisons no longer played a role in the rehabilitative process, at least not intentionally. Parole, then, was the only remaining part of the correctional system that was to play a role in the rehabilitative process. This role continued into the current call for rehabilitation. Attempts made to place prisons back into the process are struggling to succeed. An intransigent bureaucracy and prison guard/parole agent union mixed with cuts in funding and massive overcrowding prevented rehabilitation programs from taking hold. Combined, these challenges prevent a cultural shift that would enable prisons to play a role in the process. The implementation of Non-Revocable Parole and then the Realignment also created a situation where parole is now removed from the process completely for some offenders. Post-release supervision may serve the same purpose, but it is not clear the various local versions compare to a theoretically consistent statewide program. Finally, the Realignment also reinstated the notion of parole and post-release supervision as a means of addressing overcrowding.

The shift in responsibility for rehabilitation may explain the changes in how failures were viewed. When it was the agents' responsibility, and responsibility of corrections as a whole, to ensure rehabilitation, failures were viewed as a natural part of the process. Failures indicated a need for further treatment, or perhaps a different type of treatment, much the way a medical relapse would be viewed. As the responsibility shifted, failures remained a sign the parole system was successful in their job, but for a different reason. Failures indicated a threat to public safety. Catching failures, particularly when they resulted in a return to prison, showed agents were protecting the public by removing risks. At no point, however, did failures indicate a failed system.

Finally, the relationship between services and supervision also changed. During the 1940s to mid-1970s, supervision was not a tool to determine when parolees should return to prison. Instead, it was meant to illuminate when and what type of treatment was necessary. Supervision was front-loaded. Those needing the most assistance were supervised the heaviest so agents could ensure parolees had access to the appropriate services and programs. It also determined when someone was released too soon or in need of more prison-based rehabilitative programs. Thus, supervision was a tool for rehabilitation.

During the late 1970s to 1990s, this relationship flipped. Those working with parolees under the guise of rehabilitation were additional sources of information for parole agents in determining whether parolees were violating conditions of parole or too dangerous to remain in the community. Program providers became an indirect way of supervising parolees, as they were supposed to inform the parole agents if and when the parolees became a danger to themselves or the public, were violating the conditions of their parole, or were committing new crimes. Rehabilitation, then, became framed as a way of ensuring that those posing the most risk received the greatest assistance, but was really providing another means of controlling the behavior of parolees in the community and providing one more way in which the parolee could trip up (see also Werth, 2012).

Under the current version of rehabilitation, a feedback loop was created. Supervision is a way of determining the types of treatments necessary to address parolees' criminogenic needs, thereby decreasing the risk to public safety, and rehabilitation is a means of determining whether greater surveillance was necessary. In other words, supervision is a tool for rehabilitation that in turn is a tool for supervision. The two feed into each other and create a system whereby supervision and treatment are always necessary and ever expanding. The Parole Violation Decision-Making Instrument best captures this feedback loop. PVDMI was implemented to help reduce returns to prison for technical violations and divert eligible parolees to intermediate sanctions. Use of PVDMI is triggered only when a violation occurs. Intermediate sanctions add an additional condition that could be violated. If the sanction is program participation, additional surveillance occurs through the gaze of program providers, who could also report a violation. These violations once again trigger use of PVDMI, which then potentially adds another layer of intermediate sanctions. For some parolees, PVDMI is the tool by which supervision and services expand until they are finally recommended for revocation and return to prison. This feedback loop also creates a system in which early discharge or completion of the rehabilitation process became virtually impossible, thereby legitimizing the need for parole. Although the Realignment reduced the number of returning citizens caught in this feedback look, those of the highest risk are also the most likely to be caught in the loop in the first place. The new parole model attempts to break this loop by front-loading services, but the use of program providers as informants and PVDMI could aggravate the loop so that parolees are stuck on the highest level of supervision.

The shifting nature of rehabilitation was not lost on parole agents and administrators. The acknowledgement of these shifts translated into a presentation for Parole Officers' Week in July 2009, entitled "The Rehabilitation Pinball" (Figure 7.1). This presentation, sponsored by the T. H. Pendergast Parole Museum, was described as such (THP Museum representative, personal communication, 13 May 2009):

> The concept, how the parole models have changed, or not, repeating themselves in our 100 plus year history. Over the past 100 years

> parole has bounced back and forth from enforcement to Rehab, many times just dusting it off and re-using the same old model.

This description indicates that even the agents recognize the role of rehabilitation within the parole system has changed based on its position within the larger correctional system and that, through the years, very little has changed in terms of policies and everyday practices.

The most recent legislative changes, however, may be changing parole in ways not seen before by altering the reach of parole. The Realignment shifted middle- and low-risk offenders to supervision by local organizations instead of a state agency, created an avenue for early discharge for some offenders, and left state parole intact for high-risk offenders. This created a version of parole more in line with post-release supervision

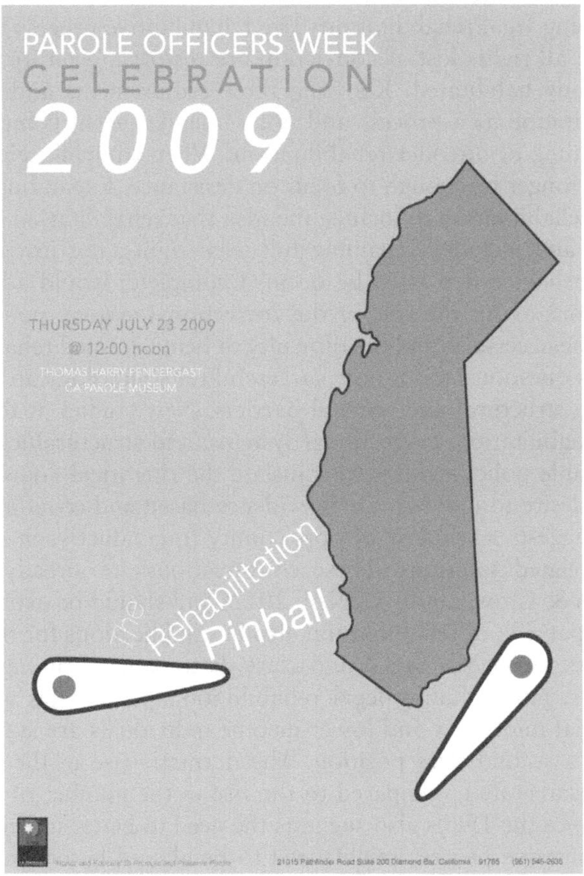

Figure 7.1 Poster for the Parole Officers Week Celebration

Reprinted with permission from the T.H. Pendergast Parole Museum

programs in other states. By also requiring the court to adjudicate all violations of parole (new crimes and technical violations), the Realignment also limited the power of the paroling authority to determine who stays in the community. These changes could signal a refocusing of parole so it provides surveillance and services to those most in need or it could be the first step in dismantling the system all together.

What Comes Next?

While multiple meanings of rehabilitation are theorized (Raynor & Robinson, 2005), discussions of and studies about rehabilitation within the criminal justice system often focus on correctional rehabilitation. As the legislative histories suggest, however, correctional rehabilitation is not the whole picture. Rehabilitation is more than just an end to criminal activities. Correctional rehabilitation is the first step and is necessary for obtaining legal rehabilitation. The rehabilitative process is not complete until all rights lost at conviction are restored, even for those who were already habilitated. Knowing these requirements and the notion of rehabilitation as a process and not a singular event complicates our understanding of offender rehabilitation. When studying rehabilitation, it may no longer be enough to focus on desistance. Expanding studies of offender rehabilitation to include the idea that rehabilitation is an ongoing event and included regaining full legal rights, not just eliminating criminal behavior if it is to be deemed complete, would address critical questions about the role of the correctional system, policy changes that may be necessary, and the difficulty of being deemed rehabilitated. It also raises questions about how successful rehabilitation can be without addressing structural and societal barriers. New studies at the intersection of rehabilitation, correctional systems, and structural/legal barriers would enable policy-makers to translate the rhetorical goals into practice. The desire to move towards evidence-based and economically wise policies suggests a window of opportunity to conduct such studies and propose related solutions. These conversations are already beginning (Robinson & Crow, 2009; McNeil, 2012) and should be expanded.

This expansion of rehabilitation also has implications for the offender population. Given the racial and class discrepancies among convicted individuals, not including legal rehabilitation perpetuates a system in which racial minorities and lower income individuals are systematically placed in a second-class position. The dramatic rise in the number of women incarcerated, compared to the rise in the number of men incarcerated, since the 1980s also suggests the need to better understand how the rehabilitative process might need to be altered based on individual needs (Kruttschnitt & Gartner, 2003; McCorkel, 2013). An expanded understanding of rehabilitation would also allow for a rethinking of reintegration policies and practices. Critically and theoretically engaged research is needed to better understand the implications of this definition of rehabilitation on offender populations.

The focus on correctional rehabilitation also suggests a disconnect between the rhetoric of correctional legislation and existing practice. This disconnect may explain why attempts at reorganizing correctional systems to implement rehabilitation are ineffective. Correctional systems are not designed to address legal rehabilitation. Being sentenced to the correctional system is precisely why legal rehabilitation is needed. Nor are they able to address social-structural and legal barriers that allow returning citizens to integrate into the community in a healthy environment and as full citizens. The correctional system could be used as one part of the rehabilitative process, but, as the Little Hoover Commission (2007) suggested, may not be the only part of the process. Given recent difficulties in adequately funding the system and maintaining constitutional compliance, it is not even clear the system as it stands can play a role.

Given all of this, understanding and supporting offender rehabilitation may require a fundamental rethinking of rehabilitation and what is necessary to achieve it. Such a reframing will likely need an expanded and interdisciplinary approach that links correctional, legal, and social rehabilitation. It may also be necessary to think ourselves out of the correctional box and envision an entirely new means of addressing rehabilitation. At the very least, it requires a reexamination of what we think rehabilitation means and what the legislation says it means if rehabilitation is to be anything other than, as Red described it, bullshit.

Notes

1 As Phelps (2011) argued, however, the actual practices of prisons did not seem to change until the 1990s.

2 Although California does provide a way of expunging a conviction, those who have served time in prison are ineligible. By definition, then, parolees are automatically excluded from the expungement process (California Courts, 2011).

Appendix

On Methods

> *To discover the character of a practice is to trace the roles it lays, the intersections with other practices it maintains, the meanings ascribed to it and that emerge from it, over the course of its evolution.*
>
> —*Todd May, 2006*

A Note on the Genealogy of Texts

This study uses Foucault's genealogical method, which questions the taken-for-granted (Smart, 1983; Kendall & Wickham, 1999) and seeks to understand universal "truths" (e.g., sexuality, punishment) (Foucault, 1984). This method aims to understand human subjectivity by studying how these "truths" emerge over time (May, 2006) and how they are influenced by various contexts (e.g., historically, politically, economically, culturally). Genealogy traces "the history of an institution or a practice by asking which forces have taken hold of it, active or reactive ones" (May, 2006, p. 64).

Genealogies are particularly useful for understanding events (Foucault, 1975/1977, 1984; Smart, 1983) and the conditions that brought them about (Garland, 1986). For Foucault (1984, p. 88), an event

> is not a decision, a treaty, a reign, or a battle, but a reversal of a relationship of forces, the usurpation of power, the appropriation of a vocabulary turned against those who had once used it, a feeble domination that poisons itself as it grows lax, the entry of a masked "other."

Reversals are key as they show a shift in prior beliefs and practices. It is during reversals that the prior beliefs and practices are brought in to relief, as they are most likely to be discussed and analyzed at the moments when they are being overturned. In this book, the event under analysis is a reversal of not just prior policy, but also of institutional discourses, practices, structures, and norms.

Unlike other uses of genealogy, historical traces are not envisioned as a tree, with a unidirectional set of causalities. Rather, it is like a web or a rhizome, "a collection of root-like tentacles with no pattern to their growth, a set of tentacles which grow in unpredictable ways, even growing back into each other" (Kendall & Wickham, 1999, p. 7; see also May, 2006). By looking at all of the possible factors that resulted in the event, it is possible to understand not only *what* a practice is, but also *how* a practice came to be and has changed over time (Foucault, 1975/1977).

Thus, understanding the (re-)emergence of rehabilitation in California requires a search of contingencies, not causalities (Kendall & Wickham, 1999). It requires "a recognition of the multiplicity of factors which lie behind things" (Smart, 1983, p. 64), particularly those that are small and ignored (May, 2006) or seemingly unrelated (Kendall and Wickham, 1999), as well as tracing the context in which historical changes emerge (White, 1973; Goodwin & Duranti, 1992). In other words, understanding the (re-)emergence of rehabilitation requires tracing the context in which it has occurred (White, 1973; Goodwin & Duranti, 1992). A reversal or rethinking implies a recontextualization (Goodwin & Duranti, 1992). Understanding modern conceptualizations of rehabilitation requires an understanding of prior contexts in which rehabilitation played a key role and the contexts in which rehabilitation fell from favor.

One way to develop this understanding is to connect what is done with what is said (Baynes, Bohman, & McCarthy, 1987). Textual analysis, the analysis of texts and the changing nature of texts, allows for an understanding of practices or events. With regards to rehabilitation, textual analysis provides the means for understanding how rehabilitation was recontextualized as a natural function of the correctional (and by extension, parole) system, the sociocultural forces surrounding the re-emergence of rehabilitation, and the ways in which rehabilitation was mandated to those working in the parole system.

Textual analysis also requires analyzing texts' intertextuality, how one or more given texts are shaped by and shape other texts (Briggs & Bauman, 1992). Intertextuality can be empirically located in the language of the texts by locating the moments of intertextual gaps and linkages (Briggs, 1993), or the ways in which a text is embedded in or separated from other texts. Intertextual gaps and linkages may be achieved explicitly (references, quotations, etc.) or implicitly. For rehabilitation, linkages and gaps provided insight into ways in which legislators drew from or distanced themselves from prior versions of rehabilitation. They also provided insight into whether the policy-makers were trying to minimize or maximize the distance between the current and prior discourses. Understanding the textual gaps and linkages also helped determine whether rehabilitation is really a re-emergence or something new entirely.

Another key aspect of textual analysis is *entextualization*, "the formal processes associated with producing particular types of texts in the service of social and political agendas" (Briggs, 1993, p. 390). As legislative histories typically include all of the documents associated with a bill, it was possible to analyze the conversations surrounding the legislation. Analyzing the process provided an understanding of support and criticism, compromises made, and aspects left out of the final bill. Analyzing these processes was particularly illuminating, as it highlighted how the historical context is impacting California's current version of rehabilitation.

A Note on Ethical Considerations

An historical study of an event requires acknowledging the countless lives involved and impacted by that history. The question of confidentiality was particularly important to this study. Maintenance of confidentiality was based on whether the information was publically available or not. For those who worked at the legislative or governmental level, names were reported as they exist in the documents. Doing so allows for connections to be made across texts and enables others to visit the original files for additional research and comparison of findings.

While the photo in Chapter 2 is also available through public archives at T. H. Pendergast Museum, I chose to obscure the identity of the alleged offender. While the face is shown, a name is not given and information associated with the inmate number is only available in the state archives and not in electronically available files, limiting the possibility of discerning his identity.[1] Thus, the risk of identification was deemed minimal. Still, this individual did not consent to his identity being used in the manner chosen by the warden nor to be included in any research projects. For this reason, I erred on the side of caution.

Names of parole agents were changed. While agents are state employees, they are not public officials and are not used to the same level of scrutiny as public officials. The agents were also speaking on their own behalf and not as a representative of the parole system, their union, or the government. Their statements are also not publically available. In order to ensure agents were comfortable speaking freely, confidentially was guaranteed.

Note

1 I double-checked this by searching the available database.

References

Addiego, W. B. (1978). *Letter to Kenneth Maddy re: Sb 1057*. Located in the Assembly Committee on Criminal Justice file. Acquired from the California State Archives.

Administrative Office of the Courts. (2012). *A preliminary look at California parolee reentry courts*. Available from www.courts.ca.gov/documents/AOC BriefParolee0612.pdf

Adult Authority. (1945, February 9). *Adult Authority report*. Sacramento, CA: Author.

Adult Authority. (1947, November). *Bureau of Paroles, Parole Officers manual*. Sacramento, CA: Author.

Adult Authority. (1966, October 31). *Policy Statement #17: Termination of parole supervision*. Sacramento, CA: Author.

Adult Authority. (1973, February 27). *Resolution of the Adult Authority. Subject: Restoration of certain civil rights to inmates and parolees*. Sacramento, CA: Author.

Adult Authority. (1973, March 27). *Policy Statement No. 24: Functions and priorities for term setting and revocation of parole*. Sacramento, CA: Author.

Adult Authority. (1975, February 19). *Resolution of the Adult Authority. Subject: Rules governing prisoners on parole*. Sacramento, CA: Author.

Adult Authority, Department of Corrections. (1945). *Philosophy, principles, and program of the California Adult Authority*. Sacramento, CA: Author.

Adult Authority, Department of Corrections. (1972). *Philosophy, policies, and program of the California Adult Authority*. Sacramento, CA: Author.

Agwin, J., Larson, J., Mattu, S., & Kirchner, L. (2016, May 23). Machine bias: There's software used across the country to predict future criminals. And it's biased against blacks. *ProPublica*. Available from www.propublica.org/article/machine-bias-risk-assessments-in-criminal-sentencing

Allen, B. F. (1976). *Letter to the Governor re: SB 42*. Located in the Governor's Chaptered Bill File. Acquired at the California State Archives.

Allen, F. A. (1959). Criminal justice, legal values, and the rehabilitative ideal. *Journal of Criminal Law, Criminology, and Police Science*, *50*(3), 226–232.

Allen, F. A. (1981). *The decline of the rehabilitative ideal: Penal policy and social purpose*. New Haven and London: Yale University Press.

Altheide, D. L., & Coyle, M. J. (2006). Smart on crime: The new language of prisoner release. *Crime, Media, and Culture*, *2*(3), 286–303.

Andrews, D. A., Bonta, J., & Wormith, J. S. (2006). The recent past and near future of risk and/or need assessment. *Crime & Delinquency*, *52*(1), 7–27.

Aos, S., & Drake, E. (2013). *Prison, police, and programs: Evidence-based options that reduce crime and save money*. Olympia: Washington State Institute for Public Policy.

Aos, S., Phillips, P., Barnoski, R., & Lieb, R. (2001). *The comparative costs and benefits of programs to reduce crime, vol. 4*. Olympia, WA: Washington State Institute for Public Policy.

Appelbaum, Y. (2016, June 27). What if America approached crime like treating a disease? *The Atlantic*. Available from www.theatlantic.com/politics/archive/2016/06/evidence-based-criminal-justice-reform/488984/

Assembly Committee on Criminal Justice. (1975, October 11). *Indeterminate Sentence Law in California, Hearing (unedited draft)*. Located in the Assembly Committee on Criminal Justice File. Acquired from the California State Archives.

Associated Press. (1979, October 12). No title. Retrieved from Lexis Nexis.

Associated Press. (1999, October 3). *Governor taking tough stance on parole for inmates serving indeterminate sentences*. Retrieved from Lexis Nexis.

Associated Press. (2004, March 15). *Parole agents angry over new budget-saving policies*. Retrieved from Lexis Nexis.

Barker, V. (2009). *The politics of imprisonment: How the democratic process shapes the way America punishes offenders*. Oxford: Oxford University Press.

Baynes, K., Bohman, J., & McCarthy, T. (1987). Michael Foucault. In K. Baynes, J. Bohman, and T. McCarthy (Eds.), *After philosophy: End or transformation?* (p. 95–99). Cambridge, MA: MIT Press.

Berecochea, J. E. (1982). *Origins and early development of parole in California*. Unpublished dissertation, University of California, Berkeley.

Blakeslee, S. (2009). *Letter to Governor Schwarzenegger re: Recommended veto of SBxxx 18 (Ducheny)*. Located in Governor's Chaptered Bill File. Acquired from the California State Archives.

Board of Prison Terms. (1988). *Parole revocation guidelines*. Sacramento: Department of Corrections.

Board of Prison Terms and Paroles. (1933). *Second annual report to the governor of the State of California, July 1st, 1932–June 30th, 1933*. Sacramento, CA: Author.

Board of Prison Terms and Paroles. (1941). *The tenth annual report to the Governor of the State of California, July 1st, 1940–June 30th, 1941*. Sacramento, CA: Author.

Board of Prison Terms and Parole. (1943). *The eleventh and twelfth annual reports to the Governor of the State of California, July 1, 1941–June 30, 1942 and July 1, 1942–June 30, 1943*. Sacramento, CA: Author.

Bock, A. W. (2009, October 23). Coping with pressures of life after prison. *Orange County Register*. Retrieved May 25, 2010 from http://articles.ocregister.com/2009–2010–2023/opinion/24659174-1-parolees-prison-shuffles

Bottomley, A. K. (1990). Parole in transition: A comparative study of origins, developments, and prospects for the 1990s. *Crime and Justice*, *12*, 319–374.

Boyer, N. D. (1976, September 13). *Letter to the Governor re: SB 42*. Located in Governor's Chaptered Bill File. Acquired from the California State Archives.

Braithwaite, H., Tatar, J. R., & Turner, S. (2012). *Impact of the California Parole Supervision and Reintegration Model (CPSRM) on parolee perceptions of supervision*. Irvine, CA: Center for Evidence-Based Corrections.

Braithwaite, H., Turner, S., & Hess, J. (2013). *California Parole Supervision and Reintegration Model (CPSRM) outcome evaluation*. Irvine, CA: Center for Evidence-Based Corrections.

Briggs, C. L. (1993). Metadiscursive practices and scholarly authority in folkloristics. *Journal of American Folklore*, *106*(422), 387–434.

Briggs, C. L., & Bauman, R. (1992). Genre, intertextuality, and social power. *Journal of Linguistic Anthropology*, *2*(2), 131–172.

Brown, J. (2013). Termination of prison overcrowding emergency proclamation. Available from www.gov.ca.gov/news.php?id=17886

Bycel, B. (1976, May 17). *Letter to John Nejedly re: SB 42*. Located in the Governor's Chaptered Bill File. Acquired from the California State Archives.

California Courts. (2011). *Self-help center: Clean up your criminal record*. Available from www.courtinfo.ca.gov/selfhelp/other/crimlawclean.htm

California Department of Corrections. (1979). *Mission, philosophy, values*. Sacramento, CA: Author.

California Department of Corrections. (1997). *Preventing parolee failure program: An evaluation*. Sacramento, CA: Author. Cited in Solomon, A. L., Waul, M., Van Ness, A., & Travis, J. (2004). *Outside the walls: A national snapshot of community-based prisoner reentry programs*. Urban Institute: Washington, DC.

California Department of Corrections and Rehabilitation Expert Panel on Adult Offender Reentry and Recidivism Reduction Programs. (2007). *Report to the California State Legislature: A roadmap for effective offender programming in California*. Sacramento, CA: California Department of Corrections and Rehabilitation.

California Secretary of State. (2006). *Proposition 83. Sex offenders. Sexually violent predators. Punishment, residence restrictions and monitoring. Initiative statute*. Sacramento: Author.

California State Personnel Board. (1958). *Parole agent job descriptions*. Sacramento: Author.

Cate, M. (2005). *Written testimony before the Little Hoover Commission regarding the reorganization for the Youth and Adult Correctional Agency*. Sacramento: Little Hoover Commission.

Citizens Advocating Legislative Leadership. (1975, April 11). *Statement to the Senate Judiciary Committee regarding SB 42*. Located in the Assembly Committee on Criminal Justice File. Acquired from the California State Archives.

Clanon, T. L. (1976, September 14). *Memo to Arlene Becker re: Length of Parole for sex offenders*. Located in the Assembly Committee on Criminal Justice File. Acquired from the California State Archives.

Coordinating Council of Prisoner Organizations. (1975). *Determined sentencing proposal*. Located in the Assembly Committee on Criminal Justice File. Acquired from the California State Archives.

Corrections Independent Review Panel. (2004). *Reforming corrections*. Sacramento: Author.

Csizmar, E., and Osterli, M. (2009). *SBX3 18 (Ducheny) analysis*. Located in the Governor's Chaptered Bill File. Acquired from the California State Archives.

Cullen, F. T., & Gendreau, P. (2000). Assessing correctional rehabilitation: Policy, practice, and prospects. *Criminal Justice*, *3*, 109–175.

Davis, E. M. (1977, May 11). *Letter to Alfred H. Song re; SB 1057*. Located Senate Justice Committee. Acquired from the California State Archives.

DeFao, J. (2003, February 18). Jerry Brown's about-face on criminal sentencing. *San Francisco Chronicle*, p. A1.

Department of Corrections. (n.d.). *Implementation report on new legislation*. Sacramento, CA: Author.

Department of Corrections. (1964a). *Requested report: Organization, operation, program, and problems, Parole and Community Service Division*. Sacramento, CA: Author.

Department of Corrections. (1964b). *One in four*. Sacramento, CA: Author

Department of Corrections. (1975). *Parole agent manual of the Department of Corrections*. Sacramento, CA: Author.

Department of Corrections. (1977). *Parole board rules*. Sacramento: Author.

Department of Corrections. (1981). *Directory: Parole and Community Services Division*. Sacramento: Author.

Department of Corrections. (1990). *Parolee information handbook*. Sacramento: Author.

Department of Finance. (1976, September 16). *Enrolled bill report, SB 42*. Located in the Governor's Chaptered Bill File. Acquired from the California State Archives.

Dill, W. (1967). *History of parole system in California*. Presented at Parole Action Study Staff Meeting, September (date unknown).

Drucker, L., Gordon, W. A., & Bixby, F. L. (1944). *Philosophy, principles and program of the California Adult Authority*. Sacramento, CA: California Adult Authority.

Dugdale, R. L. (1877). *The Jukes: A study in crime, pauperism, disease and hereditary*. New York: Knickerbocker Press.

Dunbar, W. (1965). *Parole psychiatric outpatient clinic manual of the department of corrections youth and adult corrections agency, state of California*. Sacramento: Department of Corrections.

Enomoto, J. J. (1976, March 30). *Memo to Marc Poche re: Senate Bill 42, authored by Senator Nejedly*. Located in the Governor's Chaptered Bill File. Acquired from the California State Archives.

Fairfax, R. A. (2011). From "overcriminalization" to "smart on crime": American criminal justice reform—legacy and prospects. *Journal of Law, Economics, & Policy*, *7*(4), 597–616.

Farabee, D. (2005). *Rethinking rehabilitation: Why can't we reform our criminals?* Washington, DC: AEI Press.

Feeley, M. M., & Simon, J. (1992). The new penology: Notes on the emerging strategy of corrections and its implication. *Criminology*, *30*(4), 449–474.

Feige, D. (2005, February 1). A prison without hope is a dangerous place. *Los Angeles Times*.

Fitzharris, T. L. (1975). *Letter to Nejedly re: SB 42*. Sacramento: California Probation, Parole and Correctional Association.

Fitzharris, T. L. (1976). *Letter to the Governor re: SB 42*. Located in the Governor's Chaptered Bill File. Acquired from the California State Archives.

Fitzharris, T. L. (1978). *Letter to Daniel E. Boatwright re: SB 1057*. Located in the Assembly Ways and Means File. Acquired from the California State Archives.

Foucault, M. (1977). *Discipline and punish: The birth of the prison* (A. Sheridan, Trans.). New York: Vintage Books. (Original work published 1975).

Foucault, M. (1984). Nietzsche, genealogy, history. In P. Rabinow (ed.), *The Foucault reader* (p. 76–100). New York: Pantheon Books.

Franchetti, M. (1974, December 18). *Letter to Nejedly re: SB 42*. Located in the Senate Justice Committee File. Acquired from the California State Archives.

Fries, R. T., & Schooler, R. H. (1976, July 1). *Letter to the Governor re: SB 42*. Located in the Governor's Chaptered Bill File. Acquired from the California State Archives.

Garland, D. (1985). *Punishment and welfare: A history of penal strategies*. London: Ashgate Publishing Unlimited.

Garland, D. (1986). Review: Foucault's "Discipline and Punish"—An exposition and critique. *American Bar Foundation Research Journal*, *11*(4), 847–880.

Garland, D. (1996). The limits of the sovereign state: Strategies of crime control in contemporary society. *British Journal of Criminology*, *36*(4), 445–471.

Garland, D. (2001). *Culture of control: Crime and social order in contemporary society*. Chicago: University of Chicago Press.

Gatlin, G. (1989). *Letter to James Roland, Director of Corrections*. Publication information unknown. Acquired at the T. H. Pendergast Parole Museum.

Gilmore, R. (1999). Globalisation and US prison growth: From military Keynesianism to post-Keynesianism militarism. *Race and Class*, *40*(2/3), 171–188.

Glaser, D. (1995). *Preparing convicts for law-abiding lives: The pioneering penology of Richard A. McGee*. Albany: State University of New York Press.

Gmeinder, K. (2009). *Department of Finance enrolled bill report: Prison and parole reforms*. Located in the Governor's Chaptered Bill File. Acquired from the California State Archives.

Goddard, H. H. (1912). *The Kallikak family: A study in the heredity of feeblemindedness*. New York: MacMillan Publishing.

Goodman, P. (2010). *Hero or inmate, camp or prison, rehabilitation or labor extraction: A multi-level study of California's prison fire camps*. Unpublished doctoral dissertation, University of California, Irvine.

Goodwin, C., & Duranti, A. (1992). Rethinking context: An introduction. In A. Duranti & C. Goodwin (Eds.), *Rethinking context: Language as an interactive phenomenon* (p. 1–42). Cambridge: Cambridge University Press.

Gordon, W. A. (1946). *The organization and functions of the Adult Authority of the State of California*. Presented at the California Probation and Parole Association Annual Conference, Riverside, CA, June 8.

Gottfredson, M. R., Mitchel-Herzfeld, S. D., & Flanagan, T. J. (1982). Another look at the effectiveness of parole supervision. *Journal of Research in Crime and Delinquency*, *19*(2), 277–298.

Grattet, R., Petersilia, J., & Lin, J. (2008). *Parole violations and revocations in California*. Irvine, CA: Center for Evidence-Based Corrections.

Green, D. C. (1976, August 2). *Letter to Alan Sieroty re: SB 42 (Nejedly and Way)—Oppose*. Located in the Governor's Chaptered Bill File. Acquired from the California State Archives.

Griset, P. L. (1991). *Determinate sentencing: The promise and reality of retributive justice*. New York: State University of New York Press.

Gunn, J. A. (2005, January 27). *Statement of Joseph A. Gunn, Executive Director, Independent Review Panel, Little Hoover Commission*. Sacramento: Little Hoover Commission.

Hagan, J., Hewitt, J. D., & Alwin, D. F. (1979). Ceremonial justice: Crime and punishment in a loosely coupled system. *Social Forces*, *58*(2), 506–527.

Hanks, W. F. (1989). Text and textuality. *Annual Review of Anthropology*, *18*, 95–127.

Hannah-Moffat, K. (1999). Moral agent or actuarial subject: Risk and Canadian women's imprisonment. *Theoretical Criminology*, *3*(1), 71–94.

Hannah-Moffat, K. (2001). *Punishment in disguise: Penal governance and federal imprisonment of women in Canada*. Toronto: University of Toronto Press.

Harcourt, B. E. (2007). *Against prediction: Profiling, policing, and punishing in an actuarial age*. Chicago: University of Chicago Press.

Health and Welfare Agency, Department of Corrections. (1976). *Enrolled bill report: S.B. 42*. Located in the Governor's Chaptered Bill File. Acquired from the California State Archives.

Helfgott, J. (1997). Ex-offender needs versus community opportunity in Seattle, Washington. *Probation*, *61*(2), 12–24.

Hickman, R. (2005, January 14). *Letter to James P. Mayer re: reorganization plan for the Youth and Adult Correctional Agency*. Sacramento: Little Hoover Commission.

Hickman, R. (2006, October 26). *Statement to the Little Hoover Commission*. Sacramento: Little Hoover Commission.

Hipp, J., Jannetta, J., Shah, R., & Turner, S. (2011). Parolees' physical closeness to social services: A study of California parolees. *Crime & Delinquency*, *57*(1), 102–129.

Holoubek, H. A. (1949, May 16). *Letter to Governor Warren re: Changes to parole system over time*. Located in the Governor's Chaptered Bill File. Acquired from the California State Archives.

Howard, L., Lubenow, G. C., & Lesher, S. (1975, February 10). The purpose of prisons. *Newsweek*, p. 36.

Hutchinson, S. (2006). Countering catastrophic criminology Reform, punishment and the modern liberal compromise. *Punishment and Society*, *8*(4), 443–467.

Inmate Committee for Higher Education. (1974). *Prison education: An innovated "educational-therapy" program to reduce recidivism*. Presented at Correctional Training Facility-Central Soledad, California, October 2. Re-printed in Department of Corrections. (1976). *Recommendations of the Pre-Release Committee*. Sacramento, CA: Author.

Jackson, P. C. (1983). Some effects of parole supervision on recidivism. *British Journal of Criminology*, *23*(1), 17–34.

Jacobs, A. (2000). Give 'em a fighting chance: The challenges for women offenders trying to succeed in the community (p. 44–49). In National Institute of Corrections (Ed.), *Topics in community corrections, annual issue 2000: Responding to women offenders in the community*. Washington, DC: National Institute of Corrections.

Joint Center for Housing Studies. (2007). *The state of the nation's housing, 2007*. Cambridge, MA: Harvard University.

Kenady, P. (1976). *SB 42 (Nejedly)*. Located in the Assembly Republican Caucus File. Acquired from the California State Archives.

Kendall, G., & Wickham, G. (1999). *Using Foucault's methods*. London: Sage Publications.

Keve, P. W. (1979). No farewell to arms. *Crime and Delinquency*, *25*(4), 425–435.

Kravets, D. (2002, December 17). Court: Calif. Gov. can block parole. *San Francisco Chronicle*, Retrieved from Lexis Nexis

Krisberg, B., Craine, J., & Marchionna, S. (2004). *Attitudes of Californians toward effective correctional policies*. Oakland, CA: National Council on Crime and Delinquency.

Kruttschnitt, C., & Gartner, R. (2003). Women's imprisonment. *Crime and Justice*, *30*, 1–81.

Lawrence, A. (2013). *Trends in sentencing and corrections: State legislation*. Washington, DC: National Conference of State Legislatures.

L'Ecluse, L. (1993). *Job analysis: Parole Agent I and II*. Publication information unknown. Acquired from the T. H. Pendergast Parole Museum.

Legal Action Center. (n.d.). *Housing laws affecting individuals with criminal convictions*. Washington, DC: Author.

Legislative Analyst's Office. (1976). *Analysis of Senate Bill No. 42 (Nejedly) as amended in Assembly August 3, 1976, 1975–1976 session*. Sacramento: Author.

Legislative Analyst's Office. (1978, April 17). *Analysis of Senate Bill No. 1057 (Presley). As amended in Assembly March 29, 1978, 1977–1978 session*. Located in the Assembly Ways and Means Committee File. Acquired in the California State Archives.

Legislative Analyst's Office. (1991). *The 1991–1992 budget: Perspectives and issues. Community corrections*. Sacramento: Author.

Legislative Analyst's Office. (1998). *Cross-cutting issues: Judiciary and Criminal Justice. Reforming California's Adult Parole System*. Sacramento: Author.

Legislative Analyst's Office. (2005). *Judiciary and criminal justice, 2004–2005 analysis*. Sacramento: Author.

Lester, E. W. (1952). *Parole treatment and surveillance—which should dominate?* Presented at the General Session, Annual Congress of Correction, National Probation and Parole Association, Atlantic City, NJ, October 6.

Lewis, S. (2005). Rehabilitation: Headline or footnote in the new penal policy. *Probation Journal*, *52*(2), 119–135.

Lin, J., Grattet, R., & Petersilia, J. (2010). "Back-end sentencing" and reimprisonment: Individual, organizational, and community predictors of parole sanctioning decisions. *Criminology*, *48*(3), 759–795.

Lipsky, M. (1980). *Street-level bureaucracy: Dilemmas of the individual in public services*. New York: Russell Sage Foundation.

Little Hoover Commission. (2003). *Back to the community: Safe and sound parole policies*. Sacramento, CA: Author.

Little Hoover Commission. (2005). *Restructuring government: A review of the Governor's Reorganization Plan: Reforming California's Youth and Adult Correctional Agency*. Sacramento, CA: Author.

Little Hoover Commission. (2007). *Solving California's correctional crisis: Time is running out*. Sacramento, CA: Author.

Long, G. (2005, April 20a). *Assembly Committee on Appropriations, hearing date April 20, 2005, Public Safety Policy Committee*. Located in the Assembly Committee on Appropriations File. Acquired from the California State Archives.

Long, G. (2005, April 20b). *Assembly Committee on Appropriations, hearing date April 20, 2005*. Located in the Assembly Committee on Public Safety File. Acquired from the California State Archives.

Love, M. C. (2006). *Relief from the collateral consequences of conviction: A state by state resources guide*. Buffalo, NY: William S. Hein, Inc.

Loy, H. R. (1994). *Memo to Mike Badstubner re: Cops? Or caseworkers*. Publication information unknown. Acquired from the T. H. Pendergast Museum.

Lynch, M. (1998). Waste mangers? The new enology, crime gighting, and parole agent identity. *Law and Society Review*, *32*(4), 839–869.

Lynch, M. (2000). Rehabilitation as rhetoric: The ideal of reformation in contemporary parole discourse and practices. *Punishment & Society*, *2*(1), 40–60.

Magnani, L. (1976, September 15). *Letter to the Governor re: SB 42*. Located in the Governor's Chaptered Bill File. Acquired from the California State Archives.

Marks, I., & Lander, J. L. (1983). High Control Project tests parole supervision methods. *California Peace Officer*, *3*(4), 17, 19, 35, 37.

Martinson, R. (1974). What works? Questions and answers about prison reform. *Public Interest*, *35*(Spring), 22–54.

Martinson, R., & Wilks, J. (1977). Save parole supervision. *Federal Probation*, *41*, 23–27.

Maruna, S. (2011). Judicial rehabilitation and the "clean bill of health" in criminal justice. *European Journal of Probation*, *3*(1), 97–117.

Maruna, S., Immarigeon, R., & LeBel, T. P. (2004). Ex-offender reintegration: theory and practice. In S. Maruna & R. Immarigeon (Eds.), *After crime and punishment: Pathways to offender reintegration* (p. 3–26). Portland: William Publishing.

Marvin, N. (Producer), & Darabont, F. (Director). (1994). *Shawshank Redemption* [Motion picture]. USA: Warner Brothers Entertainment.

Mauer, M. (2010). *Collateral consequences of criminal convictions: Barriers to reentry for the formerly incarcerated*. Testimony presented at the House Judiciary Subcommittee on Crime, Terrorism, and Homeland Security, Washington, DC, June 9.

Mauer, M., Potler, C., & Wolf, R. (1999). *Gender and justice: Women, drugs, and sentence policy*. Washington, DC: Sentencing Project.

Maurutto, P., & Hannah-Moffat, K. (2006). Assembling risk and the restructuring of penal control. *British Journal of Criminology*, *46*(3), 438–454.

May, T. (2006). *The philosophy of Foucault*. Montreal: McGill-Queen's University Press.

Mayeux, S. (2011). The origins of back-end-sentencing in California: A dispatch from the archives. *Stanford Law & Policy Review*, *22*(2), 529–543.

McCarthy, K. (2005). *Letter to Assembly Republican Members re: Governor's Reorganization Plan 1 (Corrections Reform and New Parole Model*. Located in the Assembly Republican Caucus File. Acquired from the California State Archives.

McCorkel, J. A. (2013). *Breaking women: Gender, race, and the new politics of imprisonment.* New York: New York University Press.

McGee, R. A. (1958). *The administration of justice: The correctional process.* Speaking at the Policy-Community Relations Institute, East Lansing, MI, May 21.

McGee, R. A. (1959). *Administrative bulletin no. 59/18: Accelerated Release Program, employment of parolees.* Sacramento, CA: Adult Authority.

McGregor, M. (1945, February 9). *Adult Authority report.* Located in the Earl Warren Papers file. Acquired from the California State Archives.

McNeill, F. (2012). Four forms of "offender" rehabilitation: Towards an interdisciplinary perspective. *Legal and Criminological Psychology, 17*(1), 18–36.

Messinger, S. L., Berecochea, J. E., Raums, D., & Berk, R. A. (1985). The foundations of parole in California. *Law and Society Review, 19*(1), 69–106.

Milford, J. (1973). *Kind and usual punishment.* New York: Knopf.

Misner, R. L. (1996). Recasting prosecutorial discretion. *The Journal of Criminal Law and Criminology, 86*(3), 717–777.

Monahan, J. (1975, April 15). *Testimony of Professor John Monahan, University of California, Irvine, before the California Senate Select Committee on Penal Institutions, Aril 15, 1975.* Located in Senate Justice Committee Files. Acquired from the California State Archives.

Morris, N. (1974). *The future of imprisonment.* Chicago: University of Chicago Press.

Murphy, A., & Turner, S. (2010). *Parole Violation Decision-Making Instrument (PVDMI) process evaluation.* Irvine, CA: Center for Evidence Based Corrections.

Nejedly, J. A. (n.d.). *Response to California Probation, Parole and Correctional Association.* Located in Governor's Chaptered Bill File. Acquired from the California State Archives.

Nejedly, J. A. (1975, June 12). *Letter to the Governor re: SB 42.* Located in Governor's Chaptered Bill File. Acquired from the California State Archives.

Nejedly, J. A. (1976, August 24). *Letter to all State Legislators re: Retroactivity Provisions of Senate Bill. 42.* Located in Governor's Chaptered Bill File. Acquired from the California State Archives.

Nelson, E. K. (1970, March 10). *Preliminary proposed draft and commentary on 1. The Adult Authority, 2. Release on Parole, 3. Violations of the Conditions of Parole.*

Nelson, M., Deess, P., & Allen, C. (1999). *The first month out: Post-incarceration experiences in New York City.* New York, NY: Vera Institute.

Newland, A. C. (1976, May). *The parole agent attitude study. A report to the Deputy Director, Parole & Community Services Division, California Department of Corrections.* Publication information unknown. Acquired from the California State Archives.

O'Malley, P. (1996). Risk and responsibility. In A. Barry, T. Osborne, & N. Rose (Eds.), *Foucault and political reason: Liberalism, neo-liberalism and rationalities of government* (pp. 189–208). Chicago: University of Chicago Press.

Office of the Governor. (2004, February 19). *Press Release: Governor Schwarzenegger appoints Jean Woodford Director of the California Department of Corrections*. Sacramento, CA: Author.

Office of the Governor. (2004, March 5). *Press Release: Governor Schwarzenegger announces Governor Deukmejian will lead an Independent Review Panel for Corrections Reform*. Sacramento, CA: Author.

Office of the Governor. (2004, August 16). *Press Release: Governor Schwarzenegger goes on fact finding mission to Mule Creek State Prison; Calls for intensified prison reform efforts*. Sacramento, CA: Author.

Office of the Governor. (2004, December 22). *Press Release: Governor Schwarzenegger grants three pardons*. Sacramento, CA: Author.

Office of the Governor. (2005, January 6). Press Release: *Governor Schwarzenegger sends government reorganization plans to Little Hoover Commission*. Sacramento, CA: Author.

Olson, G., & Cooper, A. (2009). *Assembly Republican bill analysis*. Located in Governor's Chaptered Bill File. Acquired from the California State Archives.

Ostermann, M. (2013). Active supervision and its impact upon parolee recidivism rates. *Crime & Delinquency*, *59*(4), 487–509.

Otten, M. & Lee, K. W. (1978, March 5). Why our parole system is failing. *The Sacramento Union*, *A1–2*.

Page, J. (2011). *The toughest beat: Politics, punishment, and the prison officers union in California*. Oxford: Oxford University Press.

Pager, D. (2003). The mark of a criminal record. *American Journal of Sociology*, *108*, 937–975.

Pager, D., & Quillian, L. (2005). Walking the talk? What employers say versus what they do. *American Sociological Review*, *70*, 355–380.

Parole Agents Association of California. (n.d.). *Parole revocation limits*. Located in the Assembly Committee on Criminal Justice File. Acquired from the California State Archives.

Parole Agents Association of California. (1978, February 27). *No title*. Located in the Assembly Committee on Criminal Justice File. Acquired from the California State Archives.

Parole and Community Services Division. (1969). *Executive staff meeting minutes, January 15, 16, 17, 1969*. Sacramento, CA: Department of Corrections.

Parole and Community Services Division. (1970, August 27). *Memo re: parole philosophy and policy*. Sacramento, CA: Department of Corrections.

Parole and Community Services Division. (1976, May 11). *Memo re: Annual research review 1974–1975—An evaluation of the work furlough program—Richard Bass, ASRA-Bay Area*. Sacramento, CA: Department of Corrections.

Parole and Community Services Division. (1978a). *Parole in California: A three-year evaluation and development of a new model*. Sacramento, CA: Department of Corrections.

Parole and Community Services Division. (1978b). *Parole planning report*. Sacramento, CA: Department of Corrections.

Parole Policy and Procedures Committee. (1977). *Parole procedures manual: Determinate sentence law procedures (revised per AB 476)*. Sacramento: Author.

Parole Task Force. (1967). *California correctional system study: Parole Task Force report*. Sacramento, CA: Author.
Penner, L. (2011, March 17). *Public Safety Realignment Package—CPOC support AB 109/SB85 & X1 1/ACA 2 X1*. Located in the Assembly Republican Caucus-Policy File. Acquired from the California State Archives.
Petersilia, J. (2003). *When prisoners come home: Parole and prisoner reentry*. Oxford: Oxford University Press.
Phelps, M. S. (2011). Rehabilitation in the punitive era: The gap between rhetoric and reality in U.S. prison programs. *Law and Society Review*, *45*(1), 33–68.
Piehl, A. M., & LoBuglio, S. F. (2005). Does supervision matter? In J. Travis & C. Visher (Eds.), *Prisoner reentry and crime in America* (p. 105–138). Cambridge: Cambridge University Press.
Pines, B. (1976, August 25). *Letter to the Governor re: Senate Bill 42 (Nejedly—Sentencing)*. Located in The Governor's Chaptered Bill File. Acquired from the California State Archives.
Pitchford, P. (2000, August 28). Straight talk for parolees: "You are longer ignorant," a speaker tells them. "Now you can only be stupid." *Press Enterprise*, p. A5.
Portman, S. (1976). *Letter to J. Anthony Kline re: SB-42*. Located in The Governor's Chaptered Bill File. Acquired from the California State Archives.
Price, F. H. (1949, March 26). *Letter to Governor Warren re: crimes committed while on parole*. Located in the Governor's Chaptered Bill File. Acquired from the California State Archives.
Procunier, R. (1971). *Statement by Ray Procunier, Director, California Department of Corrections*. Submitted to Congressional Subcommittee on Correctional Programs, October 15, San Francisco, CA.
Rafter, N (ed.). (2009). *The origins of Criminology: A reader*. New York: Routledge.
Raynor, P. (1997). Some observations on rehabilitation and justice, *The Howard Journal*, *36*(3), 248–262.
Raynor, P., & Robinson, G. (2005). *Rehabilitation, crime and justice*. New York: Palgrave Macmillian.
Reed, R. E. (nd). *Analysis and recommendation—Senate Bill 904 (Senator Deuel)*. Located in the Governor's Chaptered Bill File. Acquired from the California State Archives.
Reid, F. C. (1949, July 27). *Letter to Governor Warren re: Crimes committed while on parole*. Located in the Governor's Chaptered Bill File. Acquired from the California State Archives.
Remington, C. C. (2005). *Testimony of Calvin Remington to the Little Hoover Commission*. Sacramento: Little Hoover Commission.
Riles, A. (2006). [Deadlines]: Removing the brackets on politics in bureaucratic and anthropological analysis. In A. Riles (ed.), *Documents: Artifacts of modern knowledge*. Minneapolis: University of Minnesota Press.
Robinson, G. (2008). Late-modern rehabilitation: The evolution of penal strategy. *Punishment and Society*, *10*(4), 429–445.
Robinson, G., & Crow, I. (2009). *Offender rehabilitation: Theory, research, and practice*. London: SAGE Publications.

Rose, N. (2000). Government and control. *British Journal of Criminology*, *40*(2), 321–339.

Rothman, D. (1971). *The discovery of the asylum: Social order and disorder in the new Republic*. Boston: Little Brown.

Rotman, E. (1986). Do criminal offenders have a constitutional right to rehabilitation? *Journal of Criminal Law and Criminology*, *77*(4), 1023–1068.

Rotman, E. (1990). *Beyond punishment: A new view on the rehabilitation of criminal offenders*. New York: Greenwood Press.

San Francisco Chronicle. (1990, April 13). *No parole means what it says*. Retrieved from Lexis Nexis.

San Francisco Chronicle. (2000, August 20). *California's prisoners tell how they see the system*. Retrieved from Lexis Nexis.

San Francisco Chronicle. (2003, December 1). *Fresh start on parole policy*. Retrieved from Lexis Nexis.

San Francisco Chronicle. (2005, April 10). *No second chance for parole violators; Offenders to return to prison, not rehab or halfway houses*. Retrieved from Lexis Nexis.

San Francisco Chronicle. (2005, April 14). *Closing prisons' revolving door*. Retrieved from Lexis Nexis.

San Jose Mercury News. (1999, October 17). *No mercy Gov. Davis is a prisoner of the tough-on-crime mentality*. Retrieved from Lexis Nexis.

Scherb, S. (1993). The costly an vicious circle of activities of drug-addicted parole violators. *Peacekeeper: California Correctional Peace Officer*, *11*(2), 41–42.

Schlager, M. D., & Robbins, K. (2008). Does parole work?—Revisited: Reframing the discussion of the impact of postprison supervision on offender outcome. *The Prison Journal*, *88*(2), 234–251.

Schwarzenegger, A. (2005). *A government for the people for a change: Governor's Reorganization Plan 2—Reforming California's Youth and Adult Correctional System*. Sacramento: Office of the Governor.

Schwarzenegger, A. (2006). *Prison overcrowding state of emergency declaration*. Available from www.gov.ca.gov/news.php?id=4278

Senate TV. (2005). *Senate Committee on Public Safety hearing*. Publication information unknown. Acquired from the California State Archives.

Shaughnessy, M. F. (2007, September 13). An interview with Joan Petersilia: Criminology, Law and Society in the School of Social Ecology. Available from www.ednews.org/articles/17056/1/An-Interview-with-Joan-Petersilia-Criminology-Law-and-Society-in-the-School-of-Social-Ecology/Page1.html

Shah, R. (2007). *The relationship between parole revocation and mobility: A study of California parolees*. Paper presented at the American Society of Criminology Annual Conference, Atlanta, GA, November 14–17.

Shonholtz, R. (1975). *Memo to Alan Sieroty re: SB 42*. Located in the Assembly Committee on Criminal Justice File. Acquired at the California State Archives.

Sigler, R. T. (1988). Role conflict for adult probation and parole officers: Fact or myth. *Journal of Criminal Justice*, *16*(2), 121–129.

Sigler, R. T., & McGraw, B. (1984). Adult probation and parole officers: Influence of their weapons, role perceptions and role conflict. *Criminal Justice Review*, *9*(1), 28–32.

Silliman, R. (1976). *Letter to J. Anthony Kline re: SB 42*. Located in the Governor's Chaptered Bill File. Acquired at the California State Archives.

Silver, A. (1967). The demand for order in civil society. In D. Bordua (ed.), *The police: Six sociological essays*. New York: John Wiley Publishing.

Simon, J. (1993). *Poor discipline: Parole and the social control of the underclass, 1890–1990*. Chicago: University of Chicago Press.

Simon, J. (2007). *Governing through crime: How the war on crime transformed American democracy and created a culture of fear*. Oxford: Oxford University Press.

Simon, J. (2012). *Mass incarceration on trial: A remarkable court decision and the future of prisons in America*. New York: New Press.

Smart, B. (1983). On discipline and social regulation: A review of Foucault's genealogical analysis. In D. Garland & P. Young (Eds.), *The power to punish: Contemporary penality and social analysis* (p. 62–83). London: Heinemann Educational Books.

Smith, J. F. (1978, March 13). *Letter to Assembly Criminal Justice Committee re: SB 1057—Parole*. Located in the Assembly Committee on Criminal Justice. Acquired at the California State Archives.

Solomon, A. L., Kachnowski, V., & Bhati, A. (2005). *Does parole work? Analyzing the impact of postprison supervision on rearrest outcomes*. Washington, DC: Urban Institute.

Spector, D. (2005). *Testimony of Donald Specter on the Governor's Reorganization Plan 2: The Youth and Adult Correctional System*. Sacramento: Little Hoover Commission.

Stahl, D. N. (1976). *Letter to Senate Judiciary Committee, Assembly Criminal Justice Committee, Assembly Ways and Means Committee, Senator Clare Berryhill, Senator George Zenovich, Assemblyman Carmen Perino, and Assemblyman John Thurman re: SB 42*. Located in Senate Justice Committee File. Acquired at the California State Archives.

State Board of Prison Directors. (1909). *Rules and regulations for the paroling of prisoners*. Sacramento: Superintendent State Printing.

State Board of Prison Directors. (1936). *Biennial report of the State Board of Prison Directors of the State of California, for the eighty-sixth and eighty-seventh fiscal years, 1935–1936*. Sacramento, CA: Author.

State of California. (1976). *State of California Administrative Code: Title 15. Crime Prevention and Corrections. Division 2: Adult Authority and Women's Board of Terms and Parole, Parole Board Rules*. Sacramento, CA: Author.

State of California. (2001). *CDC 1515: Notice and conditions of parole*. Sacramento: Author.

State of California, Office of Legislative Counsel. (1943, May 4). *Report on Senate Bill No. 904*. Located in the Governor's Chaptered Bill File. Acquired from the California State Archives.

Stephenshaw, J. (2009). *SB 18 X3 (Ducheny) as amended August 31, 2009 analysis*. Located in the Office of Senate Floor Analyses File. Acquired from the California State Archives.

Sutton, J. (1986). *Parole outpatient clinics*. Publication information unknown. Acquired from T. H. Pendergast Parole Museum.

Swim, C. H. (1977, May 10). *Letter to Senator Song re: SB 1057*. Located in the Senate Justice Committee. Acquired in the California State Archives.

Swim, C. H. (1978). *Letter to Daniel Boatwright re: SB 1057*. Located in the Assembly Ways and Means Committee File. Acquired in the California State Archives.

Task Force on Probation and Parole. (1972). *Report to Attorney General Evelle J. Younger*. Sacramento, CA: Author.

Taylor, M. (2009). *A Status Report: Implementing AB 900's Prison Construction and Rehabilitation Initiatives*. Sacramento, CA: Legislative Analyst's Office.

Television Memories (Producer). (1957). *Parole, 1957*. Century City, Television Memories.

The Parole Reform Task Force. (2010). *Parole reform in California: An evidence-based and best practices approach*. Sacramento, CA: Author.

Travis, J. (2002). *Thoughts on the future of parole*. Available from http://webarchive.urban.org/UploadedPDF/410521.pdf

Travis, J. (2005). *But they all come back: Facing the challenges of prisoner reentry*. Washington, DC: Urban Institute Press.

Turner, S., Braithwaite, H., Kearney, L., Murphy, A., & Haerle, D. (2012). Evaluation of the California Parole Violation Decision-Making Instrument (PVDMI). *Journal of Crime and Justice*, *35*(2), 269–295.

Turner, S., Braithwaite, H., Tatar, J., Omori, M., & Kearney, L. (2011). *The impact of the California Parole Supervision and Reintegration Model (CPSRM) pilot implementation on parole agent attitudes*. Irvine, CA: Center for Evidence-Based Corrections.

Uggen, C., & Manza, J. (2006). *Locked out: Felon disenfranchisement and American democracy*. New York: Oxford University Press.

Uggen, C., Thompson, M., & Manza, J. (2006). Crime, class, and reintegration: The socioeconomic, familial, and civil lives of offenders. *Annals of the American Academy of Political & Social Sciences*, *605*(1), 281–310.

Ullman, M. (1976, June 14). *Letter to Anthony Kline re: SB 42*. Located in the Governor's Chaptered Bill File. Acquired from the California State Archives.

Unknown. (n.d. a). *Notes on SB 42*. Located in the Senate Justice Committee File. Acquired from the California State Archives.

Unknown. (n.d. b). *Staff concerns over SB 42*. Located in the Assembly Committee on Criminal Justice File. Acquired from the California State Archives.

Unknown. (n.d. c). *What SB 1057 does*. Located in the Senate Justice Committee. Acquired at the California State Archives.

Unknown. (n.d. d). *Parole*. Located in the Senate Finance Committee File. Acquired at the California State Archives.

Unknown. (n.d. e). *Assembly Committee on Criminal Justice Bill analysis, written after hearing date of February 27, 1978*.

Unknown. (1924, December 19). *Prison and the social sciences*. Publication information unknown. Acquired from T. H. Pendergast Parole Museum.

Unknown. (1942). *Statement in re Senate Bill 904 as amended March XX, 1942*. Located in the Governor's Chaptered Bill File. Acquired from the California State Archives.

Unknown. (1943, February 16). *Letter to Hon. Ralph E. Hoyt*. Located in the Governor's Chaptered Bill File. Acquired from the California State Archives.

Unknown. (1957, March 8). Adult Authority Answers IAC questions. *Communicator: California Men's Colony*. San Louis Obispo, CA: Communicator.
Unknown. (1963). *Community Correctional Center: East Bay area*. Publication information unknown. Acquired from the California State Archives.
Unknown. (1967). *California correctional system study: Parole Task Force report*. Publication information unknown. Acquired from the California State Archives.
Unknown. (1970, July 22). *Region III. Central City Community Center Program Statement*. Publication information unknown. Acquired from the California State Archives.
Unknown. (1975). *Senate Democratic Caucus Report*. Located in the Senate Democratic Caucus File. Acquired from the California State Archives.
Unknown. (1975, January 10). *Memo re: work furlough program*. Publication information unknown. Acquired from the California State Archives.
Unknown. (1975, February 25). *Letter to Nejedly re: Senate Bill 42*. Located in Senate Justice Committee File. Acquired from the California State Archives.
Unknown. (1975, April 1). *Petition to Nejedly re: Senate Bill 42*. Located in Senate Justice Committee File. Acquired from the California State Archives.
Unknown. (1975, May 14). *Senate Republican Caucus Report*. Located in Senate Republican Caucus File. Acquired from the California State Archives.
Unknown. (1975, August 14). *Bill digest: Assembly Committee on Criminal Justice*. Located in Assembly Committee on Criminal Justice File. Acquired from the California State Archives.
Unknown. (1976, April 22). *Bill Analysis: SB 42*. Located in Senate Justice Committee File. Acquired from the California State Archives.
Unknown. (1976, August 17). *Ways and Means staff analysis*. Located in Assembly Ways and Means Committee File. Acquired from the California State Archives.
Unknown. (1976, September). *Region III: Central City Community Center program statement*. Sacramento: California Department of Corrections.
Unknown. (1977, June 16). *Assembly Republican Caucus bill summary*. Located in the Assembly Republic Caucus File. Acquired from the California State Archives.
Unknown. (1978, October 10). *Senate Republican Caucus bill summary*. Located in the Senate Republican Caucasus. Acquired from the California State Archives.
Unknown. (1979, June). New parole model. *Parole Agents Association of California Newsletter*.
Unknown. (1990). *Reduction of prison bed use by developing and using alternative community based program alternatives for less serious technical violations*. Publication information unknown. Acquired from the T. H. Pendergast Parole Museum.
Unknown. (1993). *The facts: California's parole agent update 1993*. Publication information unknown. Acquired from the T. H. Pendergast Parole Museum.
Unknown. (2005, April 5). *Amendments to Senate Bill No. 737 as amended in Senate March 29, 2005*. Located in the Assembly Committee on Public Safety File. Acquired from the California State Archives.
Unknown. (2009, June 28). *Unfinished business*. Located in the Office of Senate Floor Analyses File. Acquired from the California State Archives.
Unknown. (2009, August 28). *Legislative counsel's digest*. Located in the Office of Senate Floor Analyses File. Acquired from the California State Archives.

Unknown. (2011, March 17). *Third reading: AB109*. Located in the Office of Senate Floor Analyses File. Acquired from the California State Archives.

Unknown. (2011, June 28). *Third reading: AB117*. Located in the Office of Senate Floor Analyses File. Acquired from the California State Archives

Veit, E. (1979). *Memo re: agents and guns*. Publication information unknown. Acquired from the T. H. Pendergast Parole Museum.

Veit, E. (1981). *Memo re: Expansion of parole agent activities*. Publication information unknown. Acquired from the T. H. Pendergast Parole Museum.

Veit, E. (1983). Outpatient clinics provide psychiatric help for parolees. *California Peace Officer*, *3*(4), 13, 15.

Veit, E. (1986). *Parole in California*. Publication information unknown. Acquired from the T. H. Pendergast Parole Museum.

Visher, C. A., & Courtney, S. M. E. (2007). *One year out: Experiences of prisoners returning to Cleveland*. Washington, DC: Urban Institute.

Visher, C. A., & Farrell, J. (2005). *Chicago communities and prisoner reentry*. Washington, DC: Urban Institute.

Visher, C. A., & Courtney, S. M. E. (2007). *One year out: Experiences of prisoners returning to Cleveland*. Washington, DC: Urban Institute.

Vismann, C. (2008). *Files: Law and media technology* (G. Winthrop-Young, Trans.). Stanford: Stanford University Press. (Original work published 2000.)

Vito, G. F., Higgins, G. E., & Tewksbury, R. (2015). The effectiveness of parole supervision: Use of propensity score matching to analyze reincarceration rates in Kentucky. *Criminal Justice Policy Review*. doi 10.1177/0887403415609717

Vollmer, A. (1923). *Crime and its prevention*. Publication information unknown. Acquired from T. H. Pendergast Parole Museum.

Walker, F. (1962). As others see it: The battle for rehabilitation. *The Correctional Review*, August-December, 20–21.

Warren, E. (1943, March 12). *Letter to Frank B. Belcher*. Located in the Governor's Chaptered Bill File. Acquired from the California State Archives.

Warren, J. (2005, February 13). The State; Governor aims to rehabilitation prison system; His push to reduce recidivism by preparing inmates for life outside is a break with tradition. *LA Times*. Available May 25, 2010 from http://articles.latimes.com/2005/feb/13/local/me-prison13

Warren, J. (2005, March 27). The State; State joining shift on prisons; as new strategies take hold around the nation, the governor is turning the focus of California's penal system to helping parolees join society. *LA Times*. Available May 25, 2010 from http://articles.latimes.com/2005/mar/27/local/me-prisons27

Warren, J. (2005, April 1). Victims' rights group blasts prison rehab plan: Organization that once sided with governor says parole proposals endanger the public. *LA Times*. Available May 25, 2010 from http://articles.latimes.com/2005/apr/01/local/me-victims1

Weil, J. E. (1943, March 20). *Letter to Honorable Charles H Deuel*. Located in the Governor's Chaptered Bill File. Acquired from the California State Archives.

Welsh, L. M. (1975). *Letter to Nejedly re: SB 42*. Located in the Senate Justice Committee File. Acquired from the California State Archives.

Werth, R. (2012). I do what I'm told, sort of. Reformed subjects, unruly citizens, and parole. *Theoretical Criminology*, *16*(3), 329–346.
Western, B. (2006). *Punishment and inequality in America*. New York: Russell Sage Foundation.
White, H. (1973). *Metahistory: The historical imagination in nineteenth-century Europe*. Baltimore: John Hopkins University Press.
Wood, W. J. (1943, January 6). *Letter to Governor Earl Warren*. Located in the Governor's Chaptered Bill File. Acquired from the California State Archives.
Woodford, J. S. (2004). *Memo re: new parole model*. Publication information unknown. Acquired from the California State Archives.
Woodmanswer, C. H. (1974, December 5). *Letter to Nejedly re: SB 42*. Located in the Senate Justice Committee File. Acquired from the California State Archives.
Woodward, M. G. (1943, January 4). *Letter to Governor Earl Warren*. Located in the Governor's Chaptered Bill File. Acquired from the California State Archives.
Woodworth, D. R. (1976). *Nejedly Bill (SB 42)—effective July 1, 1977*. Located in the Senate Justice Committee File. Acquired from the California State Archives.
Yi, M., and Egelko, B. (2009, September 19). State fails federal demand to cut prisoners: Assembly already rejected governor's key proposals. *SFGATE*, Available from http://sfgate.com/bayarea/article/State-fails-federal-demand-to-cut-prisoners-3286123.php
York, J. (1977). *Letter to Senator Presley re: SB 1057 (Changes in Penal Code sections relating to Parole)*. Located in the Senate Justice Committee File. Acquired at the California State Archives.
Zamora, J. H. (2002, December 23). Parolees in revolving door: California has highest rate of recidivism. *San Francisco Chronicle*, A1.
Zamora, J. H. (2003, February 28). Jerry Brown rips parole system: Indeterminate sentencing "big mistake." *San Francisco Chronicle*, A27.

Index

For Product Safety Concerns and Information please contact our EU representative GPSR@taylorandfrancis.com Taylor & Francis Verlag GmbH, Kaufingerstraße 24, 80331 München, Germany